Social History of Africa

LANDED OBLIGATION

Recent Titles in
Social History of Africa Series
Allen Isaacman and Jean Allman, Series Editors

LANDED OBLIGATION

THE PRACTICE OF POWER
IN BUGANDA

Holly Elisabeth Hanson

Social History of Africa
Allen Isaacman and Jean Allman, Series Editors

HEINEMANN
Portsmouth, NH

Heinemann
A division of Reed Elsevier Inc.
361 Hanover Street
Portsmouth, NH 03801-3912
www.heinemann.com

Offices and agents throughout the world

ISBN: 0-325-07037-7 (cloth)
ISBN: 0-325-07036-9 (paper)
ISSN: 1099–8098

Library of Congress Cataloging-in-Publication Data

Hanson, Holly Elisabeth.
  Landed obligation : the practice of power in Buganda / Holly Elisabeth Hanson.
    p. cm.—(Social history of Africa, ISSN 1099-8098)
  Includes bibliographical references and index.
  ISBN 0-325-07037-7 (alk. paper)—ISBN 0-325-07036-9 (pbk. : alk. paper)
    1. Ganda (African people)—History. 2. Ganda (African people)—Politics and government. 3. Ganda (African people)—Kings and rulers. 4. Chiefdoms—Uganda—History. 5. Power (Social sciences)—Uganda. 6. Political obligation—Uganda—History. 7. Ceremonial exchange—Uganda—History. 8. Uganda—History. 9. Uganda—Social life and customs. I. Title. II. Series.
DT433.245.G35H36   2003
967.61′01—dc22   2003056676

British Library Cataloguing in Publication Data is available.

Printed in the United States of America on acid-free paper

07 06 05 04 03 SB 1 2 3 4 5 6 7 8 9

Copyright Acknowledgments

The author and publisher gratefully acknowledge permission to use the following material:

Fondazione Sella, Biella Italy. Courtesy Panopticon Gallery, Waltham, MA.

For Simon, Músá, Enoch, Elisabeth, Daniel, Rod,
and so many other visionaries buried in the soil that was Buganda:
Weebale emirimu—*thank you for your work.*

CONTENTS

ILLUSTRATIONS

MAPS

FIGURES

ACKNOWLEDGMENTS

"Kinship is eating," the Baganda say, succinctly expressing the meaning of membership in a community. The many forms of generous assistance I have received over the past decade have drawn me into communities that I treasure, and have made this book possible.

I am indebted to the Uganda National Council for Science and Technology for permission to do research in Uganda, and to the Makerere Institute of Social Research and the Center for Basic Research for providing me with academic homes. Financial support came from a Fulbright Dissertation Fellowship, a National Endowment for the Humanities Summer Stipend, from Mount Holyoke College Faculty Grants, and from travel grants provided by the Center for African Studies and the History Department at the University of Florida. I thank helpful, patient staff of the Uganda National Archives in Entebbe, the Uganda Supreme Court, the Uganda Society Library, the Uganda Ministry of Justice, the Uganda Department of Lands and Surveys, the Public Records Office, the University of Birmingham Library Special Collections, the Bodleian Library of Commonwealth and African Studies at Rhodes House, the Royal Commonwealth Society collection at Cambridge University, the University of Chicago Library Special Collections Research Center, and the Mount Holyoke College Library. I wish to particularly thank Dorcas Kigozi and Annet K. Nuwamanya of the Makerere University Library Africana Collection for their assistance over many months, and Peter Malanchuk and David Easterbrook, Africana librarians of the University of Florida and Northwestern University respectively, for their essential contribution to my work and to African studies.

This book began as a dissertation, and I am profoundly grateful to Steven Feierman for his wise advising and teaching. I thank David Schoenbrun for his impossibly hard questions, and R. Hunt Davis for his long investment in creating an African Studies community at the University of Florida. While there, I benefited immensely from courses and interactions with Fred Kaijage, Susan Kent, Sheryl Kroen, Carol Lansing, John Mason, Murdo McLeod, and Jeffrey Needell. In my life before graduate school, I learned to think about social processes from Farzam Arbab, Hooper Dunbar, Peter and Janet Khan, Daniel Rodgers, and Ian Semple.

I am also thoroughly indebted to the historians of Buganda whom I have encountered primarily through their written work: M.S.M. Semakula Kiwanuka, Christine Obbo, Benjamin Ray, John Rowe, Michael Twaddle, Henry R. West, Michael Wright, and Christopher Wrigley. The range, insight, and vivid detail of their work allowed me to ask the questions that I pose here. John Rowe graciously allowed me to copy records of the Lukiiko and other sources no longer traceable in Uganda. Richard Waller lent me a copy of his unpublished thesis on Buganda and offered cogent suggestions on many occasions. Scholars currently working on Uganda topics have also shared sources, ideas, and commented on my work: I appreciate the generous collegiality of Holger Bernt Hansen, Neil Kodesh, Glenn McKnight, Henri Medard, Nakanyike Musisi, Mikael Karlstrom, Richard Reid, Carol Summers, Aili Mari Tripp, and Michael Tuck.

Innumerable people in Uganda facilitated my research and welcomed my family with kindness, among them Anke, Hanna, and Benjamin Alemayehu, Dawn and Rod Belcher, Mathis Onama, Judith Butterman, Nafha and Shahram Ebrahimi, Ben and Jovita Ekoot, Vinita Gilbert, Catherine Kabali, Elizabeth Kharono, Janice Lever, Kasalina Matovu, Nakanyike and Seggane Musisi, Dorothy Ngalombi, Edith Senoga, Christine Deborah Sengendo, and Richard Ssewakiryanga. For hospitality in the vicinity of various European and North American archives, I thank Sue Bremner, Andrew Olson, Cristina Romani, Bahiyyih Nakhjavani, John and Mary Rowe, Julie and Gilles Scherrer, David Schoenbrun, and Kearsley Stewart.

I am grateful to several distinct networks of people who shared my family's life in Gainesville, Florida. I am still learning from my graduate school cohort, which included Tracy Baton, Catherine Bogosian, Edda Fields, Marcia Good Maust, David Mills, Todd Leedy, Kym Morrison, Michelle Moyd, Diane Oyler, Kearsley Stewart, and James Wilson. The support of the Bahá'í community—including Jose and Jeanne Diaz, Margaret Mattinson, Vasu Mohan, Chetan and Radha Parikh, Lynne Schreiber, Joanne Schwandes, and Harriet and Sam Stafford—allowed me to meet the needs of my children and the demands of academic production at the same time. My children's friends Virginia Dzul, Cristina Risco, Keenan Topp, Erik Cook, Robbie Fitzwilliam, and Orrin and Niles Whitten and their families absorbed us into their lives in ways that allowed me to write. Cathi Hodge and Larry Hyler helped in the same way.

My colleagues at Mount Holyoke College and in the Five Colleges have both lightened and enlightened the process of turning a dissertation into a book. I have valued conversations about my work in the History Department lounge, on hikes in the Pioneer Valley, and on Friday afternoons with the Five College African Studies Council. I am particularly grateful for Eugenia Herbert's comments on the dissertation, David Newbury's thoughts about the early chapters, Wendy Watson's knowledge of Vittorio Sella's photographs, and for the Five College Social History Seminar's careful reading and stimulating discussion of a draft of the introduction. John Lemly, Michelle Markley, Lynda Morgan, Mary Renda, and Eleanor Townsley have improved my prose on short notice: thanks to them and so many others for walks, talks, meals, and intellectual companionship.

My editors Jean Allman and Allen Isaacman made suggestions that substantially improved the book, as did the manuscript's anonymous reviewers. I am grateful for Don Sluter's maps, Nancy Howard Smith's assistance with artwork, Safietou Sagna's help with French, and the editorial suggestions of Jason Cook, Jennifer Kyker, Robert Redick, and Mark Riffe.

This book developed in the context of the compassionate friendship of Kathryn Burns, Peter Von Doepp, Kiran Asher, Rebecca Karl, and Jan Shetler. My heart's thanks to them, and to Robert, Marky, Steven, and Julie Hanson. Finally, I want to acknowledge my children, Corin Olinga Vick and Rebecca Margaret Vick, who avoided stepping on all the papers on the floor for many years, and who moved to Uganda and back in middle school and high school. I thank them for their courage, fortitude, grace, and good humor.

A NOTE ON LANGUAGE

One hundred years ago, those who lived in Buganda (a kingdom that became a region of Uganda) spoke a language known as Luganda and would have called themselves Baganda. I use these terms, but have adopted the simplified adjective "Ganda" to describe people, places, and things. I ask Luganda-speaking readers to accept this ungrammatical and unattractive concession to those not familiar with Bantu language noun-class prefixes.

The modern orthography of Luganda is slightly different than that used in the 1920s and earlier, when most of the documents cited were written. By paying attention to pronunciation and context the attentive reader will recognize that the "sekibobo" in a quotation is the "ssekiboobo" of the text, the "kibari" is the "kibaale," and so on. Current punctuation standards demand that proper names be capitalized but titles remain lowercased. Since Ganda chiefly titles also served as names, readers will notice that the "mugema," the "kiimba," and other chiefs also appear as "Mugema," "Kiimba," and so forth.

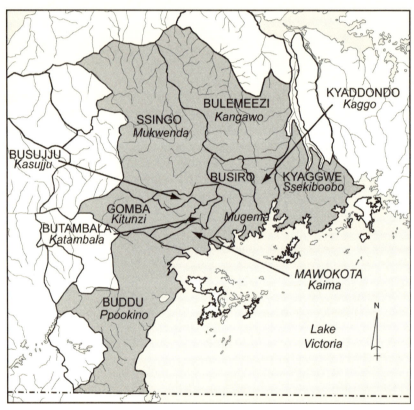

Map 0.1 Buganda Ssazas and Ssaza Chiefs.

xvi

A DYNASTIC CHRONOLOGY OF THE BUGANDA KINGDOM

King	Date of Reign According to Kiwanuka[1]	Date of Reign According to Medard[2]
1. Kintu	Beginning of 14th Century	
2. Cwa		
Probable Change of Dynasty		
3. Kimera	c. 1314–	c. 1400–1430
(generation without a king)		
4. Ttembo	c. 1374–1404	c. 1460–1490
5. Kiggala	c. 1404–1434	c. 1490–1520
6. Kiyimba	c. 1434–1464	c. 1520–1550
7. Kayima	c. 1464–1494	c. 1550–1580
Possible Change of Dynasty		
8. Nakibinge[3]	c. 1494–1524	
9. Mulondo	c. 1524–1554	c. 1580–1610
10. Jemba		
11. Ssuna	c. 1554–1584	c. 1580–1610
12. Ssekamaanya	c. 1584–1614	c. 1610–1640
13. Kimbugwe		
14. Kateregga	c. 1614–1644	c. 1640–1670
15. Mutebi		
16. Juuko	c. 1644–1674	c. 1670–1700
17. Kayemba		
18. Tebandeke	c. 1674–1704	c. 1700–1730
19. Ndawula		
20. Kagulu		

(*continued*)

King	Date of Reign According to Kiwanuka[1]	Date of Reign According to Medard[2]
21. Kikulwe	c. 1704–1734	c. 1730–1760
22. Mawanda		
23. Mwanga		
24. Namugala	c. 1734–1764	c. 1760–1790
25. Kyabaggu		
26. Jjunju	c. 1764–1794	c. 1790–1800
27. Ssemakookiro		c. 1800–1812
28. Kamaanya	c. 1794–1824	c. 1812–1830
29. Ssuuna	c. 1824–1854	c. 1830–1857
30. Muteesa I	c. 1854–1884	1857–1884
31. Mwanga	1884–1888, 1890–1899	
Kiweewa	1889	
Kalema	1889–1890	
32. Daudi Cwa	1897–1939	
33. Edward Muteesa	1939–1966	
34. Ronald Mutebi	1993–	

[1]M.S.M. Semakula Kiwanuka, *The Kings of Buganda*, 195.
[2]Henri Medard, "Croissance et crises de la royaute du Buganda au XIX siecle," 29.
[3]Christopher Wrigley argues in *Kingship and State: The Buganda Dynasty* that Nakibinge ruled after Kagulu in the mid-eighteenth century.

A Timeline for Buganda and Uganda

ca. 1000	Intensively cropped bananas become main subsistence strategy for some peoples around Lake Victoria.
after 1000	Communities growing bananas established by leaders and followers.
before 1500	Clans collaborate in Kintu worship.
	Clans collaborate in maintenance of spiritual medicine Mbajwe.
	Walusimbi kingship in central Ganda area.
ca. 1500	Innovation in spiritual practices in East African region brings lubaale worship to region north of Lake Victoria.
before 1600	Kabaka form of kingship established in Buganda heartland.
ca. 1700	Territorial expansion begins, leading to intensified internal competition, violence.
ca. 1740	Kabaka Mawanda names ssazas, creating the shape of modern Buganda.
ca. 1780	Kabaka Semakookiro ends competition among rivals for kabakaship by killing all potential kabakas.
late 1700s	Incorporation of thousands of captive women diminishes the status of free Baganda.
	Ebitongole chiefships increase; powerful men as well as kabakas create ebitongole.
early 1800s	Caravan trade reaches Uganda; kabakas attempt unsuccessfully to control it.
1868	First sale of people for cloth, as remembered by Apolo Kaggwa.
1877	Church Missionary Society (Protestant) missionaries arrive in Buganda.
1879	White Fathers (Catholic) missionaries arrive in Buganda.
1879–1884	Kabaka Muteesa holds theological debates in his court among Protestants, Catholics, and Muslims.

1870s–1880s	Competition among chiefs engaged in ivory and slave trade intensifies; kabakas' power diminishes as a result of chiefs' autonomous wealth and Muteesa's illness.
1884	Muteesa dies and Mwanga becomes kabaka.
1888	Mwanga overthrown and civil war begins.
	Imperial British East Africa Company chartered in England.
1889, 1892	Chiefs attempt to end civil war through schemes that incorporate new religions into order of chiefship.
1891	Imperial British East Africa Company agent Captain Lugard arrives in Mmengo and is drawn into land conflicts.
1893	Further realignment of land, chiefships, and chiefly titles to incorporate new religions in the order of the kingdom.
1894	British Protectorate formalized; British and Ganda collaborate in conquest of other regions of Uganda.
1897	Mwanga, in consultation with nnamasole, leads a rebellion against the Protectorate.
	Leading Ganda chiefs support British against Mwanga and against mutiny by Sudanese troops; Ganda-British alliance strengthened; chiefs rule under infant Kabaka Chwa.
1900	Uganda Agreement consolidates power of ruling chiefs under Protectorate, creates mailo land, imposes taxation.
1901	Railroad and lake steamer links undermine Ganda control of transport to Buganda.
1903–1908	Sleeping sickness epidemic kills two hundred to three hundred thousand people along shore of Lake Victoria.
1904	Cotton cultivation provides alternative to tax payment in labor.
1909	Kasanvu, obligatory paid labor, imposed by Protectorate.
1911	Ganda chiefs succeed in revoking a land law that would have facilitated land alienation during the mailo survey.
1918	Decades of heavy out-migration to avoid multiple labor demands cause Lukiiko to forbid people to move away from their homes.
1922	Kasanvu obligatory labor abolished.
	Case against mailo land heard by Kabaka Daudi Chwa.
1924	Case against mailo heard by Protectorate Commission of Inquiry into Butaka Clan Lands.
1927	Busuulu and Nvujjo law limits tenants' payments to landowners.
1949	Social turmoil and riots against chiefs in Buganda.
mid-1950s	Kabaka deportation crisis polarizes public opinion in Buganda.
1962	Uganda gains independence from Britain.

1966	Obote abolishes traditional kingdoms; kabaka flees to England and dies there.
1972	Asians in Uganda expelled.
1971	Military coup by Idi Amin leads to economic stagnation and social violence.
1979	Amin defeated by Tanzanian army and Ugandan exiles.
1980	Obote II regime characterized by massive human rights violations, war.
1986	National Resistance Movement led by Museveni comes to power.
1993	Traditional kings, including kabaka, restored.

1

INTRODUCTION

When people in Buganda thought about power, they spoke about love. The names of the oldest provinces of this East African kingdom commemorated loving services that powerful men had performed for its earliest rulers. Several centuries later, foreigners observed supplicants crowding the courtyards of important chiefs and royals, seeking signs of being loved by the powerful that would improve their standing. The vocabulary of love in governance accommodated ruthless violence, as nineteenth-century subjects knelt down to thank the king for the privilege of being stripped of their chiefships, or being sentenced to death on the king's whim. Yet even that king's reign would be judged by how many chiefs gave beads for the decoration of his tomb, because "a king died happy who had many chiefs."[1] A person rose to high chiefship, Ganda elders explained in 1906, "because the King loved him very much," and when Ganda leaders criticized British overrule in 1922, they complained that the new forms of governing "destroyed our good customs of helping and loving each other."[2]

   In the Ganda practice of power, visible expressions of love and affection created relationships of mutual obligation between people with authority and those they ruled. People in Buganda shaped relationships in this way over half a millennium and through profound transformations in the political and economic order. In the 1890s, Baganda described ceremonial exchanges that commemorated relationships of mutual obligation established among ancestor rulers and their followers many generations earlier.[3] In the mid-eighteenth century, people began to receive land because of the gratitude of a *kabaka* (king) for particular work they performed: in their love for him, they produced the king's ivory, clothes, sesame seeds for trade, and other essential commodities and services.[4] Ganda elders explained in 1906 that a nineteenth-century king would have taken care to not tax so heavily that people were unable to also give him presents voluntarily, and "to those whom he loved he gave what he chose."[5] When the colonized Buganda kingdom, as a province of the British Protectorate, improved the capital, the street leading from the new palace to the new parliament building was named "the kabaka loves me."[6] In 1990

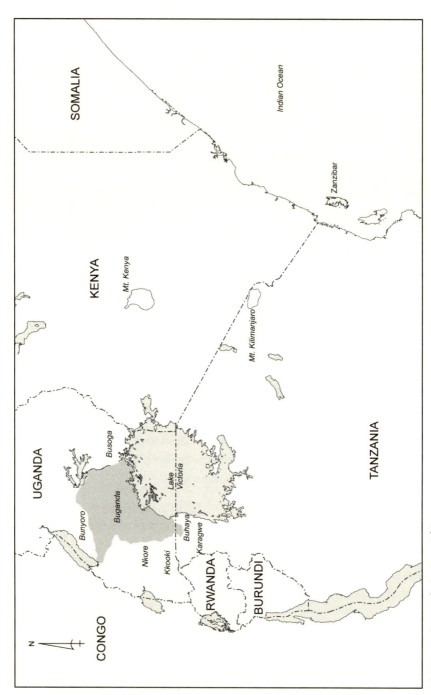

Map 1.1 Buganda in East Africa.

in the independent nation of Uganda, people living in the section of Kampala that contains tombs of the Ganda kings opposed an urban renewal project initiated by the Kampala city council, because it failed in the relational dimensions of good governance. They claimed that progress required consultation and that the proposed project showed "lack of feeling for the people," that it "would create enmity and division among families," and that for successful development "priority should be given to the social goodwill of the tenants, grassroots leadership, the elders and local residents."[7]

This book follows the Ganda association of love and power from the origins of the kingdom through the tumultuous argument over the nature of good government that occurred in Buganda in the 1920s. It examines what love in governance meant to the Baganda, and how a rhetoric of loving concern came to rationalize the extreme violence of nineteenth-century Ganda rulers. Over many centuries, people in Buganda used reciprocal obligation, pledged in land but understood as an expression of affection, to create connections, to incorporate strangers, and to vanquish competitors in an ongoing struggle for followers and prestige. Focusing on this core aspect of Ganda thought facilitates a line of inquiry that is not shaped by European experiences of social change. Mahmood Mamdani has argued that "history by analogy" deprives African societies of "an authentic future" as well as an accurate past, and Steven Feierman has observed the distortions that result because "the very categories by which we understand universal experience originate in the particular experience of the core of the capitalist world."[8]

Paying attention to the importance of love to power suggests new interpretations of familiar aspects of the history of Buganda. Evidence from ritual and from dynastic tradition suggests that kings, clan elders, and chiefs emerged as rulers with different kinds of authority through long patterns of interaction; they did not meet, fully formed, and begin to compete with each other long ago. In the distant East African past, people exercised power less by conquering than by coalition-building. The remembered history of allegiance and gift exchange suggests that followers' assent to being ruled was fundamental to Buganda: the kingdom was destabilized when followers could not leave chiefs or chiefs ceased to be able to withhold support from the king. This observation necessitates a revision of one of the most deeply held perceptions of Buganda's history. The innovations in chiefship that accompanied eighteenth- and nineteenth-century military expansion have been seen as a form of indigenous political modernization, but attention to the actual nature of the changes and the escalating violence that accompanied them suggests that the circumstances that have been described as a modernizing bureaucracy can also be understood as an imploding practice of reciprocal obligation, with drastic consequences for all the participants.

The way that Baganda wielded obligation and described it as love also affords insight into Ganda interactions with British colonizers and their economic and political institutions. Ganda leaders attached themselves to the British and then fought the British using the vocabulary of power marked in land, and when tightening British control after about 1910 distorted the exercise of reciprocal obligation on a kingdomwide scale, Baganda re-created its logic in miniature, turning small-scale land control into a new way to wield authority over clients. In the early twentieth century, Ganda chiefs and followers used the instruments of a commodified, capitalist economy, including wage labor and private property, to create social relations of obligation based on gifts of land. Power did not flow out of Ganda hands because the Protectorate authorities believed it to be theirs; rather, power derived from control of people and of resources, and colonial labor exactions and interference in the order of chiefship made it difficult and then impossible for Ganda leaders to maintain that control.

In the 1920s, as the consequences of British overrule became painfully apparent, a group of Ganda intellectuals brought a case against the exercise of power by the leading chiefs in colonized Buganda, which was heard on a colonial stage because Protectorate officials thought the issue was the wrongful alienation of clan graveyards. People who had exercised formidable authority in the decades before colonial rule, including royal women and men, the mediums of Ganda deities, and high-ranking chiefs, participated in the case. Some held the highest possible positions for Africans in the Protectorate administration, some had entirely lost their status, most of them were Christian. They argued that the arrangements of market economy enslaved people, and real social progress could be achieved through combining European knowledge with Ganda forms of power that embodied love. In order to comprehend their critique of modernity, we have to excavate their ideas from the strategies they adopted to make sense to their British listeners, and from the polarized caricatures of tradition-bound clan elders versus self-serving collaborators that have distorted our perception of their debate. The extraordinary circumstance of colonized Africans arguing with each other about the nature of good government before colonial commissioners who thought they were investigating a violation of property rights deserves more attention than it has hitherto received.

This book, then, is a study of an African habit of thought: the idea that people ought to be tied by bonds of affection, and that relationships between people became visible in gifts of land, goods, and service. It examines how people acted on that idea, from the time they used it to knit together a kingdom until the time they used it to criticize colonial practices of power. This approach emphasizes internal processes of transformation over external forces. Social and political structures were strained and sometimes broken when people lost the ability to withdraw from relationships of reciprocal obligation, which happened both before and after the beginning of colonial rule. In the eighteenth century, before Buganda's deepening involvement in a world economy, the polity knit together through bonds of reciprocal obligation frayed and almost collapsed as a result of the challenge posed by the importation of captive laborers. When long-distance trade in ivory and slaves exacerbated that process and the kingdom was convulsed by war in the 1880s and 1890s, Ganda chiefs re-created order by making innovations in the conceptual map of chiefly control over the land of the kingdom. People used the familiar and effective techniques of creating obligation to exploit emerging forms of trade, and to domesticate the power of strangers. They found ways to make colonial rulers, wage labor, and private property in land fit into Ganda categories and fulfill Ganda social purposes.

Irreparable disruptions to Ganda practices of social order came at moments when Baganda lost control of the means of creating obligation. Chiefs lost their traction over British officials and some of their authority over followers in 1901, when Ganda canoes ceased to monopolize lake transport, and the kingdom was flooded with goods brought in by train and steamer. The Ganda chiefs' inability to protect their followers from crushing demands on their labor, the Protectorate's drastic reduction in the number of chiefs, and a law that made leaving a chief illegal all undermined Ganda social order in the second and third decades of colonial rule. The protest that Ganda people launched against these conditions did not reject everything foreign and call for a complete return to the past; instead, it asked Protectorate officials to imagine the potential benefits of Ganda forms of authority combined with knowledge from Europe.

To comprehend Buganda in the past, one must imagine two kinds of essential locations. Banana gardens adjacent to every home were the most important. Bananas grew well in the consistently watered crescent of land north of Lake Victoria that became the Buganda kingdom, and in Ganda origin stories, Kintu, the first man, and Nnambi, the first woman, brought bananas to earth from heaven. Banana gardens, so abundantly productive that any amount of this staple food was always supplied freely to travelers and strangers, protected Buganda from subsistence crises and freed human labor for other activities. In the rich, green stillness of Ganda banana gardens, women produced the food that fed families, and the spirits of ancestors hovered in the play of light and shadow among the trees.[9]

Royal courts were Buganda's other essential location: wide, straight roads led from the compounds of principal chiefs to the center established by each ruler, carrying people offering tribute and labor to the king, to the queen mother, and to the other powerful figures whose authority contributed to the rule of the land. At the height of the kingdom's power in the eighteenth and nineteenth centuries, every gift was delivered and received with ceremony that registered its significance, and every hearing of a case or reception of a guest conveyed the relative status of participants. Visitors to the capital slept and ate in precise locations that delineated their allegiances to chiefs and the purpose of their visit. A few miles and a stream of running water separated the palaces of the king and queen mother, just as their distinct forms of authority contributed to the governance of the kingdom. The placement of the compounds of particular chiefs and of shrines to Ganda deities indicated their relative power and the history of their incorporation into the kingdom.

Rulers and followers created reciprocal obligation, the social glue of the Buganda kingdom, by giving gifts and by asking for gifts; and followers could dissolve relationships of obligation by refusing to participate. The imbalance in this equation is critical to understanding Ganda society. Records of tribute and histories of control over particular lands reveal dense, overlapping webs of obligation, indicating that people in power constantly competed with each other for followers, and frequently lost their followers to others. Vast numbers of authority figures had a place in the order of the kingdom, which meant that those who wielded power had to appear loving in order to hold on to their followers, or to gain prestige and the possibility of a larger following. Chiefs and rulers were constrained by the ever-present possibility that those below them could withdraw their assent to be ruled: followers might choose another patron, and chiefs could withhold the tribute and allegiance that created the ruler's power and align themselves in coalitions to pressure him.

Two examples of the creation of obligation with gifts, and two examples of the dissolution of obligation through refusal, can illustrate how people in Buganda strategized with the tool of reciprocal obligation. Henry Stanley, visiting Buganda in 1875, described gifts as a form of entrapment:

> When the traveller first enters Uganda . . . greetings with welcome gifts follow one another rapidly, pages and courtiers kneel before him, and the least wish is immediately gratified. . . . Meanwhile, however, the pages, pursuivants, messengers, and courtiers have been measuring him by rules and methods of their own. His faculties have been calculated, his abilities keenly observed and noted, and his general utility and value become accurately gauged. . . . [N]ow approaches the time for him to make return, to fulfil the promise tacitly conveyed by his ready and friendly acceptance of gifts and favours.[10]

According to Stanley, Kabaka Muteesa would ask the foreign visitor for technological assistance, in the manufacture of gunpowder, guns, cannons, ships, and brick houses, and when he admitted he did not have those skills, "why then he must pay in other coin. He has guns with him, he must 'give'; he has watches, 'give'; he has various trifles of value, such as a gold pencil-case, or a ring, 'give'; he wears good clothes, 'give'; he has beads, cloth, wire, 'Give, give, give'; and so 'give' to his utter beggary and poverty."[11] Stanley was obliged to give back because of the presents and favors he had received from the king.

How Ganda followers utilized their loyal service and the history of gifts they had received to sustain a relationship of obligation is evident in the story of a nine-year-old Ganda boy who joined the household of the Protestant missionary C. W. Hattersley sometime in the 1890s. He stayed there working for Hattersley for nine years. When the young man (whose name is not told) wanted to marry, he asked the man he had served for assistance in acquiring a plot of land. Hattersley told the young man to ask his father for help, but the young man said (as Hattersley remembered the conversation), "When I came to join your establishment I gave myself entirely to you. Since that time you are my father; I have no other. Were I to apply to my father, he would only refer me to you." Hattersley, however, did not think of himself as obliged to the young man. He had employed him for nine years, and now he was employing other boys, "and with my short pocket I cannot be always helping boys who have left me." He also explained to the young man that if he were to help him with the plot of land, the young man would also want help with the dowry, then with wedding clothes, then with the wedding feast. He told the young man, "It is very difficult to understand where such requests are going to end." Trying to get Hattersley to recognize his responsibility, the young man explained: "Sir, you altogether fail to understand the customs of the Baganda. Do you not know that the more requests we make the more we show our love for you. Were it not that I greatly love you, I would never ask you for a single thing. We never ask anybody we dislike to give us a thing." The missionary replied, "Perhaps in this particular case less love and fewer requests might suit my pocket better." The young man responded: "Sir, it distresses me much to hear you talk thus. I came to you because you are my father. You have been in Uganda many years, and I thought you knew our customs thoroughly. I hope you will never make such a remark to those who know you less than I do. At present they look upon you as a great friend."[12] Having invested nine years in a patron who chose to ignore the rules, the young man made the relationship work when he became housemaster of the Protestant missionaries' secondary school a few months later.[13]

A ruler's vulnerability to followers' choosing to exit from a relationship of reciprocal obligation is evident in dynastic tradition regarding Kabaka Kagulu, who ruled, according to M.S.M. Kiwanuka's calculations, at the beginning of the eighteenth century. According to tradition, Ganda chiefs "decided to rebel" because Kabaka Kagulu tortured people and buried them alive. They all refused to attend his court, and some of them gathered on a hill where they

could see the capital and mocked the king by saying, "Long Live Your Majesty.
We, your subjects, came here to deliberate." The king then had a drum made
with the beat "there is peace in the country, Kagulu no longer executes people.
Chiefs do come to the councils," but the chiefs still refused to attend his
councils, and this sign of rebellion motivated Princess Nassolo to lead a
revolt.[14]

The *Missionaires des Afrique,* or White Fathers, among the first foreign
visitors to Buganda, invoked the followers' capacity to exit without thoroughly
realizing what they did. Kabaka Muteesa created a small chiefship for Father
Lourdel, who had arrived in his powerful, prosperous kingdom with other
French Catholic missionaries in 1879. Kabaka Muteesa had already given the
strangers transportation across Lake Victoria, well-thatched conical houses in
a compound not far from his palace, bulls, goats, and unnumbered baskets of
cooked food, demonstrating his willingness to receive them into his kingdom.
The king's gift of banana gardens raised their status from guests to clients,
as productive land committed the receiver to provide loyalty and service to
the land granter, to attend the discussions held in his courtyard, and to serve
him. The missionaries, however, seem to have understood the land as a gift
of property rather than a contract of service: they wrote that such a valuable
present showed the king's goodness, and would be a great convenience to
themselves.

The relationship seemed like a settled thing; it was strategically wise for
the Ganda king to keep the missionaries under his control and direct their gifts
to himself and not to his rivals (the queen mother and a few central chiefs)
or his underlings. The Ganda king's intention to make Lourdel a client had
been documented: the messenger who had been appointed to show them their
land, and observers who had watched the ceremony of their receiving it, could
no doubt have been produced as witnesses. The French, furthermore, indicated
by their actions that they accepted their role. They attended court regularly,
offered gifts, and responded to the king's requests.

The missionaries' decision to leave Buganda in 1882 was a blow to
Muteesa. When they fled (having been unnecessarily frightened by unsubstan-
tiated rumors), they took their prestige and usefulness with them to Bukumbi
in Usukuma, south of Lake Victoria. Kabaka Muteesa, powerless to force them
to resume their place, sought to draw them back by asserting his appreciation. His messenger told them: "Mtesa often asked me why you left Buganda:
he does not want the whites to stay in the south. He is very surprised that
having left on good terms you did not send a greeting to him since you left,
even though you are not far. He has kept a good memory of you, he has told
me that you gave him nice presents, and that you healed him. Why have you
left?"[15] The missionaries assured the king that "nothing at all could displace
him, we are still his friends," but used their bargaining power to say they would

only return to Buganda if the king left them undisturbed as long as they chose to stay in the south. Kabaka Muteesa's weakness in relation to his French "chief" who had abandoned him illuminates the dynamic of power relations in Buganda.

The relationships of reciprocal obligation that people created using exchanges of productive land embody the history of Buganda. The kingdom held together and grew as people drew each other into these relationships, and it experienced escalating violence and disorder when the glue of obligation no longer held. The following paragraphs outline how these practices unfolded in events over the centuries, indicating the topics covered in each chapter of this book. Having established a foundation of what actually happened in this African kingdom, this introductory chapter then describes the sources used in the study and considers the usefulness of Buganda for thinking about encompassing questions in African and world history.

Social institutions which drew people into a group and placed the highest possible value on "wealth in people" can be traced in the distant African past. The people who settled in the East African lakes region more than two thousand years ago brought with them practices of incorporating strangers and attaching followers to leaders that helped people create security in environments that did not yield an abundance of food. As people gradually came to depend on intensive banana cultivation for their sustenance around the shore of the lake, sometime around A.D. 1000, the relationships of reciprocal obligation that bound people together began to be marked in land for permanently cultivated banana gardens. Predictable rainfall, rich soils, and low population densities meant that settled communities became established in conditions in which followers were in high demand and land was abundant. Chapter 2 demonstrates that in the centuries that the kingdom developed, from about 1200 to 1700, people used the vocabulary of reciprocal obligation to create the connections between multiple centers of power that became Buganda. I emphasize the slow development of the social institutions that came to be called kings, clans, and chiefs, arguing that the perception that kings arrived and took power from preexisting clans oversimplifies ancient patterns of social relations.

The record of alliance and accommodation among royals, powerful chiefs, and the representatives of Ganda deities suggests that Ganda leaders had at times succeeded in using the logic of reciprocal obligation to quell or avoid conflict. The wars of expansion of the eighteenth and nineteenth centuries, however, upset the balance of power in ways that could not be easily resolved. Large-scale importation of war captives into Buganda created social turmoil because it undermined kings' and chiefs' reliance on their followers. Ordinary Baganda experienced extreme erosion of their status, and competition for the spoils of war drastically intensified rivalry among chiefs. In an attempt to resolve this crisis, Kabaka Mawanda, who ruled early in the eighteenth century, rationalized chiefly control over territory, but his efforts did not quell internal violence or restore stability. Chapter 3 documents the successful use of the logic of reciprocal obligation to incorporate the power of *lubaale* spiritual forces into Buganda, and the failure of Kabaka Mawanda's efforts to reorder the kingdom and end the internecine bloodshed.

Kabaka Semakookiro, who reigned in the late eighteenth century, resolved this turmoil by killing all potential pretenders to the throne, an action that irreparably damaged Ganda social order and unleashed a reign of terror. When people could no longer exert pressure on a king by threatening to support another prince, kings could treat their people with brutal violence. As Buganda became involved in long-distance trade in ivory and slaves in the mid-nineteenth century, life became even more precarious. The possibilities of gaining personal power by enslaving others undermined what remained of Ganda authority. In this tumultuous and trying context, thousands of Baganda converted to Islam and Christianity. As a result, the civil war fought in Buganda after enslavement had destroyed legitimate authority had Protestant, Catholic, and Muslim factions. In order to end the war in the 1890s, Ganda chiefs inserted new religions into the conceptual map of the kingdom, imposing allegiance to a new faith onto the order of chiefship. In Chapter 4 I argue that nineteenth-century kings attempted to neutralize the threats posed by long-distance trade and new forms of production by creating new kinds of chiefships, and when that effort led to civil war, Ganda chiefs reimposed order in their country by incorporating new religions into the arrangement of control over Buganda's ten provinces.

British imperial entrepreneurs entered Buganda around the time the civil war ended, and the first decades of their presence had many of the characteristics of alliance asserted by the coalition of Ganda chiefs who had won the civil war. At a time when Captain Lugard and other officers of the Imperial British East Africa Company claimed to be in control, Baganda took actions and made statements demonstrating that they ruled the kingdom and the British were their friends. Chapter 5 explains the Uganda Agreement of 1900, which created *mailo* (private property in land) as a deliberate attempt by Ganda chiefs to reclaim the authority they lost as the burdens of British "overrule" intensified.

Baganda embraced literacy, Christianity and Islam, and the cloth and other manufactured goods that came streaming into their country from the late nineteenth century onward. This enthusiasm for the new caused foreign visitors to describe the Baganda as more eager to adopt civilization than their African neighbors, but a thorough examination of Ganda interaction with foreigners reveals them to have used new things in ways that allowed them to pursue Ganda social aspirations. The difficulties of the first decades of the twentieth century came not from processes inherent in more thorough participation in a world economy, but from deliberate, coercive interventions that British colonial authorities made in Ganda life in order to secure labor and taxes. Crushing demands wore down Ganda social institutions and changed the nature of chiefship. Chapter 6 explores Ganda uses of the opportunities created by cash wages, cash crops, and land as property and the insuperable dilemma posed by coercive colonial extraction.

Chapter 7 documents the Ganda critique of modernity. After twenty years in which the labor exactions of British colonial rule had created extreme social class differences, and the hierarchy of chiefs had been reduced from several thousand to a few dozen under tight supervision, Ganda intellectuals decried uneven land owning and a narrow political hierarchy as forms of enslavement. According to these thinkers and leaders, what ruined "the good customs of Buganda" was not the presence of the British, whom they welcomed, nor the mechanisms of a capitalist economy, which they exploited. They claimed that the highly diffuse, intricate webs of authority and obligation that had characterized their country in the past would be the best foundation for progress in the future.

The arbitrary creation of landed property in 1900 makes this study possible. Mailo—individually owned land, called mailo because it was originally allocated in square miles—was a fundamental violation of logic that forced people to document who had held land, and to put into words how power expressed in land had functioned. In an intense, politely waged power struggle, British commissioner Harry Johnston and ruling Ganda chiefs decreed that all the land of the kingdom would thenceforth be owned by the king and other royals, by the chiefs, or by the Protectorate. Johnston had originally intended to alienate most of the land to the Protectorate to encourage British settlers and create revenue, with estates for the king and a few high-ranking chiefs to ensure their prestige. The Ganda chiefs, by 1900 bitterly aware that "friendship" had a different meaning for their British "friends," insisted that each one of the chiefs and figures of authority in the Buganda kingdom would receive property in land, and that the Baganda would choose their land first. They won: the Protectorate eventually came to possess worthless swamps and rocky hilltops, and thirty-seven hundred Baganda who had controlled land because they had exercised power became owners of land. Aware of British intentions to take the land of the kingdom, the chiefs compiled a much more elaborate list of chiefs and figures of authority than they might have produced if the stakes had not been so high. The mailo allocation list therefore maps forms of authority and complex relationships of obligation that had shaped Buganda in the lifetimes of the chiefs who created the lists in 1900, at a time when the exercise of power was undergoing profound transformation. Some of the authority figures allotted land in 1900 had already lost their role in governing during the civil war of the preceding decade; only a handful retained chiefly appointments when the British rationalized chiefship some years later, and whole categories of chiefship ceased to be remembered in the following decades.

The terms on which private property was created represented a victory for the Buganda kingdom in its war over dignity with the newly arrived Protectorate officialdom, but the leading Ganda chiefs were the real winners. Having emerged victorious in the Ganda civil wars of the 1880s and backed the winning side during Kabaka Mwanga's rebellion against British rule, they used the mailo allocation to assume a kabaka's prerogative to give the best land to those he loved the most, and gave themselves massive territories, much larger than any chief had ever controlled in the past. That the ruling chiefs had prevented a massive land-grab by foreigners mattered much less to people than the appropriation of the best Ganda land by those same chiefs. Their self-serving action set the stage for an ongoing dispute about land and power in which the Baganda who benefited from the mailo allocation and those who had lost land appealed to Protectorate authorities to take their side against their opponents. These arguments, offered to everyone from district commissioners to King Edward, concerned not only who ought to control particular lands, but why their control of the land was essential to the welfare of Buganda.

Mailo land was an affront to the meaning of things, like ripping a wall off of the comfortable house of ideas people inhabit, and the result was an outpouring of statements to remember the house as it had been. The chiefs' distribution of land articulated their perception of the structures of power in Buganda, recorded with due solemnity on land certificates, surveyors' maps, and land registry lists. Those who felt their authority merited estates and who had not received them immediately attacked the mailo allocation with statements explaining their right to land and power based on generations of remembered clan or family history. Many people who had wielded power received a mailo allocation, but not the right land, and they sought the assistance of missionary allies as well as complaining to colonial authorities, documenting their connection to the particular land they had lost. British anxiety about the upheaval led to an informal inquiry in 1906, at which dozens of clan elders and chiefs explained the use of land in the Ganda system of power. Twenty years later, Ganda social discontent crystallized in a tumultuous public protest about mailo land. The culmination of this protest was a public inquiry under British colonial auspices in which people explained what Ganda society had been like in the past in order to prove that the allocation of land—and the organization of society—had been utterly corrupted by mailo, while their adversaries argued that mailo land had been a sign of the British queen's love for Buganda, and actually in harmony with the absolute sovereignty of kabakas in the past.

The massive documentation of this fight among people who had held power is valuable as a historical source because all the protagonists argued using Ganda logical categories. The conflict was not between colonized Baganda and their colonial masters, but among Baganda, who all attempted to draw Protectorate officials into their coalitions against their Ganda adversaries. While statements addressed to Protectorate officials often invoked a hazy, idealized Buganda of the past, their arguments with each other—carefully recorded by colonial clerks—centered on specific actions that marked relationships of obligation. For example, people disputed who had controlled Bussi Island in the 1880s with questions of fact. From whom had the residents received permission to hold a funeral? Who had commanded their labor? Had a messenger from the king ever had to go through an intermediary to reach them? The actions and processes they fought about point to the continuously practiced habits that created the shape of Ganda social order. Keeping alert to the issues that mattered when Baganda argued about who controlled which people, how, and when, it is possible to see the same patterns of interaction in records that span several hundred years. This analysis of reciprocal obligation in Buganda correlates the sticking points of the conflict over mailo with earlier and later conflicts over authority. These include tribute and gift obligations which probably emerged sometime after 1700, disagreements about the nature of kings' gifts to followers he particularly distinguished in the late nineteenth century, conflicts over remuneration for work and chiefs' efforts to meet colonial demands for labor between 1900 and 1920, and landowners' disputes with tenants from the 1920s to the 1950s. All these sources reveal how people in Buganda used land as an idiom for social power, and how that practice changed over time.

Ganda ideas about the meaning of things can also be discerned as a consequence of Ganda enthusiasm for literacy and conversion to Islam and Christianity, which occurred from the 1870s onward. Ganda leaders incorporated written documentation into their way of doing things in the mid-nineteenth century, creating evidence of what people were thinking in private diaries, personal papers, and published memoirs written by Ganda leaders in the 1890s and the first decades of the twentieth century. The Baganda also wrote down the records of the Ganda consultative body, the Lukiiko. Like many other African people, Baganda initiated their interactions with foreigners with the assumption that peaceful, productive, and equitable relations would result, but Ganda chiefs remained convinced of this possibility much longer than others. In their communications with Protectorate officials, whom they perceived as fellow Christians, Ganda chiefs offered advice, responded to requests, and asked for redress for unjust behavior in a way that reveals their sense of how the relationship should have been, and also how people with power ought to behave in relation to each other.

Figure 1.1   Ssekiboobo hosts Governor Bell to tea, ca. 1908. The ssaza chief of Kyaggwe Ssekiboobo, like other Ganda leaders, offered hospitality to Protectorate officials in the cultural idiom of their guests. (Royal Commonwealth Society Archives, Cambridge University)

The European visitors in Buganda, beginning with Speke in 1862, created records of their experiences that enhance our understanding of how Ganda society worked. The early explorers' efforts to be seen, to be fed, and to get what they wanted embroiled them in conflicts that reveal competition among the king, the queen mother, and other powerful figures. The detailed station diaries of the White Fathers document how figures of authority at different levels interacted with each other in relation to the kabaka. British officers sent to the kingdom gave Ganda social and political institutions greater respect, more space to continue to exist relatively undisturbed, than they granted to the institutions of neighboring polities. The military alliance Ganda chiefs forged with arriving British colonial forces clearly contributed to this, as did the skills at cultural translation that Baganda had already developed in decades of intimate interaction with Catholic and Protestant missionaries. Some Protectorate officers responded positively to the overtures of Ganda chiefs—the invitations to evening prayers and the skillfully given presents—and interacted in a way that protected Ganda institutions from direct attack. It is therefore possible to use missionary and colonial sources to observe Ganda social institutions continuing to function, and changing in subtle, incremental ways, into the period of colonial rule.

Ganda litigants, letter-writers, and diarists of the late nineteenth and early twentieth centuries knew what they thought about social order, and they valued eloquent speech. Their articulate and passionate statements regarding what mattered in the past and what they imagined for the future can contribute to our efforts to understand encompassing questions regarding African societies and their place in an interconnected world.

Baganda who explained the superiority of Ganda forms of governing with love believed what they were saying. They would have taken issue with Bourdieu's assertion that reciprocal exchange is always symbolic violence. Ganda reciprocal obligation was a set of practices that people could use to many different ends; leaders sometimes ruled through terror, but rulers also created alliances and became powerful through visible acts of generosity. When the social order was rocked by gruesome violence that sickened insiders as well as foreigners, Baganda wielded reciprocal obligation to draw people back into nonviolent relationships. It did not always work, but it never stopped making sense to people. To assert that "gentle, hidden exploitation is the form taken by man's exploitation by man whenever overt, brutal exploitation is impossible" naturalizes domination and makes it inevitable.[16] This perception impedes our capacity to recognize forms of power that may not have been coercive, and erases the possibility of nonoppressive relationships in the past or in the future. Humanity's capacity for moral choice is lost in a teleological expectation that human beings have always oppressed or been oppressed, and that only a future reorganization of social and political structures will create conditions for production characterized by moral interaction. It is more complicated, but perhaps more useful, to acknowledge that a particular habit of thought or social institution can at times oppress and at other times empower.

Baganda who interacted with missionaries and Protectorate officials never stopped hoping that their foreign visitors would learn dignified, polite behavior. They modeled appropriate actions in gifts, hospitality, and service that overwhelmed their guests, and filled their letters and speeches with praise that had an undertone of admonishment. Many strangers received Ganda names that remarked on their rudeness, lack of refinement, and appalling self-absorption.[17] Their visitors, in response, wrote home about the strangeness of Ganda hospitality and their bizarre requests; most, eventually even most missionaries, stopped reciprocating Ganda overtures of friendship. This un-resolved conflict exemplifies the enduring, subtle disagreement about whose symbols would define power, the purpose of production, and the obligations of people to each other that characterized the colonial period.

In order to unravel conflicts over meaning in colonized Africa, it is useful to keep in mind Antonio Gramsci's observation that power is exercised through unquestioned patterns of thought and action. Ganda and British decision-makers in colonized Uganda all thought they knew what they were doing, but each person's actions expressed not only his deliberate intentions, but also in-visible, unacknowledged accumulations of meanings. The commissioner's splendid dress white uniform (which one senior chief tried to purchase) or the habit of welcoming guests by sending messengers to greet them every few minutes (which Captain Lugard emulated) were statements of power that had long histories.[18] To comprehend the engagement of Baganda and foreigners in the realm of ideas, we have to keep in mind the salience of enduring hab-its of thought, as well as people's capacity to innovate and make new mean-ings. Many Baganda, some missionaries, and a few colonial officers exerted themselves to create an arena of common understanding. People became fluent with flags and barkcloth trees, amulets and crosses, books and drums. To some degree, people exercised conscious intention in the meanings they chose to attach to things, but the hidden, accumulated meanings also continued to shape people's actions.

In the complex and constantly changing struggle to make a dramatically different world make sense, people could simultaneously hold on to what they knew to be true and incorporate new things to make new realities. The story of Ganda Christianity and Islam is, in this way, similar to that of Ngwato Christianity described by Paul Landau. Ganda Christian and Muslim converts sought to reshape their beloved land following the intentions of the Word of God they had embraced. However, they understood their new faiths in deeply Ganda terms. Beginning in the seventeenth century, the rituals for installing a kabaka involved a ceremony in which the new king sharpened a brass spear on the living body of a large python, which was held in place by many people, and then the python was let go. Since East African ances-tors chose to reside in the physical bodies of snakes, especially pythons, and pythons had been the sacred emblem of cults that had predated the king-dom, this action vividly asserted the king's supremacy, and his followers' assent to it.[19] Bartolomayo Zimbe, a Christian participant in the civil war, described encountering a huge python on the path of the fleeing Christian army in 1888:

> Kisingiri Zakaliya said something that made all laugh. He said the Mos-lems say Christians eat snakes. The thing to do now is to cut this snake into

two. The tail part is to be left in the middle of the way while the other is to be taken so that when they come and see it they will think we do really eat snakes. This will really stop them from following us and they will go away making exclamations.[20]

The Christians, closely followed and attacked from the rear by the Muslims, decided to do this, but according to Zimbe, when they cut up the python, as if "one would think they were probably cutting an animal," "all . . . laughed not a lot as if out of sheer joy but sadly."[21] The sad laughter of Ganda Christians slaughtering a sacred python, and the strategies these men employed fighting a civil war and consolidating their victory, suggests the complex lineages of power that shaped social relations in colonized Africa.[22]

The Ganda insistence that ill feeling undermined good government and that rulers and followers ought to love each other illuminate an important dimension of the history of power in East Africa. Many different people came to have authority over people and territory north of Lake Victoria, and heterarchal forms of authority gave people choices. A person could be the follower of many different kinds of authority figures, could show allegiance with one mechanism or with another, could get a leader to take a desired action by calling up one line of obligation or a different one. In contrast to a habit of thought that sees power as something that is fought over, and when one group has gained it another group has lost it, power in the East African past seems to have been something that had to be assembled, and people only had it if others agreed that they had it. The evidence of heterarchal power provided by mailo documents complements work on this topic by Susan Keech McIntosh and others.[23]

Heterarchal forms of authority meant that the practice of power involved assent. Everyone, including the king, the queen mother, and the most important chiefs, could only achieve their ends in interaction with others who had the same goals. People left one patron if another patron seemed to present better opportunities; even a page in the kabaka's court could report that he had left his position in the palace because "they ruled him badly."[24] That followers exercised their ability to refuse to be ruled badly is evident in the distant past in the dense, overlapping webs of tribute that indicate extreme competition for followers in the oldest parts of the kingdom, and more recently in the mass movement out of Buganda to avoid colonial coercion in the first years of British rule. The capacity to exit, to withhold allegiance, created political accountability in Buganda in the past. Clients were vulnerable to exploitation whenever their decision to withdraw support did not matter to their patrons. The incorporation of thousands of female war captives into Buganda in the eighteenth century and the possibility of buying people in the nineteenth century made free followers less necessary to chiefs and precipitated a drastic decline in their status. Colonial authorities had to supplement their onerous labor demands with laws forbidding peasants to leave their chiefs; even so, thousands of Baganda exercised their right to refuse bad treatment and fled Buganda.

The female dimensions of Buganda's gendered forms of authority eroded in the nineteenth century and almost disappeared in the twentieth. The complex web of relationships that had comprised power in the kingdom had included queen mothers and queen sisters whose power mirrored the king's, royal wives who received tribute and maintained connections with particular regions, and princesses whose social position made them potential leaders of rebellions against a reigning king.

The loss of political complexity was among the most enduring consequences of British rule for ordinary people in Buganda. The traction people had negotiating a relationship with one of approximately four thousand chiefs and figures of authority was utterly lost when British authorities had reduced the number of chiefs to fewer than one hundred. Whether participatory democracy successfully restores the capacity to generate political accountability that people had experienced with heterarchal forms of power is a question worthy of consideration. It seems possible that habits of thought such as the image of the father as ruler, described by Michael Schatzberg, or what Goran Hyden calls the "economy of affection," had different dynamics before the precipitous narrowing of political authority that occurred in the early twentieth century. Mahmood Mamdani considers that colonial authorities "captured" what had been a free peasantry: attention to the dynamics of reciprocal obligation suggests that peasants got stuck when they lost the capacity to choose whom they would follow.[25]

This assertion of the utility of heterarchy directly contradicts the well-established perception of Ganda monarchy as a "modernizing bureaucracy." In an influential essay on chiefship in Buganda, Martin Southwold argued that in the eighteenth and nineteenth centuries Ganda kings centralized power in a way that turned formerly autonomous chiefs into a bureaucratic staff under the king's control.[26] Based on innovative research by Lloyd Fallers that contrasted overlapping forms of authority in the oldest parts of the kingdom with simpler patterns of control over land in territories acquired later, this scholarship helped to create a perception of the Ganda past in which kings with the power to appoint chiefs took land and power away from preexisting clans, demonstrating the capacity of an African polity to modernize on its own.[27] Although historians M.S.M. Kiwanuka, John Rowe, and Michael Twaddle have all noted that this narrative oversimplifies the relationship of kings, clans, and chiefs, the modernizing Baganda continue to appear in scholarly works—most recently as "defensive modernizers" in Philip Curtin's study of imperialism.[28]

   This book seeks to replace the popular image of a successfully modernizing Ganda oligarchy. A closer look at the Baganda exposes flaws in the assumption that all societies must inevitably be drawn into a process of social and political change that follows nineteenth-century Europe. Although this habit of thought sounds absurd when stated so bluntly, it can be traced from early imperial apologists, to modernization theorists, marxists, and development experts in the mid-twentieth century, to structural adjustment enforcers and both advocates and critics of globalization in the present. In Buganda it was social upheaval, not an impulse to top-down organization, that led to the reordering of chiefship that has been seen as the creation of bureaucracy, and that reordering did not yield stability. The Ganda chiefs who built two-story square houses, bought vehicles, and sent their children to college using the profits of their mailo land were not trying to be Europeans—they had other, well-defined goals.

   New patterns of accumulation and new forms of labor challenged social structures in many parts of the world in the late eighteenth and early nineteenth centuries. In Buganda, the possibility of massive accumulation of wealth for a few undermined social practices that had made rulers accountable and protected followers. This happened elsewhere in Africa; Pier Larson's work on Madagascar, for example, documents the subtle, incremental process through which the possibility of obtaining wealth through enslavement wore down political, lineage, and family relationships and transformed social structures.[29] At the same time that Ganda and Malagasy cultivators endured loss of security because of massive accumulation by a few through enslavement, British cultivators experienced a loss of security because of massive accumulation by a few through industrialization. Michael Perelman's study of classical political economy and primitive accumulation in England explores how market imagery came to rationalize the political decisions that eliminated what had been a universal right to self-provisioning.[30] Freed from an analytical framework that makes Britain's experience a model for others, these processes can be productively compared. According to Karl Polanyi, the "smashing up of social structures in order to extract the element of labor from them" happened all over the world, and involved the assent by the wielders of political power to the false notion that economic activity operated in a sphere distinct from social and political relations.[31] This observation directs attention toward the role of political power in the commodification of social relations, and to its visibility.

   To be civilized, for the Baganda, was to offer readily apparent generosity that attracted people. British visitors did not, in general, meet their standards.[32] An anxious letter from Archdeacon Walker to the Church Missionary Society passed on criticism from Reverend Samwili Mukasa regarding the Mengo Hospital practice of charging for medicine.

The people are unreasoning and look at the whole question from the point of "kindness" and they say the R.C.s [Roman Catholics] are the kinder. . . . He says the R.C.s send medicine to any one who is ill, and go and see them. They give away free of all charge their medicines. The fact that there may be no cure is not considered any objection to the medicine when it has not been paid for and when it was given in kindness and not professionally. The more I see of these people the more I see that kindness is the one thing necessary in their eyes. They do not say one man knows more than another or that he speaks the language better, or that his skill is greater, or that his religion is purer, the one thing is he is *kinder*. This is of course a childish way of reasoning but with these people it is all important. I do not mean by *"kinder"* that he gives away more but it is the manner, the unselfishness and effort to please and interest others.[33]

Roman Catholic priests made their concern for people visible with their gifts and their presence, and that visibility is essential to distinguishing Ganda goals from modernization on the British model.

Multiple, overlapping forms of authority meant that rulers in East Africa took great care to make their power visible. In Buganda, power was displayed in the seating arrangements in gatherings of chiefs before the kabaka, in the siting of buildings in the capital, and in the precise composition of gifts that flowed between representatives of Ganda deities, powerful chiefs, royal women, and the king.

For decades, Baganda fought with Protectorate authorities about whether power would be visible. British authorities attempted to make power less visible through taxation that compelled labor, in their manipulation of chiefship, and in their (unsuccessful) effort to turn uncultivated land into Crown property. Baganda attempted to demonstrate their power through visible expressions of their control over productive relationships. In the earliest years, chiefs created opportunities to demonstrate their ability to call forth labor: as Protectorate demands grew, they became less able and less willing to find laborers. People acquired land to settle followers, and engaged in competitive consumption of European goods not because they had acquired a desire to accumulate, but because they sought the prestige and social benefits associated with power over people. Wage labor and private property in land created new means to pursue those goals, while colonial threats to the Ganda practice of power, such as forced labor and the reduction in the number of chiefships, threatened people's hold on social power. The practice of reciprocal obligation had economic consequences, as Ganda land owners consistently beat the government in the competition for labor.

In 1899 the tired and irritated acting commissioner Colonel Ternan wrote of the Ganda ruling chiefs, "They are a grasping lot and want the advantages of both the old and new regimes and none of the drawbacks of either."[34] This observation was not intended to be a compliment at the beginning of the imperial era, when Europeans rationalized their presence in Africa as a civilizing mission. Forty years after the end of colonial rule, when existing practices of production are clearly not creating well-being for most of the world's people, the aspirations of Ganda leaders invite attention. This inquiry into the African past is shaped by an awareness that world-encompassing patterns of production and exchange have not yielded prosperity, and fundamental rethinking seems to be necessary. The assumption that productive activity linked to social relations is primitive while productive activity severed from social relations is progressive seems to be one fruitful arena for reconsideration. A careful examination of how the Baganda used economic activity to create social relations and political obligation, and how those strategies worked at times and failed at other times, can reveal the blind spots and borders in our perception of how things have to be. People who have created social movements insisting that love must be part of economic interactions, as some Baganda did in the 1920s, may not have been the ones looking backward.

NOTES

1. Apolo Kaggwa, *Basekabaka be Buganda,* typescript translation by Simon Musoke, Makerere University Africana Collection, 58. Slightly different translation in Apolo Kaggwa, *The Kings of Buganda,* trans. and ed. M.S.M. Kiwanuka (Nairobi: East African Publishing House, 1971), 57.

2. John Roscoe and Apolo Kaggwa, "Enquiry into Native Land Tenure in the Uganda Protectorate" Rhodes House, Bodleian Library, Oxford, 21 [hereafter cited as "Enquiry," giving the name of the informant]; Appeal to Kabaka Daudi Chwa by the "Buganda National Federation of Butaka," February 1922, Public Records Office (PRO), CO 536/133, 550. The Luganda verb *okwagala* translates into English as "want, desire, love, and like, and, as an auxiliary, to be about to do something." John D. Murphy et al., *Luganda-English Dictionary* (Washington, D.C.: Catholic University of America Press, 1972), 612.

3. For example, the many offices related to carrying for the shrines of dead kabakas in Busiro and other ancient clan privileges on Bussi Island. Bataka Land Commission, PRO, CO 536/133, Lew Nsobya, on behalf of Walusimbi, 466; Antwani Kaikuzi, 425. (Cited hereafter as "Commission," followed by the name of the witness.)

4. Among many others, "Commission," Zakayo Nkuwe, 391; Mikairi Kidza, 401; Juma Owamanyi, 429; Apolo Kaggwa, 505, 521; Danieri Serugabi, 540, 542–543.

5. "Enquiry," Tefiro Mulumba Kuruji, 34–35.

6. John A. Rowe, "The Pattern of Political Administration in Precolonial Buganda," in *African Themes: Northwestern University Studies in Honor of Gwendolen M. Carter,* ed. Ibrahim Abu-Lughod (Evanston: Program of African Studies Northwestern University, 1975), 68.

7. Aili Mari Tripp, *Women and Politics in Uganda* (Madison: University of Wisconsin Press, 2000), 181, 183.

8. Mahmood Mamdani, *Citizen and Subject* (Princeton: Princeton University Press, 1996), 9, 12; Steven Feierman, "Africa in History: The End of Universal Narratives," in *After Colonialism,* ed. Gyan Prakash (Princeton: Princeton University Press), 50.

9. Ham Mukasa explained the visible presence of ancestors' spirits in butaka to Audrey Richards. January 7, 1956, Audrey I. Richards fieldnotes, Box 32, Folder 12, Lloyd Fallers Papers, University of Chicago Library.

10. Henry M. Stanley, *Through the Dark Continent,* vol. 1 (1878; rev. ed., 1899; reprint, New York: Dover, 1988), 318–319.

11. Ibid., 319.

12. C. W. Hattersley, *The Baganda at Home* (1908; reprint, London: Frank Cass, 1968), 189–190.

13. Ibid., 190.

14. Kaggwa, *Kings,* 63.

15. White Fathers *(Missionnaires des Afriques), Chronique Trimestrielle,* vol. 24, March 12, 1884 (Center for Research Libraries, Cooperative Africana Microfilm Project MF 2530), 241.

16. Pierre Bourdieu, *Outline of a Theory of Practice,* trans. Richard Nice (Cambridge: Cambridge University Press, 1977), 192.

17. George Wilson, fluent in Luganda and beloved by Baganda, was known as "Bwana Tayali" because his first question, on arriving in camp, was "Chakula tayari? Whisky soda tayari?"—"Are my food and drink ready?" Bell also mentions an assistant district commissioner known as "Mr. One Plate" for his marked disinterest in entertaining guests. Sir Hesketh Bell, *Glimpses of a Governor's Life: From Diaries, Letters, and Memoranda* (London: Sampson Low, Marston, n.d.), 193.

18. W. J. Ansorge, *Under the African Sun* (London: Heinemann, 1899), 136; Margery Perham, *Lugard: The Years of Adventure, 1858–1898* (London: Collins, 1956), 307–308.

19. Robert P. Ashe, *Chronicles of Uganda* (New York: Randolf, 1895), 112–113; David Lee Schoenbrun, *A Green Place, a Good Place: Agrarian Change, Gender, and Social Identity in the Great Lakes Region to the Fifteenth Century* (Portsmouth, N.H.: Heinemann, 1998), 197.

20. Bartolomayo Musoke Zimbe, *Buganda ne Kabaka* (Mengo, 1939), typescript translation, "Buganda and the King," Cambridge University Library, 211.

21. Ibid., 217.

22. Nancy Rose Hunt, *A Colonial Lexicon of Birth Ritual, Medicalization, and Mobility in the Congo* (Durham, N.C.: Duke University Press, 1999).

23. Susan Keech McIntosh, ed., *Beyond Chiefdoms: Pathways to Complexity in Africa* (Cambridge: Cambridge University Press, 1999).

24. "Commission," Danieri Serugabi, 540; Sir Apolo Kagwa, *Ekitabo kya Kika Kya Nsenene* (Mengo: AK Press, n.d.), manuscript translation seen courtesy of John Rowe, 14.

25. Michael G. Schatzberg, *Political Legitimacy in Middle Africa: Father, Family, Food* (Bloomington: Indiana University Press, 2001); Goran Hyden, *Beyond Ujamaa in Tanzania: Underdevelopment and an Uncaptured Peasantry* (London: Heinemann, 1980); Mamdani, *Citizen and Subject,* 17.

26. Martin Southwold, *Bureaucracy and Chiefship in Buganda: The Development of Appointive Office in the History of Buganda,* East African Studies no. 14 (Kampala: East African Institute of Social Research, n.d.).

27. Lloyd Fallers, "Social Stratification in Traditional Buganda," in *The King's Men,* ed. Lloyd Fallers (New York: Oxford University Press, 1964), 64–113.

28. M.S.M. Semakula Kiwanuka, *A History of Buganda from the Foundation of the Kingdom to 1900* (New York: Africana, 1972), 120–121; John Rowe, "Revolution in

Buganda, 1856–1900" (Ph.D. diss., University of Wisconsin, 1966), 25–26. Michael Twaddle observes that the one time when a distinction among bakungu, batongole, and bataka might make sense is in the 1880s, when kabakas attempted to regain control of the polity by creating many new *ebitongole* chiefships. Michael Twaddle, "Muslim Revolution in Buganda," *African Affairs* 71 (1972): 54–72, 58. Philip D. Curtin, *The World and the West: The European Challenge and the Overseas Response in the Age of Empire* (Cambridge: Cambridge University Press, 2000), 116–127.

29. Pier Larson, *History and Memory in the Age of Enslavement: Becoming Merina in Highland Madagascar, 1770–1822* (Portsmouth, N.H.: Heinemann, 2000).

30. Michael Perelman, *The Invention of Capitalism: Classical Political Economy and the Secret History of Primitive Accumulation* (Durham, N.C.: Duke University Press, 2000).

31. Karl Polanyi, *The Great Transformation: The Political and Economic Origins of Our Time* (Boston: Beacon Press, 2001), 172.

32. Rowe, "Revolution," 122.

33. Walker to Baylis, November 11, 1899, Church Missionary Society Papers at the University of Birmingham, G3 A7/0 1900, no. 3.

34. Ternan to Clement Hall, June 27, 1899, PRO Foreign Office (FO) Series FO 2/202, 261–267.

2

CREATING RELATIONSHIPS
WITH GIFTS OF LAND:
LINEAGES, CHIEFS, AND
ROYALS INTERACT TO
MAKE THE STATE,
CA. 900–CA. 1700

Neatly cut, thickly thatched grass bundles rose in a smooth dome to a tufted pinnacle to form the large, dramatic buildings that so impressed early visitors to Buganda. Three concentric roof rings, each named and decorated with red, black, and natural papyrus fronds, supported a structure of reed poles on which the thatch was laid. People built houses from the roof rings outward: builders placed the rings on temporary supports, attached the framework of reeds (and further, unnamed roof rings) until it was large enough to reach the outer circle of posts, and then lifted the structure, something like a funnel-shaped spider's web, onto its permanent posts. For some important buildings, construction began with the roof ring placed on the head of the chief in charge of the building. The central rings could not be used again when a house was dismantled, and the specialists who made them for the king were exempted from taxation.[1] The pinnacle on a large house was two feet tall and three feet wide, made of concentric circles of thatch with the tallest circles in the middle.[2] Thatch was laid from the lower edge, where the roof touched the ground, up to the pinnacle: bundles had to be placed carefully and tightly next to each other, because no stitching was used to hold the thatch onto the framework of reeds. A Ganda home was remarkably like the Ganda kingdom: it had an essential and obvious center, but hundreds of connections in the structure gave it strength, and thousands and thousands of elements, held together tightly, gave it substance.

Ganda people made a connection between buildings and political order: the pinnacle of a building was a *kitikkiro,* and the prime minister of the kingdom was the *katikkiro.*[3] A map of the kingdom as it existed in the nineteenth century would have resembled the inside view of the walls and ceiling of a home: broad, well-maintained roads led in straight lines from the court of every provincial chief to converge on the palace of the kabaka, the central roof ring of the kingdom.[4] Kabakas lived at the center of the kingdom, at the top of Buganda's patterns of power and exchange. In the 1880s, people told the missionary Alexander Mackay that "the axis of the earth sticks visibly out through the roof of the conical hut of their king."[5] Tribute in labor and in goods, and the respect and obedience of subordinates, flowed toward the king like the perfectly aligned strands of elephant grass that made the walls and roofs of Ganda buildings. Many people's work, many people's voices, and many people's authority as decisionmakers made the Ganda kingdom.

In oral traditions, the world had always been that way: Kintu, the first king, brought Nnambi, his wife, and the first banana shoot from heaven to establish the kingdom.[6] Stories explain how some clans received their land from Kintu or a following king, and how others had welcomed the kings and therefore been granted the land they already occupied. Chiefly authority came from the king also: "[I]n the beginning of the world the King called the people together to receive their chieftainships. He sent out messengers to call them, and among others he sent the dove to call the moon, and the bat to call the sun."[7] These stories explained the present (that is, the present at the time the stories were written down, about one hundred years ago), but spoke less clearly about the processes through which kings came to be the center of Buganda.

Although the roads in Buganda eventually pointed to the king's palace like the straight lines of grass in a Ganda roof, the polity grew out of much more complicated connections between communities. Eventually, kings did call people and give out chiefships, but in earlier generations, people had become chiefs by leading the process of opening new land, and several different kinds of people had the capacity to muster the necessary labor. In order to comprehend the beginning of Buganda, it is important to step back from the recorded oral tradition and pay attention to other sources as well, such as ethnographic descriptions of the customs of the kingdom, historical linguistics, and the farming dynamics of intensive banana agriculture. This allows us to move beyond the most commonly accepted version of this past—that kings came from outside, found clans, then took the land from clans and gave it to their favorite chiefs, creating a centralized bureaucracy. Apolo Kaggwa, the architect of Ganda-British cooperation, explained Ganda history in this way in

1906, only a few years after he led a comprehensive reallocation of Ganda land in which he was the biggest winner and clans were the biggest losers. His explanation raises suspicions because it so perfectly rationalized his own actions, and because people who had not benefited from colonial rule remembered the past differently. Furthermore, the evolutionary quality of this interpretation is also problematic. To see clans as archaic institutions and kingship as more advanced obscures the political character of clans, and the ways that clanship, chiefship, and kingship as institutions affected and developed each other.[8] It also ignores the important role played by religious practice in the creation of the polity. The story of kings vanquishing clans assumes a kind of dominating power—that one entity (kings) wanted to take power, authority, and resources from another entity (clans) and succeeded in doing so. This does not fit with what we know about the exercise of power in ancient East Africa, which seems to have been much more oriented toward assembling coalitions of capacities. It also does not fit with the character of social institutions in Buganda, which showed much more compromise and much more attention to relations among participants in a field of power than a story of kings winning over clans would explain.[9]

I argue in this chapter that the people who became Baganda created a kind of vocabulary of reciprocal obligation, marked on land, to define relationships among sets of people, and that they used the connecting capacity of those relationships to assemble the Buganda polity. In its earliest stages, this process involved a gradual reshaping of familiar Bantu social institutions such as marriage, lineage, and chiefship in response to the permanent, fixed-in-space, and highly productive characteristics of intensive banana cultivation. The next stage involved the creation of coalitions among units of people. At this time, roughly after 1200 and before 1700, chiefs, clans, and kings had different characteristics than they assumed later, but the earliest names in the king list probably refer to this period. Some of the forms of association, such as the Mbajwe cult and the Kintu cult, crossed what would become the geographical boundaries of the Buganda state; others, such as kingship with a leader named Walusimbi at its head, appear to have been practiced exclusively in regions that became Buganda. The Ganda kingdom in its familiar form developed through the intentional interaction of leaders who had various forms of chiefly status and a new kind of king who was probably an outsider, but may have been an insider who put himself forward with foreign innovations. People drew the new king into their spheres of activity through strategic deployment of the logic of reciprocal obligation, and the new king and his successors adopted the same language.

Ganda clans, chiefship, religion, and monarchy took their familiar shape from these interactions, which are remembered in rituals, in clan traditions, and in patterns of tribute and obligation. This chapter explores how clanship, chiefship, and kingship evolved as the people living north of Lake Victoria incorporated permanent cultivation of bananas into the structures of their lives. By making an effort to look beyond the recorded dynastic tradition, we can see more clearly the participants who were not kings, and the interactions that were not submission to central power. The dense, overlapping lines of authority that characterized Buganda recorded the many participants and the multiple struggles that had made the state.

INTENSIVE BANANA CULTIVATION AND THE SHAPE OF SOCIETY

The long, slow process through which people who lived north of Lake Victoria intensified their cultivation of bananas probably began around the turn of the first millennium. We know it happened between A.D. 1000 and 1500 because Luganda has almost one hundred terms for banana varieties and processing that speakers of its grandparent language did not use.[10] Over these centuries, banana gardens became a necessary part of establishing a marriage, connecting to ancestors, and being a chief or a follower. The patterns of interaction of the Ganda polity seem to indicate that the kingdom was assembled out of structures of relationships marked in banana gardens.[11]

In the centuries before intensive banana cultivation, people in this region maintained themselves through a combination of labor-intensive activities. They farmed tubers and beans in intercropped fields, and may have grown sorghum and finger millet. We have a glimpse of this time in the origin story of the Yam clan, which explains that members of the clan do not eat yams because their ancestor Sedumi tried to steal yams from his wife's relatives, but was discovered and committed suicide out of shame.[12] For root crops, people formed mounds in the fields and kept them weeded. Harvested yams had to be peeled and pounded to make meals. Grains had to be weeded several times in a season, threshed, and pounded. People prepared their fields with iron hoes and wooden digging sticks. Since soil fertility was low, they had to practice rotational cultivation, opening new fields every few years; staying close to worked fields would have forced people to move and rebuild their homes every few years. They also kept cattle, fished, and hunted and supplemented their diet with gathered wild food.[13] David Schoenbrun has hypothesized that severe rainfall fluctuations between 950 and 1100, combined with reduced soil fertility and increased erosion caused by overcultivation and deforestation, made productive agricultural land less available than it had been at any time before or has been since.[14]

A transition from mixed farming to intensive banana cultivation would have involved a period of time in which members of a household allotted their time among many different kinds of work. In the gendered division of labor we know from later ethnographic observation and a few historical linguistic hints, men cleared fields, women weeded, young men herded, everyone participated in harvesting, and women threshed grain and prepared food. Since untended banana plants continue to grow and can be returned to productivity quickly once they are weeded, women may have paid attention to bananas during the slack times in the agricultural calendar when root and grain crops had been harvested and men concentrated on hunting.[15] It is possible to imagine that women devoted more energy to banana cultivation in seasons when inadequate rainfall or soil exhaustion reduced the need to weed their other crops. More production from banana gardens, and less from root and grain fields, would have gradually changed people's eating habits toward bananas as a daily food. Since growing bananas involved less men's labor than grain and tuber crops, a transition toward banana cultivation would have meant that men spent less time on agriculture, leading gradually to a shift in perceptions of gender roles.

Women's work of banana cultivation eventually became so central to the ancestors of the Baganda that it defined marriage: the terms for marriage in the grandparent language (spoken before A.D. 500) had been *kuswera,* "to marry a woman," and *kuswerwa,* "to be married (by a man)." In Luganda a man married with the action *kuwasa,* "to cause (someone) to peel bananas," and a woman married with the action *kufumbirwa,* "to become the cook (for someone)."[16] Marriage rituals reveal the incorporation of banana cultivation into people's concepts of what marriage was about. The gift exchanges that marked a marriage were all things of value in a mixed-farming agricultural system. The groom gave an initial gift of salt, beer at the engagement, a brideprice that people remembered as having included beer, salt, meat and tobacco, and later cowries as well as presents of bark cloth and goats to members of the bride's family.[17] When the bride first visited her parents in a ceremony called "taking back the butter," she carried the package of butter that her mother had smeared on her on her wedding day. The two last wedding rituals stated the wife's obligation to cook and cultivate bananas. She returned from her father's home with a procession of her relatives carrying food for a feast, including bananas, salt, chickens, goats or a cow, sesame, and mushrooms, which she was supposed to cook. The bride then visited her husband's parents' home, where she was rewarded for doing each of the tasks of a daughter; she had to continue hoeing in the banana garden until her mother-in-law called her to stop, and her mother-in-law gave her a knife for cutting down and peeling bananas.[18]

By the nineteenth century, access to banana land was an essential dimension of marriage practice. In order to marry, a man had to obtain land for a home and for his wife's banana garden by aligning himself with a chief. A woman indicated her willingness to marry with a form of the verb *kusenga* ("to join a new chief") in the statement *"nefunide obwesenze bwange"* ("I have found my master/my home").[19] In the most common form of marriage, a

Figure 2.1 Ganda home from banana garden, 1906. Baganda built houses from the top down by tightly layering broad-bladed grass on a framework of reeds placed on pillars. A family's banana garden surrounded their home. (Vittorio Sella)

woman's control of her productive capacity followed the logic of reciprocal obligation: a woman went "on a tour of exploration" to choose a husband, and a woman could withdraw from marriage if she felt she was being mis-treated.[20] Women who had been given to their husbands in some forms of marriage without bridewealth could convert their marriage to one with a follower's rights in a relationship of reciprocal obligation through a practice called "treating one's relatives-in-law with disrespect." This process, *okweebuula obuko,* involved the wife returning to her own family until her husband made the necessary gifts.[21] In marriage, women exchanged hard work for social esteem: a woman whose hoe handle broke because it had been worn through by hard use received the gift of a goat from her husband.[22]

Reliance on banana cultivation affected people's lineage and clan practices, just as it had worked its way into marriage. People who devoted more and more attention to banana groves around A.D. 1000 must have gradually altered their deeply ingrained habit of moving homes to stay close to worked fields. In the distant past African farmers maintained the fertility of their relatively poor land with long fallow periods; in the forest, the ancestors of the people who came to live around the East African lakes broke new fields every three years and moved their homes about every decade. The pole and tied-grass construction of their dwellings facilitated this habit, because homes needed to be replaced every few years. We can imagine that women trekked back to banana groves from their homes when bananas were one among many significant food sources. As people came to derive more of their food from bananas, they might have decided they could tolerate the lower yields that would come with reduced fallows for their other crops, and the period between moves might have grown longer. It is also possible to imagine that people became fixed in one location without really intending to, when they kept their home near a productive banana grove that had become more important to their diet. Eventually, Baganda stopped moving their homes. Only the king's capital continued to be moved every few years, a residual of the earlier practice.[23]

Living in one location and cultivating the same land for long periods of time, even whole lifetimes, changed the transcendent aspects of life as well as the material ones. People developed new practices for remembering ancestors and elaborated the relationship of the living and the dead. Among the ancient beliefs of the Bantu language speaking peoples around the lake was that the life force of a person, *mwoyo,* was indestructible and continued to exist after death. The Baganda said, *"Omwoyo tigumera nvi"*—"The soul does not have white hair."[24] At death the soul became a *muzimu,* an ancestor spirit.[25] Ancestor spirits needed living people to remember them in order to continue to have a presence in this world, and (one thousand years ago) living people needed the active assistance of their ancestors. Since religious practices changed radically around five hundred years ago and again in the colonial period, we have to look carefully for evidence of the role of ancestor spirits in earlier centuries. The Otter clan's tradition regarding their ancestor Mwanga-Kisole, whose ghost had taken a medium when he died and who "looked after the well-being of the clan, multiplied their cattle, and made their women fruitful" suggests what people may have expected from ancestors in general.[26] A nineteenth-century practice in which a wealthy man or chief offered a feast for a particular ancestor spirit also suggests the responsibility of ancestors to the living. In these feasts, the ancestor spirit received beer and the blood of a sacrificed animal, family and friends ate meat, and in return the spirit increased the donor's wealth, children, and influence.[27] Writing about the *cwezi* form of spirit mediumship in Kitara, a region that is now northern Uganda, Renee Tantala has argued that daily, small-scale offerings and petitions, and a sense of reciprocal obligation, characterized the relationship between spirits and living people in earlier centuries.[28]

People who lived around Lake Victoria remembered their ancestors through sacrifices at graves and shrines and through practices of spirit possession, in which an ancestor "seized the head" of a living person and spoke through that person.[29] Ethnographic evidence suggests that sacrifices happened periodically: people held a feast to remember ancestors at least once a year north of Buganda in Bunyoro, and south of Lake Victoria in the Western Serengeti, some peoples returned to sites associated with important ancestors periodically to make sacrifices or to obtain special material for rituals; others went to these places at the initiation of a new age set, or to ask for assistance in a crisis.[30] People north of the lake also made periodic sacrifices for ancestors buried in banana groves, but the presence of the graves in a place that people stayed for decades seems to have added a dimension to the way they remembered ancestors. The work of maintaining a banana grove in which ancestors were buried became in itself a way of remembering those ancestors. Julien Gorju, the insightful missionary whose ethnography described his observations of Uganda between 1895 and 1919, described how this happened at the turn of the twentieth century: "And what to say of those who stay in the village, in the shadow of the tomb, living the name, and in intimate communion with the person who carried it before? Because this is not a distant memory, the essential cult of the religion is domestic, invocations and ritual offerings to the departed, the influence which is attributed to them, all of this constantly brings their names to the lips of the living."[31] All the people who cultivated land on which ancestors were buried did the work of remembering, and, we can assume, expected to benefit from doing so. When an ordinary man died and was buried in a banana grove, one of his widows with children had to stay there, maintaining that grove, and remembering him.[32]

The continuing, daily usefulness of buried ancestors to the descendants who lived and worked around their graves created *butaka,* the lands associated with clans that people consider to be the origin of Buganda. It is important to keep in mind that these fertile lands with clan graves did not come into being about one thousand years ago because clans buried their members on land that belonged to them, but rather because the buried ancestors claimed the land for their descendants. As the Baganda said, *"Ensi engula mirambo"*—"Land is acquired through tombs."[33] Jan Shetler has observed a similar way of thinking about land for people in Mara, south of Lake Victoria, who shared until about A.D. 100 a common language with the people who became Baganda. In Mara, even land that was not cultivated was occupied by the spirits of ancestors who were propitiated in sacrifices, and stranger ancestors had to be expelled or co-opted for successful occupation of an area.[34] In the presence of permanent banana gardens and permanently maintained graves, this relationship became much more concrete: the people who benefited from the attentions of those ancestors, and who had the responsibility of maintaining their memory, had moral and instrumental obligations connected to the banana gardens with their ancestors' graves.

The butaka was a crystallization on productive land of a relationship between living people and an ancestor who had been exceptionally influential during his or her life. Sometimes the living people remembered both the ancestor and a heroic deed: in Ganda folklore, a man who succeeded in capturing the monster python Kalungu, who had been killing all the people in a region, was made a chief and the garden the python had occupied became a butaka for his descendants.[35] The place where Princess Nassolo and her servant captured and killed the wicked Kabaka Kagulu became a butaka for the servant's lineage.[36] People chose to gather in a place that became butaka because of the power of the buried ancestor, and generations of active remembering made the space butaka.

A butaka came into being when people chose to live in the vicinity of the grave of an important or powerful person: it was not a three-generation mechanism for creating absolute rights to control land, which is how it is often understood in scholarship on Buganda.[37] In the 1906 investigation of Ganda land tenure practices, Apolo Kaggwa told John Roscoe that three generations of ancestors buried on land created a butaka, but Roscoe's notebook records Ganda elders' statements that "this applies to chiefs and not to peasants," "the body must be of a chief who was in charge of the land," and "this was not often done, only to a few chiefs."[38] The rarity of butaka allocation, quite at odds with Roscoe's view, is evident in one prince's explanation: "It makes a difference as to the length of time between burials, it should last over the reign of two or three kings. A good butaka should contain about 10 bodies of chiefs, the length of time also makes a difference, some butakas have 50 or 60 bodies in."[39] According to Prince Rasito Kawaga, Kaggwa had a personal motive for claiming that butaka could be created in three generations because he had convinced the vacillating Kabaka Mwanga to create a butaka for his lineage on land that contained the grave of Kaggwa's peasant grandfather and two other relatives.[40]

Over the centuries, the burial of important people became a way of assembling transcendent and material power for coalitions of people, and a component of the negotiation of power relationships between those who competed for authority. Continuing cultivation of a grove with ancestors buried on it maintained a relationship between the living and the dead. The work of remembering carried out on butaka asserted people's connections to ultimately powerful individuals and defining moments in the history of the kingdom. Those ties legitimated their control of the best lands for banana production. The power of important buried ancestors to draw followers to the land around their graves helped to establish the pattern of access to land that came to characterize the Ganda state. Gradually, the coalitions of people that are present-day clans came to claim the butaka lands now associated with each clan (see Map 2.1).

The power of the dead over land became the major instrument in the ideological battle over who would control the most fertile lands. Baganda traveled

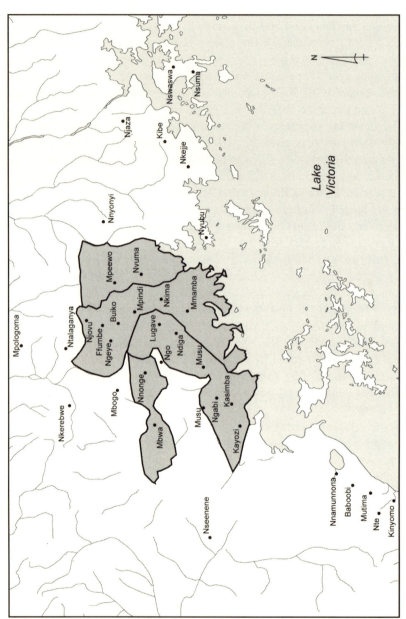

Map 2.1 Principal Clan Butaka. (Derived from L.A. Fallers, *The King's Men*, 77)

to take the body of an important person to the appropriate location for burial if he (or she) had died in another place, and also exhumed the bodies of significant members of the lineage who had not been buried in the butaka. Men who had been leaders in the late nineteenth century described this kind of disinterment as normal; witnesses before the Butaka Land Commission in 1924 described both reburials and the tragedy of important men who had been buried in inappropriate places.[41] Thousands of people might gather in a butaka for the funeral of a clan head: in 1906, Nsimbi, a chief of the Lungfish clan, said eight to twenty thousand would gather for an important funeral.[42] Eventually, kings became part of the process of butaka creation by naming—ratifying—an area with generations of significant graves as butaka, an action that would gain them the gratitude of the favored clan and reduce the resources of whoever had controlled that land previously. Kings did not wield authority over buried ancestors even after the monarchy became powerful: graves had to be removed from any area that a kabaka intended to use as his capital. Since kings came to have sovereignty over all the land, it seems likely that graves had to be removed in order to eliminate the power of the buried ancestors to thwart the kabaka's actions.

People used land differently as they gradually replaced mixed farming with intensive banana cultivation, and the changes in land use led to innovations in patterns of political authority. The settled, fixed quality of intensive banana cultivation gave people a way of naming and developing relationships of obligation between people, just as it had enabled an elaboration of connections between the living and the dead. In contrast to the gift of crop land that would be fallowed after three or four seasons, the space given for a banana garden established a relationship between the ruler who gave it and the follower who received it that could last for decades. Like any other gift, the gift of a banana garden made the connection between ruler and follower visible, but this gift produced much more food per unit of land than yams and grains, and facilitated the enduring prosperity of follower and chief. Over time, the allocation of banana land became the way that Ganda people defined relationships that involved the power of some people over others.

Evidence of the naming power of gifts of land for banana gardens can be gleaned from an oral tradition referring to the early eighteenth century. Nkalubo rose in influence through being given three successive plots of land, before the most important part of the story (in which he saves a future kabaka from death in the womb):

> There were two brothers who went to live under Nawandugu at Lubu, having immigrated from Sese. Their names were Nkalubo and Miingo. Nkalubo decided to leave Nawandugu and to become the Kabaka's man being presented before the throne by Sewankambo, and receiving a plot of land near the palace from the Kabaka then reigning—Ndawula. From day to day

Nkalubo paid a visit of respect to the Kabaka and soon he gained favour the outward sign of which was: a new plot nearer to the palace where Sebugwawo now resides.[43]

Each stage in Nkalubo's progress was documented in a plot of land: first he was a follower of the chief Nawandugu, then he became a follower of the king and received land, then he became more favored and received land whose exact location was still remembered approximately two hundred years later.[44]

Banana gardens gave people a new vocabulary for relationships: in marriage, with ancestors, and between givers and receivers of land. These relationships were highly visible, extremely productive, and potentially stable. As the polity developed, people assembled the parts of the kingdom using expectations of reciprocal obligation between chiefs and followers.

A COALESCING POLITY

Before the reign of the first kabaka, the people north of Lake Victoria organized their communities under various kinds of rulers who had the capacity to allocate land, and the people attached to those rulers also created broader forms of collective endeavor. This section examines clan eldership, the rule of a "big man," and cult authority as forms of leadership that preceded chiefship under the kabaka. It explores evidence for the Mbajwe cult, the Kintu cult, and Walusimbi kingship, and considers how Buganda grew from these diffuse forms of overlapping social organization into a kingdom with clear boundaries under a king entitled kabaka.

Several kinds of authority figures and their followers created forms of association that began the Ganda polity. A careful examination of the available evidence suggests that the rulers who allocated land included people who would later be seen as clan heads and people who would later be seen as chiefs. In other words, the perceptions that clans held the land of Buganda before the first kings is too simple—it imposes characteristics that clans developed in their interaction with kings into the past.

The most ancient forms of polity in Buganda assembled out of coalitions of people who had authority as the "fathers" of clans and others who were members of clans but probably had authority because of their wealth and ability to mobilize followers. As Schoenbrun points out, the Great Lakes Bantu word for "chief," *kungu,* comes from a word that means "to gather up, assemble," and it seems likely that the ability of *bakungu* to assemble the resources to maintain people in new communities created their political power.[45] Clans had been amorphous, non-contiguous groups before the transition to intensive banana cultivation, and patterns of authority over land seem to indicate that this did not change. People of any clan could live on land associated with the graves of a particular clan, and the clan elder who controlled the land had the responsibility of ruling all the people on the land, of whatever clan, as well as carrying out clan responsibilities for a dispersed clan group.[46] The "father" of a clan who controlled land with clan graves could invite people into his area but could not keep people on his land who chose to find another place to live. People who left created communities with other leaders, whose ability to attract followers might have come from spiritual power, from the attractive power of an exceptional buried ancestor, or from charisma or well-massed material resources. A place for alternative leaders to assemble power existed because land was abundant.

In order to establish a community on a ridge that was not already occupied, people would have had to marshal considerable human capital. Since the impulse for intensive banana cultivation seems to have come from an environmental crisis in which land had been worn out from overcultivation, the people establishing new communities dependent on banana agriculture may well have been clearing mostly elephant grass, not forest, to establish fields.[47] Even if a new community began in a very small way, the work of clearing fields and building homes would have been vast. Banana suckers take eighteen months to three years to come to fruition. Beginning communities would have had to rely on gifts of food, and on crops of sweet potatoes and grains, during that time. Some new communities must have been established with the help of clan relatives, a process that is evident in the way grave sites for minor lineages radiate out from those of superior, older lineages.[48] An important or wealthy man may also have mobilized followers to establish a new community. A nineteenth-century confirmation of the capacity of the wealthiest individuals to create communities using their own resources is evident in the statement "it is the usual custom for the Katikiro to open up new land."[49] With a sufficiently large number of followers, a powerful man could muster and feed the labor force necessary to open land, settle people on it, and maintain them until they had sufficient crops. A concerted effort by people following a religious movement might also have established new communities.[50]

In the several hundred years during which intensive banana cultivation became firmly entrenched, population densities increased and people opened new land to banana cultivation. The patterns of political and social activity people established profoundly influenced the shape of the future Ganda polity. Two ecological factors—the abundance of land and the differing potential of that land—gave people the capacity to move out into new land and the motivation for doing so. An almost infinite number of new small chiefships could be formed in this process, and as a result, competition among chiefs for followers characterized the practice of power in Buganda.

The multiple forms of authority that later characterized the Buganda kingdom developed in a geographical context of abundant land that was not all

equally suitable for banana cultivation. Flat-topped hills and ridges that extend like long fingers into Lake Victoria make up the landscape of the region. These land forms have a characteristic soil structure: on the top of the
hills are thin gray soils that grow short grass, good for cattle but not for
crops. Banana gardens are planted in the middle and upper slopes of the hills
in rich, productive soils, called "red" or "chocolate" loam. Neither the sandy,
acidic soils of the lower slopes nor the wet, clayey soils of the valley bot-
toms are very productive.[51] The ancient Bantu word for "settlement area,"
tala, came to mean a settlement spread out a long a ridge or hill in the area
rich in "red" soil, but this word also came to signify uncultivated land.[52] That
"settlement" and "unoccupied land" have the same root suggests both that
unoccupied land becomes a settlement and that ridges on which people are
settled have unoccupied land. Social practices were premised on land availability. For example, a woman could withdraw from marriage and receive
land to cultivate from a brother, and young men who reached adulthood
sought a chief to whom they would attach themselves and from whom they
would receive a plot of land.[53]

Since bananas could support a higher population density than mixed agriculture, the population must have increased in the several centuries that accompanied the transition to banana cultivation. The same land would have
accommodated more people, and we can surmise that gradually higher food
yields would have led to population levels that required some people to move
out from the *ekyaalo,* the settled ridge that was their home, to another place.
One story of the semi-mythical Kintu is that he left the area of Mangira, which
was populated, well-cultivated, and under the control of a clan leader, for the
Mabira forest.[54] A synthesis of remembered clan histories suggests that the
areas that are remembered as being settled first are those where banana agriculture would have been most successful: Kyaddondo, which has a long shore
on Lake Victoria, Mawokota, which is also on the edge of the lake, and
Butambala, immediately behind Mawokota. The areas farthest from the lake
were the last to be settled.[55]

While there is no evidence that people in the region that became Buganda
ever experienced an absolute shortage of arable land, the region has some areas
that are distinctively better for growing bananas than others. One reason for
this is that some regions have a higher percentage of productive soil than other
regions. In southern Buganda, up to 80 percent of the land surface is "red"
loam; in the north only 65 percent of hillsides are "red" earth, and a higher
percentage is less productive lower slope soil.[56] The other factor that deter-
mines how good land is for growing bananas is rainfall. Banana plants need
consistent rainfall all year long in order to yield fruit constantly. The ridges
and hills closest to the lake provided the best land for bananas, because warm
wet air rising from the lake, and cooling on the hillside, provided reliable

rain.[57] Two rainfall zones have adequate precipitation for continuous banana production: a short zone immediately on the lake shore that receives forty-five to seventy inches of rain in nine out of ten years, and a zone next to it that receives forty to sixty-five inches of rain in nine out of ten years. People seeking a place to establish themselves clearly wanted to settle in these areas, rather than in the dry belt. This area receives twenty-five to forty inches of rain most years, runs from the southwest to the northeast of the country, and was much more sparsely populated.[58] However, it is essential to keep in mind that even in southern Buganda, where the soil was best for bananas and the rains were most reliable, the hilly landscape caused rain shadows and subtle but essential differences in moisture available to gardens from the path of mists rising from the lake every day. In the mid-twentieth century, people had a keen sense of which land was best for banana cultivation.[59]

Since allocating land to followers established the authority of a chief, these environmental conditions allowed an almost infinite elaboration of small chiefships. More than four thousand figures of authority were recognized in the mailo allocation in 1900, and during the negotiation between Protestants and Catholics regarding how to share the main chiefships in 1891, six hundred chiefships were discussed.[60] The abundance of land meant followers could always leave to find other land to cultivate; the variable quality of the land gave people with the less-productive plots a reason to do so, even if their leader was ruling well. That people did move frequently is evident in the pledge husbands were asked to make to their wives upon marriage, "to not be always seeking new situations and wandering from one chief to another."[61] This meant that conflict over the resource of particularly good land happened between rulers, not between rulers and people.

We have evidence that competition among authority figures for followers on the land was part of Ganda political order from the beginning in a description of the establishment of the shrines of lubaale deities on clan land: "One Lubari was Lubari of 4 or 5 clans and they would build a Kigwa (great temple) in some place, and as the Lubari was established there members of his 4 or 5 clans would come and build around, possibly the Kitawi of the clan originally in possession might object, but the mandwa (or head priest) would say 'You'll die if you don't let them stay' and so he had to do so."[62] A clan leader could not refuse when the priest or medium settled followers on his land and threatened him with death if he displeased the lubaale by turning them out.

Before the Buganda kingdom emerged, members of clans lived throughout the region, some of them under clan leaders, but others under leaders who were not seen as leaders of clans, but leaders of people. Some people followed chiefs who controlled land as leaders of branches of clans, other people followed chiefs who controlled land as gatherers of people, and still others followed leaders who controlled land because they connected people to spiritual forces. Enduring patterns of tribute and rituals of allegiance suggest that people accepted all these forms of authority as legitimate: when competition occurred, it happened between alternative legitimate authorities over who would control followers.

The people who lived in the region that became Buganda created forms of association, such as Mbajwe and Kintu practices, that linked them together in ties beyond clanship and allegiance to a chief.[63] Six different clans participated in the care of the spiritual object named Mbajwe, which was the "strongest medicine" of the kingdom. The "father" of the Sheep clan was in charge of it and a man from the Bird clan thatched its temple. A man of the Seed clan carried it, a man of the Yam clan carried its stool, and it had a male priest and female spirit medium from the Leopard clan. Members of the Bushbuck clan beat drums for it, and the Grasshopper clan provided a wife for it.[64] Since two of these clans claimed to have been in the region "from time immemorial" and two claimed to have arrived with the first semi-mythical king, it seems probable that this spiritual medicine came into existence before the familiar Ganda kingdom.

The continuously reenacted memories of contributions to Kintu suggest that people created connections through gifts and services that created obligation. Worship of Kintu at Magonga brought together people associated with the oldest core area of Buganda and people of clans that were also clans in Bunyoro. As Christopher Wrigley has observed, the locations of Kintu worship and the range of ways that Kintu was understood suggest that Kintu as a spiritual force came first, and later people telling the history of Buganda made him the father of the kingdom.[65] The carefully delineated tasks of remembering Kintu were carried out by officers whose names and functions succeeded in particular lineages of eight clans. Mwandje, a chief of the Leopard clan, was in charge of the shrine. A man in the Pangolin clan had the task of building Kintu's house with twelve assistants. Each month a man of the Vervet Monkey clan and a woman of the Bird clan had the task of taking cooked food from the priest into the forest for Kintu to eat.[66] Two of these (Pangolin and Bird) are clans that claimed firstcomer status in Buganda and two others (Vervet Monkey and Leopard) were among the most powerful in relation to the kabaka, once the kabakaship was established. Furthermore, according to Wrigley, fifteen Ganda clans had representatives at or near Magonga, and people of the Buffalo, Bushbuck, and Grasshopper clans, which all have Nyoro associations, had important functions in the ritual. It is clear that worship of Kintu at Magonga drew people from a broad region, only part of which became Buganda.[67]

These spiritual practices were ancient. Kintu worship probably began after A.D. 500, when the people who eventually settled all around Lake Victoria shared the West Nyanza language, since a Kintu figure was honored by people ranging from the Haya west of the lake to the Soga in the northeast. The Mbajwe spiritual medicine probably started after A.D. 1000, when Luganda became a separate language, but before the establishment of the power of kabakas. Unlike the worship of lubaale deities, which entered Buganda several hundred years later, Mbajwe and Kintu practices are remarkable in the way that the rituals required the participation of people of many different clans. (As lubaale deities gained popularity in Buganda a few centuries later, various clans asserted primacy in the worship of different lubaale.) These practices had the quality of deliberate confederation: they enacted and maintained spiritual well-being through the combined endeavor of people who had diverse clan allegiances. The well-defended rights to perform particular aspects of each ritual suggests that clans used a vocabulary of gifts and services to assert their place in Kintu worship and in the Mbajwe cult. Undoubtedly participants sought the spiritual protection and prestige that the cults provided, but it is also possible that these forms of association created ties between people that had economic, social, and political or military dimensions.[68]

Buganda's earliest practice of kingship also involved a number of clans whose members performed clearly prescribed ritual roles. A coalition of clan-based units is remembered in the traditions regarding the ancestor of the Civet clan, named Buganda-Ntege-Walusimbi, who ruled Buganda before Kintu. (The question of whether Buganda had kings before Kintu became part of Apolo Kaggwa's bitter fight with clans in the early twentieth century; some people said there had been seven earlier kings, the Catholic Bishop claimed to know of nine more, and other authors published longer lists.)[69] A kernel of memory of authority before Buganda's nominal first king is a folk tale in which God sent the moon to report on how well Walusimbi was ruling, which made the sun jealous, causing a fight that gave the moon its dark spots. In his insightful analysis of the Ganda dynastic traditions, Christopher Wrigley suggests that Walusimbi controlled a center of ritual activities directed toward fertility and agricultural prosperity at Bakku in Busiro.[70] In the Bakka ceremonies for "confirming" the king, leaders of the Civet Cat and Lungfish clans in royal regalia had elaborate exchanges with the king being installed, and named officers of the Vervet Monkey, Mushroom, Seed, and Colobus Monkey clans also participated. Like the Mbajwe and Kintu cults, the Walusimbi kingship drew apparently autonomous groups into association through the contribution each made to ritual with connotations of prosperity.

KINTU, KIMERA, AND THE AUTHORITY OF FIRSTCOMERS

Sometime between 1200 and 1700, the Ganda polity underwent a radical transformation. A new kind of kingship with new royal rituals inserted itself at the center of the polity, establishing a form of monarchy quite different from other practices of kingship in the region. The character of these differences, particularly the primacy of chiefly power and the lack of power of princes, suggest that a stranger king did indeed come to Buganda, but could not import all the dimensions of royal prerogative because of the well-embedded practices of power that already existed in Buganda. It is also possible, however, that a new indigenous dynasty sought to establish itself using the prestigious royal practices of Bunyoro and claiming Nyoro origins. Whatever his origins, the historical record demonstrates that the new king made a place for himself in the polity by creating relationships of reciprocal obligation with the coalition of leaders who already held power in the region. *Obwesengeze,* which literally means "from service," an archaic form of chiefship in the nineteenth century, provides insight into how the king's system of chiefs developed alongside other forms of authority. Clanship, chiefship, and kingship all changed as the new king, the kabaka, sought to establish himself in relation to the many already existing centers of authority in the area.

Remembered lists of the kings of Buganda do not reveal these changes: to the contrary, they show an unbroken line of kabakas stretching back from the present to the fourteenth century.[71] The earliest remembered rulers on this list would not have been called kabakas in their own time, but the new kind of king called kabaka had been established by the rule of Kabaka Kimbugwe, around 1600.[72] We know this because of the story of a central chief's outstanding service to Kabaka Kimbugwe, which caused the name of his office to be changed from Wolungo to Kimbugwe in commemoration. The office of Wolungo existed in Bunyoro and probably entered Buganda as part of kabaka kingship.[73]

The kabaka was a new kind of ruler, an innovation from or an imposition on top of the practice of kingship that was already there. Some of the evidence of this is linguistic—Schoenbrun points out that in related languages, *mwami* means "king" and *mukungu* means "chief under the king," but in Luganda these words (plural *bakungu* for the latter) both mean "chief under the kabaka." Since the hierarchical usage of the words is more widespread, the people speaking Luganda probably thought of bakungu being inferior to a mwami at one point, but then changed to think of both mwami and bakungu as inferior to the kabaka. That Luganda has its own word for "king," instead of using the more common terms *mwami* or *mukama,* is another indication that the Ganda form of kingship developed later than its neighbors.[74] A myth of the origin of kingship with widespread currency in eastern Africa also provides a hint that the Ganda kabaka was superimposed onto an earlier practice of kingship. Many eastern African societies have an origin story concerning a ruler or first king who arrives from the wilderness and wins people as followers by hunting and giving them meat. In the Ganda tradition, Mulanga, who was wealthy, generous, and taught people to eat meat, was not the hunter/

ruler he is in other versions of this origin myth; instead he is the hunter/son of the mythical first kabaka, Kintu.[75]

The special sovereign status accorded to particular people in Buganda provides further evidence of the layering of a new kind of kingship over older ones. According to Apolo Kaggwa, twenty-three figures of authority who "had a considerable voice in the country" never saw the king in person, and conducted all their business with the king through representatives. They wore brass rings on their legs and hair crests in their hair that distinguished them from other people. They could not be arrested for any offense, and if a king wanted to put one of them to death, he had to arrange to make it look like an accident.[76] By the twentieth century, explanations of this phenomenon were highly partisan: the clan version was that ancient chiefs who were also clan elders had not been interested in ruling, and asked the kabaka to relieve them of chiefly duties. The royalist version was that the chiefs who stayed away felt indignant because the king had usurped their power.[77] In practice, they "had considerable voice in the country" and their avoidance of the king may have been a statement of the importance of keeping distinct powers separate.

The dynastic traditions of Buganda, which have been carefully analyzed by M.S.M. Semakula Kiwanuka, Christopher Wrigley, and others, contain stories that explain the new form of power in Buganda as the arrival of an immigrant king, but also contain hints of conquest through war or internal revolution.[78] The first king, Kintu, is said to have come from heaven, or from a port named Podi, in Bunyoro, and to have killed a tyrannical ruler named Bemba, who is said to have been a python. Kabaka Kintu established capitals all over the center of the kingdom before disappearing in a forest. His son and successor also disappeared. His grandson, Kimera, is said to have been born in Bunyoro and returned to rule after an interregnum caused by his father's mysterious departure into a forest.[79] The fight with King Bemba and the disappearances are signs in the dynastic history of political turmoil and social change, and give weight to interpretations that focus on internal transformations of the evolving polity. However, clan histories as well as the dynastic history indicate that people came into Buganda from the direction of Bunyoro. For example, an elder of the Crow branch of the Otter clan explained in 1906, "Before Kimera's reign there were not many people in Uganda; he brought a lot in from Unyoro."[80] Either the prosperity of people north of the lake attracted settlers, and those settlers brought with them a form of political order different than the system that had been developing in the region already, or the prestige of Bunyoro led an indigenous innovator to style himself as a Nyoro prince.

The anomalous status of *balangira* (princes) in Buganda suggests that immigrants or innovators brought a new pattern of royal power that did not entirely "take hold" in the host country. The ancient leaders who are remembered as Kintu and Kimera would have brought from "the north" Rutaran concepts of royal power. Royal people, including the king (*mukama* in Haya, Nyambo, Nyoro—all Rutaran languages) and princes (*balangira*) had authority over land and people. Royals also possessed noble bearing and qualities of generosity and goodness by virtue of their high birth.[81] In the nineteenth century in Busoga, Buganda's neighbor to the east, princes were distinguished from commoners through strongly marked differences in speech, behavior, and power.[82] In Buganda, people of royal birth had some marks of distinct status—they spoke differently and royal women flaunted norms of female behavior—but in many ways they had less power than other people, rather than more. Princes and princesses controlled land (until the trouble in the kingdom that accompanied expansion, they appointed chiefs on their land whose titles matched the titles of the main chiefs of the province), but their holdings were smaller than those of important chiefs, and by the nineteenth century they were kept far from the center of power.[83] Why were balangira so unimportant in Buganda? They might have had significant power at one time, and lost it, but it seems unlikely that princes' power would have entirely dropped out of the deep and well-preserved memories of control over land.[84] Another possibility is that a form of royal power that involved princes' rights over land was not acceptable to people in Buganda because when this practice of royalty and nobility arrived in the area, people already had a functioning vocabulary of power expressed in control of land. In an ideological struggle over who had the power to allocate land to others, influential buried ancestors and rulers with active ties of reciprocal obligation won over newly fashionable princes. Julien Gorju observed that the kings of Buganda, whom he perceived to have come into the country from the north, established and created legitimacy for themselves by creating graves of their own.[85]

Rituals and clan histories that link the king and clans in Buganda suggest that people required the new kabaka figure to conform to habits of the practice of power that already existed in Buganda. Strategies of invoking reciprocal obligation permeated the publicly performed statements of the relationship of groups in the kingdom to the kabaka. In the ceremonies installing a new king, successive clan heads stated their service to earlier kings and offered the new kabaka gifts that defined their relationship to him. For example, the *mugema,* head of the Monkey clan and chief of the province that contained the graves of deceased kings, placed a bark cloth and calf skin on the new king and said, "I am your father, you are my child. Through all the ages, from your ancestor Kimera, I am your father. This skin with which I clothe you was worn by your ancestor Kimera when he took possession of Buganda."[86] The rites of "confirming the king" took place at Bakka, where the Walusimbi rituals had been located, about six months after this installation. The new king received instructions and confirmation of his role as king from the heads of the clans who had been part of the Walusimbi kingship rituals. The king trespassed and had to pay fines, demonstrating the clan leaders' prior authority. They met him wearing royal regalia, and gave him pieces of it, asserting the royal power they had wielded in the past and their assent to the kabaka's rule.[87]

In addition to his precisely enacted dependence on the people who had participated in the Walusimbi kingship rites, each kabaka had to enact his relationship with other clans. The king's debt of obligation to the Elephant clan was reenacted early in the reign of a new king through a ritual in which the chief herdsman of the king, a titled position in the Elephant clan, brought cows into the king's enclosure, and made the king play on a flute that Kimera had played on and herd the cows for a short time. Members of the Reedbuck clan, who hunted elephants and gave the king tribute in ivory, brought a new king an elephant tusk, which he had to jump over, in order to increase the size of elephant herds.[88] Each of these rituals required the new king to acknowledge his indebtedness for the transfer of authority or for the service performed for kings by the people who preceded him in the land. The original participants in these ceremonies would not have been heads of clans with the characteristics clans came to have several hundred years later: it is possible that some clans coalesced around the relationship to royalty that was being remembered.

Many of the services provided by clans maintained the spiritual health of the king—he could not be well or rule without the contributions made by the clans. The Mushroom clan served as gatekeepers, presided over the temple of the god Nende, and cared for the royal stool and the royal drum, Kawagulu. The Buffalo clan carried the king and were responsible for the temple of Musoke. The Bird clan took care of powerful spiritual medicines, including one named Buganda, and provided the chief who guarded the king's sacred fire and a drum that informed people of the king's health. The Sheep clan kept the powerful spiritual medicine Mbajwe, and took care of the temple of the god Kibuka.[89] Since Ganda kings had to have the support of the gods to rule successfully, clan responsibilities for the gods increased the king's indebtedness to clans. The only clans that did not provide gifts and services that contributed to the king's spiritual well-being and power to rule were those who were integrated into the kingdom in later centuries.

Material gifts that flowed from people to the kabaka also created relationships of obligation: various peoples provided the kings' bark cloths, built named canoes, and supplied beer, musical instruments, drummers, and servants for particular tasks.[90] Service to any king in the history of the dynasty could create bonds of connection and obligation with the ruling king. A new king had to visit the land on which the Seed clan herded for kings since the time of "Kabaka Nakibinge, who planted a tree there for us to tie on his cow which we look after there and which is called Nakawombe; moreover the present Kabaka Daudi Chwa came to this place and saw this very tree and he also gave us his own cow to look after."[91] People guarded the right to provide these gifts and services, because each action explicitly stated the giver's connection to royal power, and implicitly asserted the king's obligation to reciprocate. As someone who had been a high-ranking chief in the mid-nineteenth century explained, "no duty was lower than another; all were in the king's reward and any kind of work done for him was an honour."[92] Even in the early twentieth century, Mugema, chief of Busiro, where all the deceased kabakas were buried, did particular building work for the king in the capital "with his own private people, not with everyone in his saza."[93] The work was not labor the king demanded of a provincial chief, but a statement of a relationship of obligation between the king and his "father" that could only be made by Mugema's own followers.

Since many of the services that created ties of obligation have been commemorated with butaka land, some scholars have perceived the interaction between firstcomer clans and arriving kings to be a conflict over who would control valuable land.[94] A careful examination of the character of the relationship created between kings and clans suggests that this is not an accurate representation of their relationship, especially for the first several hundred years of the kingdom. The statements made by clans in ritual and in clan histories emphasize their intention to participate in the attractive, enticing practice of the kingship, with the rewards of prestige it yielded. What the kings initially gained from the association was a place in the center of a network that had more to do with prestige than with material wealth. The gifts given to the king could not be stored, so what the king had was the power to redistribute.[95] While more research into early Ganda history is necessary, it seems possible that the kabaka king figure had the effect for Buganda that David Newbury describes for the arriving Basimbula royalty on Ijwi Island. There, "new patterns of interaction among groups on the island and new concepts of group belonging" made the people on Ijwi receptive to the new king figure.[96]

The structures of the Ganda kingdom developed out of a practice of chiefship that expressed the recipient chief's service to the king. By the late nineteenth century, obwesengeze had become an archaic, relatively insignificant aspect of the Ganda chiefly hierarchy, but chiefly titles and recorded oral histories indicated that the chiefly hierarchy began in relationships that commemorated the king's recognition of services performed for him. A chief "from service" held a title that described his work for the king, and controlled land with followers on it that had the same name. The personal dimension of this service is evident in titles such as "Mulimyambuga," "He who cleans the courtyard of the palace," and "Mukebezi," "He who calls upon the king," a chief who "looked after the king's latrines and gave him his bath."[97] In the earliest period, these chiefships might have been partly created by kings who had the human resources to enable a favored follower to open new land. Other, much more substantial chiefships in the hierarchy of the kingdom came into being when people who actually already had authority over land and people associated themselves with the king by offering a service. M.S.M. Semakula Kiwanuka has pointed out that the rulers of the ancient central areas of Buganda, who had status as elders of clans and rulers of people, became chiefs with titles that indicated work in the royal household. Kaggo, the leader of the Seed clan who controlled much of Kyaddondo, became the chief called Sabaddu, "chief of the servants," who supervised people who worked in the household, and his immediate subordinate was called Sabakaki, "chief of the palace guards." While these chiefs controlled large, important provinces (that had previously been their independent territories), they also continuously carried out the work of their office for the king. The vocabulary of *kusenga,* attachment through reciprocal obligation, connected their authority to the king's.[98] Even though these chiefs had brought their land and people into the kingdom, rather than being given the land and authority over people by the king, in popular memory, "the great Chiefs together with the Bataka started as the Kabaka's servants."[99]

The extent to which chiefship in the oldest part of the kingdom derived from relationships of pledged obligation is evident in Lloyd Fallers' research contrasting chiefship in Busiro and Buddu. In Busiro, the ancient heartland of the kingdom, almost all chiefships had some dimension of remembered relationship to the king, and in the nineteenth century these chiefships were claimed by various clans. In Buddu, which was annexed to the kingdom after kabakas had become powerful, the kabaka appointed almost all chiefs (see Map 2.2).

The familiar structures of the kingdom developed slowly as existing rulers and existing forms of association became connected with the kabaka. Just as the Ganda polity before the arrival of kabakaship had involved the authority of leaders of clan branches, the authority of chiefs who gathered people around them, and the authority of leaders who mediated spiritual forces, the structures of the kingdom under the kabaka drew together leaders who had followers for different reasons and chiefships that had different kinds of origins. Chiefship came to mean not only control over land and authority over people, but also a place in the gathering of "all of Buganda" in the court of the kabaka, and the prestige was considered to be the most important part.[100] As chiefship under the king became the most significant location of power, between approximately 1400 and 1700, clans became the means through which people sought influence in the kingdom. Far from losing their power to chiefs, as some historians have argued, clans grew into centers of political mobilization as part of a political system of chiefs and authority figures serving a king.

Map 2.2 Chiefship in Busiro and Buddu. (Derived from L.A. Fallers, *The King's Men*, 78–81)

As Christopher Wrigley has observed, Ganda clans grew out of forms of association that had been cults, lineages, and groups of people under a leader. The constitutive, identity-creating aspect of clans evident in clan rhetoric and symbols lends itself to an interpretation of clans that understands them as a timeless reality that had been part of Buganda since its beginning or before. But clan histories of their achievements also clearly state the power-gathering and power-brokering capacities that clans developed.[101] The highly political character of clans is revealed in the 1906 explanation of etiquette: it was never polite to ask a person's clan, only his name, but in the presence of the king, a person's clan had to be mentioned. The complex history of clans hiding in other clans to escape the wrath of a king or to circumvent restrictions placed on them is further evidence of clan power in a kingdom structured by chiefships.[102]

The political power of clans operated through the institution of the *nnamasole,* the queen mother. In many societies across Africa, queen mothers were women rulers who exercised power by doing for kings the things that mothers did for their sons. As Sandra Barnes has pointed out, queen mothers engaged in governing through "supporting, advising, defending, protecting, punishing, and nurturing" their sons who were kings.[103] The Ganda manifestation of this pattern of gendered political power developed after the people living around Lake Victoria broke into different language families in about A.D. 1500. We know this because the languages in the region have entirely different words for the position of queen mother, and queen mothers engaged the political process in different ways in different kingdoms.[104] In Buganda, the position of queen mother became the vehicle for the political ambitions of clans, since every clan offered women to the king as wives, and any wife could (in theory) bear the child who would be the next king and therefore ascend to the most powerful position in the kingdom next to the kabaka, that of nnamasole.[105] A woman became nnamasole through having a male child by the kabaka, amassing enough personal influence to put her son forward among dozens of others, and building a coalition of support behind her son. Since one clan did not provide a sufficiently large number of supporters to win the throne, the successful queen mother and her allies in her own clan had to align with other clans in order for her son to come to power.[106]

A queen mother had her own court near the king's capital (*kibuga*) but on another hill, separated from the kibuga's hill by a stream of running water. The nnamasole was served by a coterie of chiefs in all parts of the kingdom that mirrored the set of chiefs serving the king.[107] A kabaka visited his mother, but the nnamasole never entered the kibuga; when she wished to communicate with a kabaka, she sent messengers. A kabaka had deep, continuing obligations to the clans who had placed him in power. The queen mother's influence over her son, and her autonomous power marked in her independent control of land and people, held the king accountable to his supporters.

The nnamasole's brother, who had the chiefly title *ssaabaganzi* ("father of the favorites") was also among the most influential people in the kingdom. Queen mothers substantially limited the power of kings: Ham Mukasa (a Ganda chief who rose to power in the nineteenth century) wrote, without a queen mother, "there would be no one to check him [the king] if he behaved too evilly."[108] If a kabaka wanted to remain in power, he had to act in a way that pleased the nnamasole.[109]

Clans triumphed over princes in the making of royal power in Buganda through the value that was placed on royal offspring born to women of the clans. This involved a deviation from regional social practice by having the children of a king take their mother's instead of their father's clan. It makes sense that marriage would be the center of a battle over power between newly arrived kings and preexisting rulers, because, as we have seen, marriage was one of the tools people in the region used to incorporate strangers. New kings would have wanted marriage alliances to develop links with the preexisting rulers who carried significant authority and controlled most material resources; those people would have found marriage of their daughters useful in making claims to some of the prestige found in the presence of the newly arrived king. Clear evidence of this comes from memories of a decision made in the time of Kateregga, who began to rule around 1600, about one hundred years after the disjuncture in dynastic traditions that suggests the arrival of the new kind of king. People remembered that "Kateregga and his chiefs decided to demand of the prominent and wealthy chiefs taxes in the form of goods, to be given to the wives of the king."[110] From then on, specific chiefs were assigned the responsibility of collecting taxes to be delivered to particular wives, all of whom held titles that passed down within their clan. Clans that had been most powerful in the pre-kabaka kingdom controlled the chiefships and other royal offices responsible for the care of pregnant royal wives and raising of the king's children, which gave them great influence in the production of kabakas. It seems reasonable to assume that the relative strength of existing rulers in relation to king with a royal cachet (but not too many other resources) led to the Ganda royal practice in which the king was at the center, but a coalition of clans, organized around potential queen mothers, put him there.

The new moon ceremonies provide further evidence of the claims made by rulers who already had authority in Buganda on the powers of the attractive but parvenu person of the kabaka. In the new moon ceremonies, each ruling kabaka had to acknowledge and embrace his predecessors' "twins" (highly decorated objects containing each king's umbilical cords).[111] Since the successor of the chief who had been in charge of the "twin" during the deceased kabaka's reign presented it to the living kabaka, this event required the ruling kabaka to acknowledge his debt to the most significant chiefs who had served his predecessors. Clans continued to appoint successors to these individuals, who carried out the work of remembering their clan member's service in the vicinity of the grave of the kabaka they had served.

Kings, clans, and chiefs, in the form that we recognize, did not exist when the immigrant or innovator king who became known as kabaka established

Figure 2.2 Women drummers at Ssuuna's Tomb, ca. 1908. The principal wives of a deceased kabaka continued to live by his shrine, remembering his actions; clans provided successors when these women died. (C. W. Hattersley, *The Baganda at Home,* 22)

himself in Buganda. Chiefship under the kabaka emerged from the relationships built between people who already lived there, and had some kind of kingship, with a new kind of king who was either an immigrant or an indigen advancing a new and foreign form of kingship. A new thing—chiefship that defined a relationship with the kabaka—developed out of, and then alongside of, an older thing—chiefship that defined a relationship between a superior and his followers on land. The already established authority figures evolved into clan leaders who might or might not be chiefs under the kabaka, and chiefs who did not lead clans but did serve the kabaka and used their connections to the king to advance the interest of their groups. The distinct qualities of clans, the stories they told about themselves, and their habits of action as a group developed in interaction with the power and obligations of the kabaka. A pattern of many nodes of power, with many links between them, came to characterize the Buganda kingdom.

CONCLUSION

Around A.D. 1000, banana gardens became a way that people marked relationships of obligation—the obligation of wives to husbands, the obligation of descendants to ancestors, and the obligation of followers to leaders. The capacity of banana gardens to name connections between people contributed to the shape of Ganda clans, and to the character of Ganda chiefship, and it provided one of the mechanisms through which people assembled the network of allegiances that became the kingdom.

In the Ganda polity, a king occupied the center, but leaders of people who had independent claims on their followers made him powerful through their allegiance. The statements about power inherent in the pattern of interaction of chiefs and authority figures in the courts of the king and queen mother strongly suggest that participants understood the state to be a coming together of multiple sources of authority. Groups of people organized as clans controlled essential spiritual power and functioned as collective centers of political power through the institution of the queen mother. The rituals of a new king's installation asserted each clan's contribution to his power, and the new moon ceremony reminded the reigning king of his debts to clans for the services performed by their members in previous reigns.

Power in the early Ganda kingdom was diffuse, always visible, and constantly negotiated. Using the language of chiefship as a statement of reciprocal obligation, authority figures built a complex and comprehensive network of allegiances. In its earliest centuries, these alliances led in many directions: toward Magonga, the location of the Kintu cult, toward Bakka, where Walusimbi reigned, and toward connections that promoted strength of Buganda through Mbajwe. The establishment of kabaka kingship sometime before 1600 drew these various forms of connection more toward one center, the kabaka's capital. Like the tightly aligned reeds that made the walls and roof of a Ganda home, gifts, labor, and respectful participation flowed through chiefs to the kabaka from all the regions of the kingdom.

NOTES

1. John Roscoe, *The Baganda: An Account of Their Native Customs and Beliefs* (1911; reprint, New York: Barnes and Noble, 1966), 126, 369–374; Lucy Mair, *An African People in the Twentieth Century* (1934; reissue, London: Routledge and Kegan Paul, 1965), 118–119.

2. Roscoe, *The Baganda,* 373; Julien Gorju, *Entre le Victoria, L'Albert et L'Edouard* (Rennes: Oberthur, 1920), 136.

3. Gorju, *Entre le Victoria,* 136. The root of these words is *tikka,* "to put a load on the head." Murphy, *Luganda-English Dictionary,* 546.

4. In the nineteenth century, the kibuga (palace) was a vast fenced region several miles in circumference that contained more than five hundred buildings. Peter C. W. Gutkind, *The Royal Capital of Buganda: A Study of Internal Conflict and External Ambiguity* (The Hague: Mouton, 1963), 14.

5. Alexander M. Mackay, *A. M. Mackay, Pioneer Missionary of the Church Missionary Society in Uganda* (London: Hodder and Stoughton, 1890), 214.

6. Roscoe, *The Baganda,* 463.

7. Ibid., 483.

8. David Newbury, *Kings and Clans: Ijwi Island and the Lake Kivu Rift, 1780–1840* (Madison: University of Wisconsin Press, 1991), 4.

9. The transformation of power to a more dominating form in the late eighteenth and early nineteenth centuries is the subject of Chapter 3.

10. Schoenbrun, *Green Place,* 80.

11. Christopher Wrigley argues for a later date for the adoption of intensive banana cultivation, but I think the social changes are too profound, too thoroughly worked into people's way of being in the world, to have happened in a quick unfolding of Ganda statehood in the sixteenth or seventeenth centuries. Christopher Wrigley, *Kingship and State: The Buganda Dynasty* (Cambridge: Cambridge University Press, 1996), 235.

12. Schoenbrun, *Green Place,* 72–73; Roscoe, *The Baganda,* 161.

13. David L. Schoenbrun, "We Are What We Eat: Ancient Agriculture Between the Great Lakes," *Journal of African History* 34 (1993): 1–31, 26.

14. Schoenbrun, *Green Place,* 194; Schoenbrun, "Ancient Agriculture," 23.

15. Hattersley, *The Baganda at Home,* 101; John Tosh, "Lango Agriculture During the Early Colonial Period: Land and Labour in a Cash Crop Economy," *Journal of African History* 19:3 (1978): 415–439.

16. Lucy Mair, *Native Marriage in Buganda,* Memorandum no. 19 (London: Oxford University Press for the International Institute of African Languages and Cultures, 1940), 13.

17. Mair, *An African People,* 80–82.

18. Mair says the bride's aunt, *sengawe,* actually supervised the feast. Mair, *An African People,* 87.

19. Ibid., 155, 80.

20. Hattersley, *The Baganda at Home,* 108; Mair, *An African People,* 98; Roscoe, *The Baganda,* 92.

21. E. S. Haydon, *Law and Justice in Buganda* (London: Butterworths, 1960), 80.

22. Roscoe, *The Baganda at Home,* 93.

23. Kaggwa, *Kings,* 44.

24. Gorju, *Entre le Victoria,* 164.

25. Schoenbrun, *Green Place,* 198.

26. Roscoe, *The Baganda,* 143.

27. Ibid., 288.

28. Although Tantala writes about people's relationship with cwezi spirits, her argument regarding the loss of positive and pervasive interaction between people and spirits would apply to ancestor spirits as well. Renee Tantala, "The Early History of Kitara in Western Uganda: Process Models of Religious and Political Change" (Ph.D. diss., University of Wisconsin, 1989), 282, 291–293. Regarding the positive influence of ancestors in the past, see also Schoenbrun, *Green Place,* 198, 213 n87.

29. Schoenbrun, *Green Place,* 198–199; Fallers, "Social Stratification," 90.

30. Tantala, "Early History of Kitara," 272; Jan Bender Shetler, "The Landscapes of Memory: A History of Social Identity in the Western Serengeti, Tanzania" (Ph.D. diss., University of Florida, 1998), 327–329, 342.

31. Gorju, *Entre le Victoria,* 87.

32. Cf. Kingdom of Buganda, *Customary Law Reports 1940–1955,* comp. E. S. Haydon and I. S. Lule (Nairobi: E. A. Printers, 1956), Civil Case 38/46, 41–44, which excoriates families who disturb widows.

33. Gorju, *Entre le Victoria,* 132.

34. Shetler, "Landscapes of Memory," 339.

35. Roscoe, *The Baganda,* 477.

36. Kaggwa, *Kings,* 65.

37. Roscoe, *The Baganda,* 134; Morris Carter, "The Clan System, Land Tenure, and Succession Among the Baganda," *Uganda Protectorate Law Reports* 1 (1904–1910): 99–120. Roscoe's and Carter's interpretation has been taken as authoritative by other scholars.

38. "Enquiry," Teofiro Mulumba Kuruji, 44; "Enquiry," Ham Mukasa, 19; "Enquiry," Nuha Mbogo, 16.

39. "Enquiry," Rasito Kawaga, 27.

40. Ibid., 27.

41. Mugwanya to Apolo and Kisingiri, Rubaga, January 24, 1906, Apolo Kaggwa Papers, AR KA 1, CA 22, Makerere University Africana Collection; "Commission," Zedi Zirimenya, 357–358; "Commission," Sulumani Mivule, 361; "Commission," Antwani Kaikuzi 425; "Commission," Saulo Lugwisa, 448.

42. "Enquiry," Nsimbi, 28.

43. Kaggwa, *Basekabaka,* trans. Musoke, 73.

44. The story provides further useful information for understanding how power became embedded in allocation of banana land, because a chiefship was created to honor Nkalubo for saving the unborn king, and successors to that chiefship assumed his name as their title of office.

45. Schoenbrun, *Green Place,* 187; David Lee Schoenbrun, *The Historical Reconstruction of Great Lakes Bantu Cultural Vocabulary: Etymologies and Distributions* (Koln: Koppe, 1997), 139–142.

46. Fallers, "Social Stratification," 88–89.

47. Christopher Wrigley, *Crops and Wealth in Uganda: A Short Agrarian History* (Kampala: East African Institute of Social Research, 1959), 1. J. M. Fortt points out that the areas that had been transformed from forest into elephant grass, indicating the longest period of cultivation, were the areas with most constant and reliable rains. J. M. Fortt, "The Distribution of the Immigrant and Ganda Population Within Buganda," in *Economic Development and Tribal Change,* ed. Audrey I. Richards (Cambridge: W. Heffer and Sons for the East African Institute of Social Research, 1954), 85.

48. Fallers, "Social Stratification," 87.

49. "Commission," Aligizande Mude, 338.

50. Schoenbrun, *Green Place,* 203–204.

51. J. M. Fortt and D. A. Hougham, "Environment, Population, and Economic History," in *Subsistence to Commercial Farming in Present-Day Buganda,* ed. Audrey I. Richards, Ford Sturrock, and Jean M. Fortt (Cambridge: Cambridge University Press, 1973), 18; Wrigley, *Crops and Wealth,* 2–3.

52. Schoenbrun, *Historical Reconstruction,* 103.

53. Roscoe, *The Baganda,* 13, 96, 426. Women's access to land on divorce is implied in Haydon, *Law and Justice,* 83, and Mair, *An African People,* 97–8, and is stated explicitly in the records of the Lukiiko of Buganda, translated into English by the East African Institute of Social Research, seen courtesy of John Rowe.

54. "Commission," Zedi Zirimenya Bugo, 438.

55. Gorju, *Entre le Victoria,* 97; M.S.M. Semakula Kiwanuka presents a slightly different timeline in *History of Buganda,* 41.

56. Wrigley, *Crops and Wealth,* 2–3; Fortt and Hougham, "Environment, Population, and Economic History," 18.

57. H. B. Thomas and Robert Scott, *Uganda* (London: Humphrey Milford, 1935), 50.

58. Fortt, "Distribution of the Immigrant and Ganda Population," 83–84.

59. Ibid., 87.

60. Ashe, *Chronicles,* 163.

61. Roscoe, *The Baganda,* 87–88.

62. "Enquiry," Apolo Kaggwa, 5.

63. Wrigley, *Kingship,* 79; Schoenbrun, *Green Place,* 207.

64. Roscoe, *The Baganda,* 327.

65. Wrigley, *Kingship,* 118–119.

66. Kaggwa, *Empisa za Baganda,* 1907, partially translated by Ernest B. Kalibala under the title *The Customs of the Baganda,* ed. May Mandelbaum, Columbia University Contributions to Anthropology no. 22 (New York: Columbia University Press, 1934), 9.

67. Wrigley, *Kingship,* 119.

68. Uganda's President Yoweri Museveni, observing these practices, said, "In the same way our ancestors in Buganda and other kingdoms used all creative means to weave unity among the clans, we should use similar creative measures to unite the different peoples of Uganda and the different religions in order to achieve similar goals." *New Vision,* July 30, 1993, quoted in Mikael Karlstrom, "The Cultural Kingdom in Uganda: Popular Royalism and the Restoration of the Buganda Kingship" (Ph.D. diss., University of Chicago, 1999), 315.

69. Benjamin C. Ray, *Myth, Ritual, and Kingship in Buganda* (New York: Oxford University Press, 1991), 94, 101; Wrigley, *Kingship,* 28, 83; Kiwanuka, *History,* 94–95.

70. Wrigley, *Kingship,* 83–86.

71. M.S.M. Semakula Kiwanuka prepared a chronology of Ganda kings based on the dynastic tradition recorded by Apolo Kaggwa in *Basekabaka be Buganda (The Kings of Buganda).* The list of kings presented here retains Kiwanuka's dating but attempts to indicate moments of change in dynasty and in the structure of the kingship. Alternative chronologies are proposed in Wrigley, *Kingship and State,* and in Henri Medard, "Croissance et crises de la royaute du Buganda au XIX siecle" (Ph.D. diss., University of Paris, 2001), 28–29.

72. Further research on clan histories and in historical linguistics will undoubtedly illuminate this period, for example, the research of Neil Kodesh, "Beyond the Royal Gaze: Ganda Clans and the Construction of an African Metahistory" (unpublished dissertation proposal, Northwestern University, November 2000).

73. Gorju, *Entre le Victoria,* 136; Roscoe, *The Baganda,* 235–236.

74. Schoenbrun, *Green Place,* 187, 194.

75. Kaggwa, *Kings of Buganda,* 6; Wrigley, *Kingship,* 104.

76. Kaggwa, *Customs,* 87.

77. Michael Wright, *Buganda in the Heroic Age* (Nairobi: Oxford University Press, 1971), quoting Kalikuzinga, 4; Kaggwa, *Customs,* 87.

78. Kiwanuka, *History of Buganda;* Kiwanuka notes in Kaggwa, *Kings;* and Wrigley, *Kingship.*

79. Kaggwa, *Kings,* 1, 13–14.

80. "Enquiry," Isaiah Kunsa, 92.

81. Schoenbrun, *Green Place,* 190, 194–195; Schoenbrun, *Historical Reconstruction,* 112.

82. David William Cohen, *Womunafu's Bunafu: A Study of Authority in a Nineteenth-Century African Community* (Princeton: Princeton University Press, 1977), 155.

83. Roscoe, *The Baganda,* 189; "Commission," Aligizanda Mude, 332–333; Paulo Kaliro, 419; Lewo Nsobya, 464, 466; Mikairi Kidza, 515.

84. Christopher Wrigley sees evidence of the overthrow of a royal clan in the dynastic traditions regarding Kabaka Kagulu. Wrigley, *Kingship,* 187–191.

85. Gorju, *Entre le Victoria,* 133; Schoenbrun, *Green Place,* 194; Kiwanuka, *History of Buganda,* 97.

86. Mair, *An African People,* 191; Roscoe, *The Baganda,* 197–199. Although the description is written in the past tense, I observed the ceremony at the installation of Kabaka Ronald Mutebi in July 1993.

87. Benjamin Ray, *Myth, Ritual, and Kingship,* 91–93. The killing of the son of the head of the Frog branch of the Lungfish clan was part of this ritual.

88. Roscoe, *The Baganda,* 147, 168.

89. Ibid., 143–144, 152–155.

90. Ibid., 143–144, 163–167; Gorju, *Entre le Victoria,* 117; "Commission," Semei Sebagala Kyadondo, 442; "Commission," Danieri Sendikadiwa, 475b.

91. "Commission," Semei Sebagala Kyadondo, 442.

92. "Enquiry," Teofiro Kuluji, 39.

93. "Enquiry," Zachariah Kisingiri, 11.

94. Schoenbrun, *Green Place,* 182, 203, 213; C. P. Kottak, "Ecological Variables in the Origin and Evolution of African States: The Buganda Example," *Comparative Studies in Society and History* 14 (1972): 372. Fallers and Kiwanuka emphasize the issue of prestige. Kiwanuka, *History of Buganda,* 6; Fallers, "Social Stratification," 96.

95. Richard Waller, "The Traditional Economy of Buganda" (M.A. essay, University

of London, School of Oriental and African Studies, 1971); Newbury, *Kings and Clans,* 182.

96. Newbury, *Kings and Clans,* 235.

97. "Commission," Nkuwe, 388–392; "Enquiry," Temeteo Bujomba, 20.

98. Kiwanuka, *History of Buganda,* 112–113; Gorju, *Entre le Victoria,* 136.

99. "Commission," Danieri Serugabi, 540.

100. According to the Ganda proverb *"Abantu magoma gavuga aliwo"*—"The drum beats for the office, and not for the person who holds it." Roscoe, *The Baganda,* 489.

101. Wrigley, *Kingship,* 189; "Commission," Malaki Musajakawa, 342; Fallers, "Social Stratification," 97–98.

102. "Enquiry," Tefiro Mulumba Kuruji, 42; Roscoe, *The Baganda,* 138, 164, 171–172; Wrigley, *Kingship,* 64–65.

103. Sandra T. Barnes, "Gender and the Politics of Support and Protection in Precolonial West Africa," in *Queens, Queen Mothers, Priestesses, and Power: Case Studies in African Gender,* ed. Flora Edouwaye Kaplan, Annals of the New York Academy of Sciences vol. 810 (New York: New York Academy of Sciences, 1997), 13.

104. Schoenbrun, *Green Place,* 192–193; *Historical Reconstruction,* 114, 151.

105. "Enquiry," Stanislaus Mugwanya, 9; Roscoe, *The Baganda,* 236.

106. Martin Southwold has pointed out that the necessity of finding broad-based support for one woman's son over another's gave Ganda succession democratic elements and "some of the virtues of both a monarchy and a republic." Martin Southwold, "Succession to the Throne in Buganda," in *Succession to High Office,* ed. Jack Goody (Cambridge: Cambridge University Press, 1966), 96–97.

107. Lawrence D. Schiller, "The Royal Women of Buganda," *International Journal of African Historical Studies* 23:3 (1990): 455–473; Holly Hanson, "Queen Mothers and Good Government in Buganda: The Loss of Women's Political Power in Nineteenth-Century East Africa," in *Women in African Colonial Histories,* ed. Jean Allman, Susan Geiger, and Nakanyike Musisi (Bloomington: Indiana University Press, 2002), 213–236.

108. Ham Mukasa, "Some Notes on the Reign of Mutesa," *Uganda Journal* 1:2 (1934): 128.

109. Ibid. Among many examples of the power of queen mothers over their sons are Kaggwa, *Kings,* 92; Mackay, *Pioneer Missionary,* 162; Wright, *Buganda in the Heroic Age,* 3.

110. Kaggwa, *Customs,* 68.

111. Gorju, *Entre le Victoria,* 112; "Enquiry," Tefiro Mulumba Kuruji, 55; Ray, *Myth, Ritual, and Kingship,* 208. New moon ceremonies called "sacrifices for the lineage" happened elsewhere in the region. Tantala, "Early History of Kitara," 289, 325.

3

KABAKAS STRUGGLE TO HOLD THE CENTER: THE DESTABILIZING CONSEQUENCES OF STOLEN PEOPLE AND UNOBLIGATED POWER, CA. 1500–CA. 1800

Expansion of the kingdom in the seventeenth and eighteenth centuries profoundly destabilized the practice of power in Buganda. On the most obvious level, expansion created new avenues to prestige and control of resources, and therefore intensified the kabaka's task of maintaining balance through redistribution. Thirteen kabakas held power inside of five generations, as brothers and cousins and their factions fought each other for control of the spoils of expansion. A more encompassing and even more challenging consequence of winning wars was the partial unraveling of the practice of reciprocal obligation. In order to utilize newly conquered territory, kabakas created *ekitongole* chiefship (plural *ebitongole*), in which mostly nonfree people, captives of war, served a particular interest of the holder of the captives. Power over people without the bonds of reciprocal obligation undermined the coherence of the polity, because participants who had lost their capacity to influence the kabaka's actions attempted to install more compliant kings. Even worse, chiefs began to use war captives to create ebitongole of their own, which threatened the kabaka's control of the center. The vast numbers of captives brought into Buganda with the wars of expansion seriously diminished the status of followers in relation to chiefs, as thousands of nonfree people lessened chiefs' need to compete with other chiefs for the goodwill of followers.

The wars of expansion brought political conflict and social crisis to Buganda, evident in escalating internal violence: the short life span of kings, and also brutal, coercive violence against ordinary people. It is possible that an end to expansion and to Buganda's military dominance of the region in the nineteenth century would have led to a resolution of the social crisis engendered by the wars, but the eighteenth-century dilemma of unobligated power fed into a nineteenth-century crisis of further forms of unobligated power and of people for sale.

This perception of the eighteenth and early nineteenth centuries as a time of crisis, in which the kabaka's place at the center of the kingdom was threatened by institutional change and masses of stolen people eroded the status of followers, strongly contrasts with predominant interpretations of the Ganda past. Most historians of Buganda see the wars of expansion as a period of consolidation and centralization, from which kabakas emerged much more powerful.[1] Expansion, according to this interpretation, allowed kabakas to take power away from clans and create a set of chiefs who were "king's men"— the beginning of a modern bureaucracy. Differences in both theoretical framework and in choice of evidence suggest a process of dissolution of social order and disintegrating power where others have seen social development and expanding royal power. If we make an effort to understand how participants in the Ganda polity interacted in the past, without imposing categories and practices that came to exist later, the eighteenth-century changes defy simplification as a process in which kings took power from clans to create a new kind of bureaucracy. All those who wielded authority in the kingdom, including chiefs with ancient responsibilities and newly appointed chiefs over recently added territories, enacted an unwritten constitution of the kingdom in the way they gathered in the capital, gave and received gifts, and performed work for the king. These practices did not change with the wars of expansion, and to see the social stresses the wars caused, we have to look further than memories of chiefly appointments, or the records of the violent actions of Ganda kings in the nineteenth century.

How to manage the labor of newly acquired nonfree dependents and maintain the allegiance of free followers was the critical social dilemma faced by Ganda people as the kingdom expanded.[2] The problem posed for chiefs and the kabaka is evident not only in the period's political violence, but also in the histories of particular ebitongole chiefships, remembered as part of the disputes over land granted to those chiefships. The problem posed for free and nonfree followers is evident in the increasing coercion of dependents that appears to have accompanied the expansion. The dynastic history regarding this period recorded a higher level of violence against followers than had occurred earlier and it is important to note that the dynastic history condemned that violence. A gap opened up between the social power of followers asserted by Ganda proverbs, stories, and expressed views regarding social relations, and the character of those social relationships described by nineteenth-century visitors and participants. Either Baganda wrongly believed their society to allow women to choose their husbands and people to choose their chiefs, or the influx of nonfree people with the expansion wars seriously disrupted practices of reciprocal obligation that people considered to be ordinary and unremarkable.

This chapter documents social and political upheaval in eighteenth- and early-nineteenth-century Buganda in three sections. The first section demonstrates the place of the kabaka at the center of a visible, continuously enacted competition among chiefs over people, power, and prestige. This pattern had been established as the kingdom gradually coalesced before 1500. It explores the contradictory ideas inherent in the Ganda practice of power: that kabakas were both supreme and entirely obligated to their followers. The second section shows how rulers in Buganda accommodated and negotiated with competing sources of power through exploring the arrival and incorporation of lubaale spiritual authority, beginning in the sixteenth century. The third section shows how expansion in the seventeenth and eighteenth centuries undermined kabakas' ability to stabilize the kingdom at the center. This happened through escalating competition between chiefs and the kabaka unleashed by the unobligated quality of ekitongole chiefship, and in the deterioration of social relations caused by the incorporation of nonfree people.

LOVE, COMPETITION FOR FOLLOWERS, AND THE ORDER OF BUGANDA

Incessant competition among chiefs for followers and for the prestige that consolidated a chief's hold over followers characterized Ganda politics. An examination of patterns of tribute and allegiance demonstrates that as the kingdom developed, the critical axis of conflict in Buganda had been between chiefs for followers, and people relied on kabakas to mediate that conflict. People continuously and visibly enacted the centrality of the kabaka: he was physically at the center of the kingdom, politically the designator of some people's power over others, and materially the point of redistribution of goods. Placed at the conceptual and material center of the kingdom, kabakas balanced the contending interests championed by literally thousands of chiefs, elders, royals, and priests, and the followers of all those figures of authority.

The essential dynamic of power in Buganda was that chiefs needed followers and followers could leave their chiefs. Inherent in *kusenga,* the action of attaching to a superior, was *kusenguka,* the action of leaving a superior. In theory, a ruler could also *kusengusa,* cause people to move away, but since a ruler's standing was dependent on having lots of followers, the terms of kusenga favored the followers. Ganda proverbs speak of followers as people who had choices. *"Musenze alanda"*—"The follower often changes his master," and *"Busenze muguma: bwe bukonnontera n'osongola"*—"Service is like the digging stick: when it has become blunt, you point it again."[3] Zachariah Kisingiri, one of the most powerful chiefs at the beginning of a British presence, explained, "A new kitawi (controller of clan land) would not turn out such a cultivator [a nonclan member] without reason as he would be afraid that other cultivators would run away and so the estates become waste land."[4] People with authority needed to keep their followers.

The forms of exchange marking kusenga expressed the reciprocity people expected to experience in the relationship.[5] In the nineteenth century, a chief's men built elaborate reed fences that encircled his compound as part of their service to him; a chief protected his men from other powerful people who might claim their labor or service. Followers took their chief part of every brew of beer they made and some of the game they caught, and expected gifts from him.[6] Oral traditions recorded the limits of appropriate exchange in kusenga. The consequence of beyond-reasonable extraction, and the impossibility of deceiving followers, was told in the tale of the disaster of chickens' overlordship of cats. Because the chickens demanded four-fifths of all of the flying ants the cats caught, and made them bring the ants in large packages for inspection, the cats wanted to rebel, but were frightened by the chickens' threat to burn the cats with their combs. However, the dissatisfied cats discovered that the combs had no fire, and the chickens lost their power and had to take refuge with humans.[7] On the other hand, the Ganda epic tradition recalls a chief of Kabaka Tebandeke (the eighteenth kabaka, who probably ruled just before 1700), who lost his position as keeper of the royal tombs and was killed because he asked too often for gifts, instead of waiting to receive them.[8]

The discourse of love in relations of power in Buganda has been a problem for some historians, who have assumed that since people invested labor in banana land over generations and the land became more valuable, exploitation had to have been the result. We do not want to make the mistake of assuming that people wanted to be independent economic actors and were forced into being the people of a chief against their will. It makes more sense, and shows more respect for the evidence of Ganda people's own ideas, to see people using the rich land north of Lake Victoria and the agricultural technology of permanent banana cultivation to create a pattern of interaction that had material and political usefulness and also great intrinsic meaning. The aesthetics of chiefship and followerhood were clearly expressed in Ganda culture. It was a good thing for a chief to have many people, and it was a good thing to be the man of a chief. The Baganda likened chiefship to the light of torches that burned at night. Ganda chiefs were said to initially dismiss paraffin lamps, saying: "What will become of our torches? How will a chief be able to hang onto a torch? Surely it is the lamp-torch which is adhering to the chief?"[9] Chiefs, like torches at night, collected people around them.

People of a chief claimed their status in the work they did, in drumbeats, and in where they stayed in the capital and where they slept on a campaign. The claim, made during the butaka controversy in the 1920s, that "we have always been fishermen for the Namasole (Queen Mother) from time immemorial," asserted for the claimants the status of the nnamasole. Fishing for the nnamasole was not just the tribute they gave for the land they held, but a way of defining who they were and how they fit into the kingdom.[10] The social statements people made of association with a chief disturbed Europeans who observed them in the late nineteenth century. Writing about fighting a fire in the capital, John Roscoe wrote, "As they went to the royal enclosure each man called the name of his chief, and the stamp of hundreds of feet, added to the sound of hundreds of voices, was such as to produce a most disquieting effect upon the nerves in a dark night. No one who has heard the war-drum beat, and has witnessed the assembling to the chief, will readily forget the scene."[11] The connection between followers and chiefs, intensely meaningful and politically powerful, was the critical social relationship in Buganda.

Ethnographic evidence suggests that a chief had to be constantly alert to the possibility that his followers might desert him because they decided another chief in the same neighborhood treated his people better. Chiefs had to be generous and gracious: Lucy Mair observed that in the 1930s Ganda people expected "meat, beer, and politeness" from their chiefs, and a follower who had been given gifts might list them to his superior when asking for something else.[12] According to Roscoe, "when a chief called his men servants they often replied *'wampa'* 'You have given to me,' meaning 'it is you who have given me all that I have, my wife, food and clothing.'"[13] This greeting stated the expectation that the chief would continue to give those gifts. Effective chiefs had to be skilled in resolving disputes in ways that seemed just to all parties; they had to be able to obtain and redistribute goods in ways that satisfied their superiors and their followers; they had to develop working relationships with other rulers so that their control of their people would not be threatened.[14]

Since followers had the capacity to leave rulers because of the abundance of land and the consequent abundance of people controlling land and allocating it to others, those with authority could not exert pressure on their own followers to advance their position. Instead, people in power tried to attract away the followers of other rulers. This happened not only in the most obvious way, in which a ruler's success or reputation for generosity convinced people to leave another chief to become his follower. It also happened in a more complex way, in which people stayed in the area of one authority figure, but became the followers of another authority figure.

The densely complex and overlapping patterns of tribute obligations remembered for the nineteenth century suggest many successive contests, probably over generations, regarding chiefly control of followers. Obligatory gifts of bark cloth, produced goods, and labor flowed through chains of allegiance from tribute givers to their particular superiors, who were not always the superiors of their neighbors.[15] For example, people remembered in 1906 that only some of the people giving tribute in the territory of Kyaggwe in the nineteenth century gave it directly to the *ssekiboobo,* the chief of Kyaggwe. Others paid directly to his deputy, because they were the followers of the deputy, not followers of the chief. Other people residing in the same area gave tribute only to the leader of a clan, and in order to obtain tribute destined for the king from those people, a chain of collectors, representing the king, the chief, and his deputy, would appeal to the clan elder to collect tribute. When chains of collectors asked for tribute in a group, each authority figure represented kept a portion of what was collected.[16] These complex and overlapping chains of tribute suggest that new figures of authority (tribute receivers) had been inserted among older figures of authority for a long period of time.

A person could live in the area of one chief but be the follower of a different chief. A follower's allegiance to the chief who was nominally in control of a region depended on a consensus regarding that chief's authority over the specific land the follower occupied. For example, blacksmith Erenesti Kakoza claimed that in the 1880s he had not been a follower of the *kimbugwe,* keeper of the king's twin figure, even though he had been "under" (living in the territory and of lower status than) the kimbugwe. He demonstrated his autonomy by claiming that no intermediaries came between the holders of his title and the kabaka: "All the kabaka's messengers sent to Kakoza used to come straight from the Kabaka to myself, but did not come through the Kimbugwe; and when the Kabaka used to come to my workshop to [ask me] to do some blacksmith work he used to come straight to me not through the Kimbugwe; and he would not have paid such visits to a private tenant."[17] A person might be independent of the chief's authority because he or she was a follower of the kabaka directly, of a lubaale deity, of the nnamasole or another royal woman, or of a different chief who controlled some land inside that particular area. For example, the people of Busamba, the men of a leader called Kasamba, owed their allegiance to a subsidiary chief in Bulemeezi, even though the land they lived on was in Busiro. Lloyd Fallers observed that "a veritable jungle of overlapping and interdigitating authorities" characterized the oldest part of the kingdom.[18] These dense webs of overlapping authority represent old conflicts over followers that eventually were resolved in working agreements over divisions of tribute and allegiance.

Testimony about control of Bussi Island from about 1880 to 1900 demonstrates that chiefly authority over followers had to be enacted as well as proclaimed, and a person with a high chief's title might not actually be able to command the labor of the people nominally beneath him. The island had been given to Gabunga (a Mamba clan elder with responsibility for the kabaka's canoes) by Kabaka Mwanga in 1884, but not all the land came under his authority.[19] A witness before the Bataka Land Commission explained, "When Gabunga was given power to rule the islands of Sesse he found some important bataka who had power over their own land and he did not take away that power from them. But [he] took possession of all the estates which belonged then to some less important bataka and converted them into his own private estates."[20] A series of clan elders testified that even though the island had been given to Gabunga, they had never become his followers. They proved their independence from the chief by describing their actions. Zedi Zirimenya said, "When my father died we were about 150 men who attended the funeral, but we never went to Gabunga first to apply for permission to bury him."[21] Malaki Musajakawa challenged the katikkiro (prime minister), "Let Chief Gabunga point to any one of us [bataka from Bussi] who was his private tenant and who worked for him."[22] Before it was given to Gabunga, Bussi Island had been territory controlled by Guggu, the priest of the shrine of the god Mukasa. Witnesses discussing the issue of authority on Bussi pointed out that no nineteenth-century kabaka had ever tried to call up the canoes controlled by Guggu for service on the lake. Kabaka Mwanga gave Bussi to the chief, Gabunga, but large groups of people who lived in his territory gave their allegiance, tribute, and labor to others and not to Gabunga.

Kings mediated the competition among chiefs for followers from their court at the conceptual and physical center of the kingdom.[23] Many of the battles among chiefs for prestige happened in the courtyard of the king, and the physical layout of the capital itself reflected the outcome of the ongoing struggle for power at the center. A kabaka had to mediate between chiefs in competition with one another in a way that maintained chiefs' allegiance to him.

A study of the names kabakas chose for their capitals and for their twin figures suggests that people valued a force so powerful it could eliminate conflict beneath it. For example, King Kigala (fifth in the dynastic list, which means he would have ruled around 1400, according to Kiwanuka) named his house "A White Chicken," referring to the fact that a white chicken cannot conceal itself from a preying animal, implying that "the king cannot conceal himself, but meets everything, public or private, openly, whether or not it is good," and he named his twin Lutimba, "Long Net," meaning that the king, like a long net, reaches everywhere and therefore "the king conquers not by himself but through those men everywhere who support his cause, so that he triumphs over every one of his enemies."[24]

Decisions that went in favor of one chief or clan at one time were decided in favor of another party at a later date, when their relative strength—the love the kabaka felt for them—had shifted.[25] A kabaka balanced and coordinated the actions of chiefs: he could not rule without them. The chiefs who met in the gathering place in the center of the kingdom had the power to offer or withhold tribute and labor, and to choose the peers with whom they would align. A kabaka's capacity to secure the allegiance of chiefs depended on his ability to reallocate prestige, but he had to constantly be aware of the power of groups of chiefs who might favor one of his brothers over him.[26] When kabakas moved the kibuga every few years, they were able to consolidate the allegiance of some chiefs and make others more remote and less powerful depending on where they placed the kibuga in the kingdom, and how they rearranged the order of the compounds of particular chiefs within it. Though ritual and proverbs celebrated the absolute authority of kabakas, in practice they were obliged to cultivate the cooperation of chiefs.

Everyone who had authority in the kingdom—the kabaka, nnamasole, lubuga, priests of lubaale deities, and all manner of chiefs—engaged in highly strategic exchanges of gifts and services in the capital. Evidence for this practice before 1800 comes from chiefship and place names, and from incidents in the dynastic tradition. Nineteenth-century visitors described formal and wildly enthusiastic presentations of gifts and labor that demonstrated the devotion of the chief for his superior and the commitment of his followers to the chief. The strangers were fascinated, and frightened, by these displays of love and power. For example, James Grant observed a ceremony involved in presenting tribute in 1860:

> [A]ll were under officers, perhaps a hundred in one party. If wood is carried into the palace up the hill, it must be done as neatly as a regiment performs a manoeuvre on parade, and with the same precision. After the logs are carried a certain distance, the men charge up hill, with walking sticks at the "slope," to the sound of the drum, shouting, and chorusing. On reaching their officer, they drop on their knees to salute, by saying repeatedly in one voice the word "n'yans." . . . Each officer of a district would seem to have a different mode of drill.[27]

In theory, people said *n'yans* in thanks for having had the privilege of doing the work, but their enthusiasm was also a reminder to observers of the work they had done. The drumming and energetic proclamation of ownership of the work that accompanied cut trees brought for building the Protestant cathedral in 1894 so frightened British agent Dr. Ansorge that he thought a war was starting.[28] C. W. Hattersley, an early missionary, described the work of repairing a royal building before 1908: "When the squad of men belonging to a given chief had finished their part of the work they seized a reed and came before their chief, and before the Katikiro, to announce the completion of their portion, and danced up and down chanting peculiar refrains and behaving generally like madmen."[29] This "madness" conveyed the importance and satisfaction inherent in being men of the chief and of the king, and it also made a claim for the presenting chief in relation to all other chiefs.

Gifts from the king had the same ceremonial, documentary quality of gifts to the king. In the earliest centuries of the kingdom, kabakas drew followers to themselves with gifts and demonstrations of affection, and what a particular chief would receive was never fixed, to enable the king to demonstrate his particular "love" for his favorites.[30] Kings always looked at the food that would be served to the people at the palace, but until the struggles over prestige and favor described below, few chiefs had the privilege of eating with the king.[31] We know that in the nineteenth century, a person who had received a gift from the king "left with great pomp, as everyone saw how he had been favored," and spoils from a raiding expedition were distributed by the king in a large gathering in which all participants recounted their activities.[32] Before the wars of expansion of the eighteenth century, kings controlled prestige, and distributed it in a way that mitigated the competition between chiefs, who controlled followers.

Chiefs fought each other primarily through the practice of *okusala omusango,* cutting cases. People sought justice by presenting their complaint in the presence of the person being complained against, before a chief or other authority who was superior to both litigants. Everyone who was present could listen and participate.[33] Alexander Mackay noted in 1881 that "there is a never-ending amount of *musango* (trial) going on."[34] Bringing and arguing cases shaped people's experience of conflict. According to legend, one of the Christian martyrs warned his executioner that Kabaka Mwanga would face a case with God if he did not repent, and in response Mwanga had his ashes desecrated and said, "How can he now plead against me?"[35] Mackay described a disagreement he had with Kabaka Muteesa that the members of the court played out as a case, choosing people to represent Muteesa's and Mackay's views, and assigning victory to Mackay. The pervasive place of cases in daily life is evident in the English-language exercise book of a rising Christian chief in 1898. In a very neat hand are the translations into English: "The dog wants a bun." "Shall we have cakes for tea?" On the facing page are the learner's own sentences: "He has cut a difficult case." "How will he argue the case?"[36] A chief always heard a case against his own follower, no matter where the offense had been committed. Furthermore, an appeal was against the ruler who made a decision that a complainant disagreed with.[37] Cutting cases, a ubiquitous dimension of Ganda life, constantly set chiefs against each other. Their eloquence, fairness, and the esteem in which they were held by superiors was publicly displayed in every case in which they participated. The endless cases that consumed the energy of Ganda chiefs created a clear means of assessing chiefs' strengths relative to each other.

A kabaka was expected to mediate impartially. According to Christopher Wrigley, ancient kings in interlacustrine Africa were "architects of consensus." "The role most commonly ascribed to them is that of judge, or rather arbiter, or, still better, mediator of disputes."[38] Implicit in the movement of people, allegiance, and things toward the kabaka was the kabaka's obligation to re-ciprocate by distributing prestige and judging well between chiefs in conflict with each other. If a kabaka failed to do this to their satisfaction, individual chiefs or coalitions of chiefs could, and did, withhold their support. Passive opposition to a king could be extremely effective because the kabaka was not alone in the center of the kingdom: not in the layout of the capital, nor in the structures of authority, nor in the collection and redistribution of tribute. The alignment of dissatisfied chiefs with one or more of the powerful people who held autonomous power constrained the action of kabakas. People in Buganda asserted the supreme, encompassing power of kabakas at the same time that they acted in coalitions that circumscribed and shaped the actions a kabaka might take.

The physical layout of the Ganda capital in the nineteenth century suggests the deliberate incorporation of separate sources of authority that must have occurred as the kingdom coalesced: the palace itself became a physical state-ment of alternative forms of power reconciled (see Map 3.1).[39] One side of the huge oval city was the palace of the kabaka, and immediately in front of the palace was a large courtyard where "all of Buganda" gathered to greet the king and listen to cases. Two very large compounds faced the kabaka's across the courtyard; these belonged to the katikkiro and the kimbugwe. According to an oral tradition, the holder of the office of keeper of the king's twin figure, which previously had been called *wolungo,* bought the right to change the title of the office to commemorate his service to the Kabaka Kimbugwe, who probably ruled around 1600.[40] Since the katikkiro and the kimbugwe (wolungo) also existed in the kingdom of Bunyoro, and since they were not attached to a par-ticular Ganda territory, it seems likely that these two offices came into exist-ence at the same time a kabaka became king over an earlier hierarchy in Buganda. The physical places of the kabaka, the katikkiro, and the kimbugwe are together at the very center of the capital, and of the kingdom.

Sources of authority that preceded the kabaka, and could challenge the kabaka, asserted themselves physically in compounds that were part of the capital, but separated from the king's palace by a stream of running water. The largest and most important of these belonged to the nnamasole (queen mother), who, as we saw in Chapter 2, mobilized support for her son but also served as a check on his power, and lived in a palace that mirrored the kabaka's. The *lubuga* (queen sister), who had the title of kabaka and wielded autonomous authority and the *nabikande,* a sister of the nnamasole who over-saw the birth and ensured the legitimacy of the king's children, also had com-pounds in the capital separated from the king's by a stream of running water. According to Roscoe, this was because the queen mother and queen sister were also kings and "two kings could not live on the same hill."[41] The lubuga ad-vised the king on a daily basis.

Two people who had had substantial power in the kingdom before the ar-rival of kabakas also had compounds on the edge of the capital, with a stream between them and the king. One was the mugema, a leading clan elder and chief of Busiro, called the "father" of the kabaka, who had a powerful role in the installation and burial of kabakas. A kabaka could not gain the throne without the mugema's willingness to sanction the use of the drum Mujaguzo. As the "katikkiro" of the deceased kabakas, whose tombs were all in his ter-ritory, the mugema could speak with a voice of authority that challenged the reigning kabaka. The mugema was the only chief who stood instead of kneel-ing in the presence of the kabaka, and he did not eat food prepared by the kabaka's cooks.[42] The *katambala,* the head of the Sheep clan, who tended Mbajwe, the strong spiritual force that had been one of the vehicles of unity for the pre-kabaka polity, also had a compound in the capital separated from the king's by a stream.[43] The katambala and the mugema supported Buganda under the kabaka, but the flowing streams that divided them from the kabaka's part of the capital asserted their ancient and enduring authority.

Gorju described power in Buganda as like a beehive, made up of many cells.[44] The assembled, linked quality of power in Buganda emerges through an exami-nation of habits of exchange. The kabaka's function of balancer is evident in practices of giving to and receiving from the kabaka, which reveal the intense competition among chiefs, and in the ubiquitous habit of hearing cases, *omusango,* which provided the means of mediated conflict among chiefs. A contradictory philosophy of power is evident in a careful study of how people with authority behaved: everyone in Buganda proclaimed the absolute power of kabakas, but people seemed to have valued the kabaka's power for its ability to limit competition among chiefs, and very many forces in Ganda society had the capacity to ensure kabakas filled that function adequately.

Gatherings of "all of Buganda" had tremendous import. In them, the kabaka made choices that could mitigate the roiling tension among chiefs compet-ing with each other for followers. Figures with significant autonomous power—such as the royal women Nnamasole and Lubuga, and the powerful chiefs Kimbugwe, Katikkiro, Mugema, and others, could put pressure on the king to take particular actions. People built up and expended obligation in the tribute and labor they brought, and in the cases they "cut." The careful place-ment of powerful people's establishment in the capital, and the seating

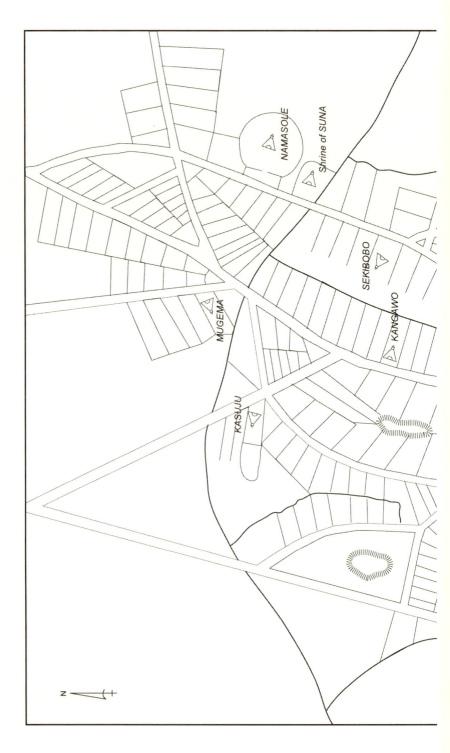

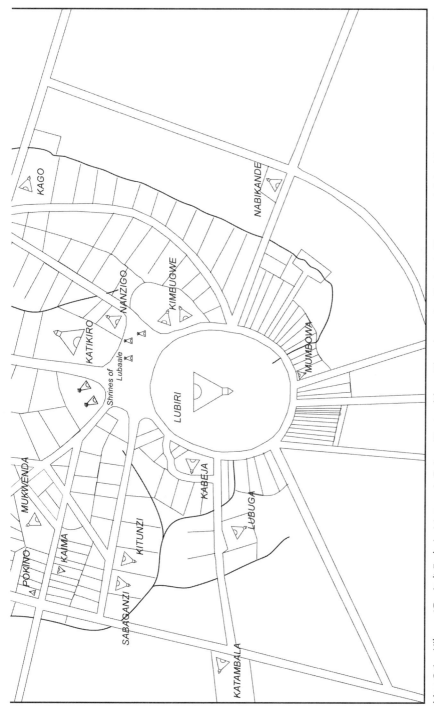

Map 3.1 Kibuga (Capital) Early in Muteesa's Reign. (Derived from Plan drawn by Sir Apolo Kagwa, published in John Roscoe, *The Baganda*)

71

arrangements in the king's courtyard, attested that power was constantly under negotiation.

LUBAALE DEITIES AND KABAKAS NEGOTIATING REALMS OF AUTHORITY

Oral traditions regarding kings' relations to lubaale deities offer further evidence of the tenuousness of kabakas' power. At a very early stage in the coalescence of a Ganda polity, a process of accommodation using the language of reciprocal obligation created a place for lubaale deities in the structures of the kingdom. Lubaale were spiritually powerful beings capable of influencing human affairs, who accepted the active worship of devoted followers and might also accede to the requests of occasional petitioners.[45] Lubaale gods captured the attention of people living north of Lake Victoria around 1500, several hundred years after the adoption of intensive banana cultivation had given them the means to settle densely and establish the connections among groups of people that became the Buganda kingdom. Since *misambwa,* the ancient spiritual forces associated with rivers, waterfalls, great trees, and other natural phenomena, could also be approached with offerings and spoke through mediums, lubaale and misambwa worship were probably related, but the broadly accessible character of lubaale gods, in contrast to the specific-place and particular-people quality of misambwa, suggest that lubaale were part of an innovation in spiritual practice that spread throughout the East African interlacustrine region around five hundred years ago.[46] The arrival of lubaale deities is remembered as having occurred during the reign of Nakibinge, the eighth kabaka, around 1500, but the acceptance of new spiritual forces probably took hold gradually over a long period of time, and engagement between lubaale deities and kings would only have occurred once many people had shown interest in the new kind of worship.[47]

Lubaale worship in Buganda had a closer relationship to the state than other East African forms of spiritual practice, but the lubaale deities had not been co-opted by kabakas and lubaale worship was not a state religion in that the king did not control lubaale deities or their priests.[48] Kabakas and lubaale forces were involved in a continuously negotiated relationship in which the participants demanded an independent realm of action and had definite expectations of the other. The conflicts between kabakas and lubaale deities remembered in dynastic tradition do not convey a quest for domination by kabakas and submission by lubaale forces: rather, they describe the failures of one side or the other to meet its responsibilities in a balanced interaction in which each relied on the autonomous authority of the other. Ethnographic evidence and nineteenth-century accounts of kings interacting with lubaale priests and mediums also suggest that Ganda kings deployed the social tool of creating mutual obligation to connect the power of lubaale to the power of the king.

Dynastic tradition remembers that Kabaka Nakibinge (who probably ruled around 1500) asked for the god Mukasa's help to fight the Banyoro, and received the assistance of the god Kibuka. This story explains how the Baganda drew closer to the then distant world of the Ssese Islands, which was the home of Mukasa. It also remembers the creation of enduring relationships between Ganda rulers and lubaale forces. In contrast to the bonds of obligation that articulated kabakas' dependence on preexisting chiefs, exchanges between kabakas and lubaale priests and mediums clearly expressed the autonomy of the participants. Lubaale deities, not the king, controlled lands dedicated to them, and people who lived there did not pay taxes or owe service to the king. Furthermore, kabakas could not intervene in the succession of clan elders who had official responsibilities to specific lubaale deities. The gods had the title of kings, their temples were built on the same model as the kabaka's palace, and they controlled vast wealth.[49] Mukasa, the highest-ranking lubaale, referred to the kabaka as his son-in-law. As sons-in-law, the kabakas offered gifts, politely asked for the gods' assistance, and gratefully received what the gods gave them.

Kabakas and lubaale priests and mediums defined their relationships through precisely prescribed gifts, given at specified times and sent by the king whenever he needed assistance. Each year the kabaka gave Mukasa sets of nine women, men, white cows, white goats, white fowls, nine loads of bark cloth, and nine loads of cowries, and each year Mukasa sent the kabaka an offering of all the kinds of fish in the lake. All the king's chiefs observed the arrival of Mukasa's gifts, and the king entertained the bearers for several days. A representative brought the kabaka's gifts to Mukasa accompanied by Gabunga, the high-ranking chief in charge of the lake area, but in a striking departure from normal protocol, the king's messenger and Gabunga had to travel alone on a road shown to them by the lubaale priest who welcomed them—the priest took a shorter road and arrived at the temple before they did, a clear assertion of the priest's autonomous authority. Kabakas provided the means for maintaining and rebuilding the temples for all the lubaale deities, following rituals that stated both the kabaka's power to provide the material support for the building of the temple and the lubaale's willingness to accept the gift. When a kabaka needed assistance, his request to a lubaale had to be accompanied by gifts of people and cattle. Lubaale forces also actively asserted their connection to the king by spontaneously offering warnings and advice.[50]

Dynastic tradition records tension and conflict in the practices of gift-giving between kabakas and lubaale forces. In each of the remembered conflicts, kabakas attacked lubaale forces for inappropriate demands for gifts from the

king, but the gods triumphed in the end. Kabaka Tebandeke, who probably
ruled in the last quarter of the seventeenth century, became involved in a conflict with priests of the lubaale Mukasa because he felt they had charged too
much for helping him with an infertility problem. Tebandeke killed the priests
and pillaged Mukasa's shrines, but the god drove him insane, and the kabaka
was only cured by becoming a medium himself.[51] A successor who commemorated Tebandeke's worship of Mukasa took office with each subsequent
kabaka.[52] Kabaka Mawanda, who ruled in the early eighteenth century, had
tried to build his capital on a sacred hill, but became blinded until he left the
place.[53] Kyabaggu, who ruled during the troubled times of eighteenth-century
expansion in the generation following Mawanda, made mediums of Mukasa
angry because he did not give them a large enough share of meat at the feast
he made to celebrate his health when they had cured him of being haunted
by the spirit of a competitor. Kabaka Kyabaggu was angry at their complaints,
killed the mediums, destroyed some temples, and sent people to kill Guggu,
the chief priest of Mukasa. At first it seemed the kabaka had succeeded in
punishing the people of the god, but a few years later Mukasa responded by
sending a plague of rats to the capital, and Kyabaggu was forced to rebuild
the temples and give the god significant wealth, including one of his daughters,
in order to end the plague.[54] In each of these circumstances, recorded in the
dynastic tradition, a kabaka failed to properly acknowledge what was due to
a lubaale, attempted to encroach on a lubaale's power, and suffered such dire
consequences that he had to back down.

Marriages of princesses with lubaale deities expressed kabakas' continuing debt to the lubaale and created a substantial check on kabakas' power, since
princesses spearheaded rebellions. Princess Nassolo, the chief of the princesses, was the wife of Mukasa; she had been given to Mukasa as compensation for the death of Kibuka. It was a Princess Nassolo who led the
successful rebellion against Kabaka Kagulu, the tyrannical twentieth king.
According to Robert Ashe, one of the more inquiring nineteenth-century missionaries, "Every Mumbeja (princess) is . . . nominal wife of a Divinity."
Princess wives for each lubaale held a particular title which was passed down,
a different royal woman holding each title under successive kabakas. Unlike
the celibate lubaale wives who tended the shrines, princesses were sexually
aggressive and "notorious for their amours."[55] The expectation that princesses
would attempt to establish a sexual relationship with whomever they chose,
and their ability to call on the moral and material resources of their lubaale
husbands, made them powerful actors in Ganda political life.

Nineteenth-century chroniclers observed interactions between kabakas and
lubaale representatives that suggest a continual engagement over authority and
prerogatives. King Muteesa had to build elaborate structures to accommodate
visiting representatives of the god Mukasa in 1879; the meetings of lubaale

representatives and kabakas entailed extensive competitive displays of wealth. Because the lubaale Mukasa controlled Lake Victoria, the priest of Mukasa could powerfully intervene in Ganda trade and diplomacy by allowing or forbidding canoes to cross the lake.[56] A confrontation between Kabaka Ssuuna, who ruled from 1824 to 1857, and Kigemuzi, a famous spirit medium of the lubaale Kiwanuka, arose when Ssuuna ordered people not to defecate in the capital on pain of death. It may be that Ssuuna intended public health improvements, but since Ganda capitals did have sanitary arrangements, he may have made this impossible demand as an attempt to reassert control at a time when trade with the coast had begun to erode the kabaka's power. According to Apolo Kaggwa, Kigemuzi objected to the new law and sent a message to Ssuuna through the tax collector: "Ask him, where does he defecate?" The horrified tax collectors took him to the palace, but Kigemuzi refused to be humble. When the kabaka's men stuck his lips with sticks to make him be quiet, he said, "You also will be stuck"; when he was burnt with irons, he said, "You also will be burnt." According to the remembered tradition, only a few hours passed before Kabaka Ssuuna was struck by lightning and his capital burnt down. Kigemuzi, who had been held in stocks, was released and taken to the kabaka. He told Ssuuna, "Punishing a child does not mean hatred, you will soon recover," after which the nnamasole and Kabaka Ssuuna made sure that Kigemuzi got everything he might want.[57]

While dynastic tradition remembered conflicts in which kabakas persecuted the lubaale's people and were punished by the lubaale in return, the material support provided by kings to the priests and temples of lubaale suggests that at some point in the distant past, Ganda rulers had established relationships of mutual obligation with lubaale deities. The regulated exchange of gifts between kings and lubaale forces, and the constant evaluation of the adequacy of those gifts, demonstrates the importance of interaction and balance in Ganda politics. Kabakas had the power to raid lubaale temples, but they more often gave gifts, because of their fear of retribution.[58] In the lived world of social exchange, kabakas sought the assistance and approval of lubaale representatives, and lubaale establishments relied on the people, cattle, and labor supplied by the king and other powerful chiefs.

THE DILEMMAS OF EXPANSION

When Bunyoro and Buganda fought centuries ago in the reigns of Nakibinge and Kateregga, many things changed. Julian Gorju, the missionary chronicler who lived in Buganda for several decades at the beginning of the twentieth century, thought that this war provoked the Baganda into a pattern of territorial expansion. Wrigley observes that "the center of gravity" of the Ganda kingdom shifted from the inland areas that would have been most vulnerable to Nyoro attack to the regions closer to the Lake. According to M.S.M. Semakula Kiwanuka, the royal power became stronger and clan power became weaker, and Martin Southwold has explained the transitions in kabakas' relation to chiefs as the beginning of a "modernizing bureaucracy."[59] It makes sense to imagine that war in the distant past caused people to regroup in different territory, to develop military capacity, and to innovate with social structures. It is important to recognize, however, that war and expansion posed challenges and required accommodation within the practice of power that already existed in Buganda. Conquered land gave kabakas an ability to create chiefships they had never had before, and the coalitions of rulers who had held power in the kingdom strongly objected to the loss of their prestige that newly created chiefships entailed. Even more destabilizing, the importation of war captives into Buganda profoundly eroded the bonds of reciprocal obligation that tied free followers to chiefs and chiefs to the king. Brutal, bloody conflict between coalitions of lineages and ruling kings ended only when Kabaka Semakookiro began a policy of killing all princes in the late eighteenth century. This destroyed the balance of power and turned Ganda kings into despots.

The Ganda hierarchy of important chiefs almost doubled through the incorporation of Butambala, Ggomba, Busujju, and southern Ssingo in the early seventeenth century, and of Kyaggwe, Bulemeezi, and Buddu over the course of eighteenth-century wars of expansion (see Map 3.2). The new territories enabled kings to assume a kind of power that had previously belonged to chiefs, of creating dependents through allocating land. In the late seventeenth century, kings began to allocate regions as chiefships in the same way that chiefs allocated gardens for cultivation to their followers. Some chiefships, such as the *ppookino* of Buddu, were assimilated into the Ganda hierarchy; others were newly created. This represented a new role for kings, who had distributed prestige, but not land, in earlier generations. New chiefships had to be accommodated in the order of prestige of the kingdom enacted in the gatherings of chiefs in the court of the kabaka. As more chiefships were created, the share of the kingdom's power wielded by the chiefs of older provinces was somewhat diminished.[60]

Apolo Kaggwa described the creation of chiefships on unoccupied land as a conflict between kings and clan leaders, and this may be the origin of the perception of a modernizing process in Ganda chiefship:

> King Mawanda found the whole of the land in the hands of the Bataka. He cut off a bit of land (uncultivated) from a butaka and made it *butongole* (a chiefship created by the king). . . . The king wanted to get reports from his own man from various parts of the country so he put them in to a corner of the butaka and told the mutaka you needn't worry to come to see me

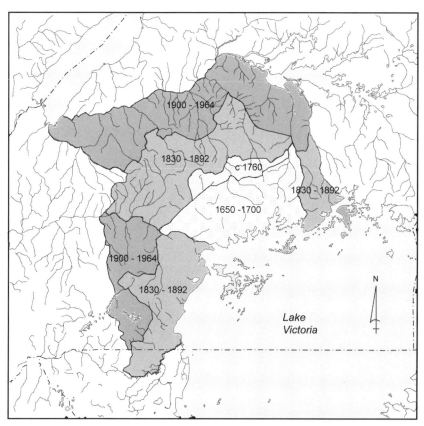

Map 3.2 The Expansion of Buganda. (Derived from Henri Médard, "Croissance et crises de la royauté du Buganda au XIX siécle," 53, 55, 57, 61)

and report, my man will do it, this was the beginning of the *basaza* (chiefs of provinces appointed by the king), just as now the Government are giving milos.[61]

Kaggwa's explanation may accurately point to the desire kings had to increase their autonomy, but it fails to describe the actual consequences of their actions. The new chiefships created new kinds of conflict, but they did not re-create power in Buganda as something held by kings and "king's men" whose only loyalty was to the king who appointed them. In the first place, the older regions still had the greatest prestige and a significant voice in decisionmaking. The chief of Kyaddondo, for example "was often surpassed by others in wealth, because he could not raise as much in taxes," but he was one of the

highest-ranking chiefs.[62] Furthermore, newly appointed chiefs in recently
conquered areas might be favorites of the kabaka, but they still had to win
the allegiance of the people who lived there through a long, slow process of
creating relationships: David Cohen estimates that constructing authority took
forty years in Busoga.[63] The dynastic tradition records kings making innovations in rituals to connect people to the center of the kingdom and to clarify
patterns of prestige at the same time that they created new chiefships.

Many people with factions behind them competed to receive the new
chiefships created through expansion: in this time of intense competition, some
clan elders lost the "love" of the kabaka and lost positions, but others succeeded in making the kabaka so obligated to them that their chiefships were
created as hereditary.[64] An example of kabakas' new ability to allocate land
for chiefships comes from the dynastic tradition regarding Kabaka Ndawula,
who reigned in the generation before Mawanda. He created a chiefship in this
way: "He at this time gave the ladies who are sisters to his mother the village of Kikaya. The leader of these ladies put here to grow food for him, was
Nakaberenge and to whomever that village is given, she bears the title
Nakaberenge."[65] Since the *nnakaberenge,* "the mother who is entrusted," came
from the family of his queen mother, the king may have been trying to consolidate their support, but this chiefship also had the function of organizing
production of food for the palace.

The accelerated creation of chiefships as the kingdom expanded led to conflicts over prestige. As we have seen, chiefs relied on the kabaka to mediate
in conflicts of competition for status and for followers. The incorporation of
the newly made chiefs of recently acquired lands into the *Lukiiko,* the gathering of chiefs in the courtyard of the king, entirely upset the balance of prestige. This gathering had a definite order of precedence depending on "the
service provided by the first title holder, or the size of the population, or, the
date at which the province was annexed by the Kingdom"; chiefs who experienced their status as diminishing seem to have attempted to withdraw support from the king.[66]

Kabaka Kateregga began the period of Ganda expansion by incorporating
the territories of Ggomba and Butambala (center of the Mbajwe cult), to the
west of the Ganda heartland of Busiro. Kateregga used marriage to create
alliances, and he established the practice of requiring particular chiefs to bring
tribute to particular royal wives.[67] The three important chiefships Kateregga
created were hereditary, and he died of natural causes. Kateregga's son Mutebi
added Ssingo, to the north of the center of Buganda, and part of Mawokota,
to the east. Kabaka Mutebi attempted to dismiss the chiefs Mugema and
Kaggo, in order to appoint his "favorites," but his chiefs refused to allow it.
According to the dynastic history, "the chiefs kept him from this because of
the precious dignity and honor of these men," and "partly due to the vigor-

ous opposition of the chiefs, and partly due to the fact that the dismissal of the mugema would have violated a traditional custom, the king yielded."[68] However, a few days later, Mutebi was informed by a soothsayer that he had to have a particular tree cut down to make a new royal drum, Kaulugumo: Mutebi may have elaborated royal ritual at this moment in order to regain his authority, which had been undermined by his defeat in relation to the mugema and the *kaggo,* chief of Kyaddondo.

Mutebi seems to have bargained with the Oribi Antelope clan: he first removed the clan's head from his position and placed a different man of the clan in the position of Mukwendo, chief of Ssingo. This chiefship did not become hereditary in the Oribi Antelope clan. Instead, the Oribi Antelope clan people received the important hereditary position of the *kibaale,* a chiefship that required the holder to voice objections to unacceptable actions of the kabaka. A proverb stated: *"Mpaawo kinene kyeetwala: ne Kabaka afugibwa Kibaale"*—"None is beyond the law: even the kabaka is governed by Kibaale."[69] The kibaale took the kabaka's place when he was absent, and was the only person who could try the kabaka. According to Zachariah Kisingiri, one of the most powerful chiefs of the early colonial period, the kibaale in the past "could find the king was in the wrong, but he had no authority to punish him."[70] Succession to this position followed a unique procedure: the Oribi Antelope clan selected fifteen candidates from the appropriate lineage, then the kabaka chose four of those, and the final decision of who would succeed to the position of kibaale was made by "all of Buganda"—the chiefs who gathered to hear cases in the kabaka's court.[71] It seems possible that Kabaka Mutebi created the office of kibaale as a form of compensation, since the kibaale's office was to reveal the kabaka's mistakes, and Mutebi had removed the clan head from the position of the *mukwenda,* and had failed to appoint clan members to the position. Mutebi died naturally, but the dynastic tradition remembers that his two brothers both reigned and both died in fights over succession.[72] Juuko, the kabaka who followed Mutebi, had to deal with the disruption to the order of prestige in the Lukiiko caused by the creation of powerful new chiefships. According to dynastic history, before the installation of Juuko, "diviners prophesied that there would be a rebellion" and told him to create order in the Lukiiko with a new ritual for seating the chiefs. A child of Mugema (the prime minister to all deceased kabakas and "father" of the living kabaka) was to whip the chiefs who acted in a disorderly way using a whip made of the sinews of a person sacrificed during the kabaka's installation. According to Kaggwa, "This position was very much respected, and parliament became much more dignified by the exercise of this power in preserving order."[73] The need for a new method of keeping discipline, and the fact that this task was given to the son of the chief and clan elder with the greatest autonomy from a kabaka, suggests that chiefs had ceased to be able to determine their relative importance.

New ritual functions added by Kabaka Kayemba, the second brother of Mutebi, suggest an attempt to draw some lineages into closer association with the center of the kingdom. Previously the *kinyolo* (a chief with particular ritual duties who was always a son of Mugema) had had the responsibility of giving a new king his first wife. From the time of Kabaka Kayemba, the kinyolo also oversaw the preparation of a home for a wife from the Grasshopper clan, with donations from relatively autonomous people who lived in the cattle-raising areas adjoining Buganda. Kabaka Mutebi had previously dispossessed an autonomous Grasshopper clan ruler; Kabaka Kayemba may have been trying to regain the clan's goodwill through creating the named Grasshopper clan wife Nakimera and arranging for her to be honored. From the time of Kayemba, the kinyolo also began to take actions that connected the Vervet Monkey clan, the Colobus Monkey clan, the kabaka, and the shrines of all the lubaale deities in preparation of protective medicine for the king.[74]

Kabaka Kagulu, the grandson of Juuko, spent his entire reign defending himself against at least six princes who conspired to rule. Kagulu's unstable reign is remembered as a kind of anti-government. He made people carry reeds for his fences with the points sticking up, and kneel down where he had planted needles in the ground. He also made them dig trees out of the ground, including the roots, which caused some people to be buried alive. The tradition explains, "When the chiefs and the rest of the people came to hate being pierced by needles or buried alive, they rebelled against Kagulu." People gathered on a hill adjacent to the kibuga and jeered the Kabaka, saying "Sir, we your men have come to pay you a visit, Busiro greets you.'" Another factor in the revolt was that Kagulu murdered the mugema. "When word of this went through the kingdom, the people rose in revolt and deserted the king and his kingdom."[75] When Kabaka Kagulu saw the people refusing to come to him, he made a drum and ordered it to be beaten: "Buganda is at peace: Kagulu does not now kill people: come and visit him." But the people did not come, so Princess Ndege Nassolo called the princes to organize the overthrow of the king. She sought help in blood brotherhood with a chief who had been her lover, and enlisted the assistance of a powerful healer. Kagulu so thoroughly lost authority that all his people left him, no one would feed him, and he had to kill a man to obtain a goat to eat. The rebellion faltered when all the princes refused to be installed as kabaka because Kagulu was still alive. Eventually, Princess Nassolo drowned the kabaka herself, an action that is commemorated with butaka land by Lake Victoria. After Kabaka Kagulu's death, people of the Elephant clan were killed for having produced such an evil kabaka, and clan members had to hide themselves in another clan.[76] Since Kagulu was the last kabaka before a significant reconceptualization of the kingdom by his brother and successor, Mawanda, it is not surprising that his wrongdoing and the rebellion against him have the quality of a charter of good government for Buganda.[77]

Mawanda strategized with reciprocal obligation in his ultimately unsuccessful efforts to remain alive and in power. According to Wrigley, he attempted to consolidate his authority by utilizing his marriage connections to the Magonga shrine to arrange to meet with his ancestor Kintu.[78] He built allegiances with wealthy and powerful chiefs. For example, he carved off the province Bulemeezi, in the north, from the wealthy, older province Kyaddondo, and created a separate chiefship with the name "to break off a branch" in order to thank Mwogozi, a wealthy man who had built a very large house for the king in the royal enclosure.[79] Kabaka Mawanda's creation of a high-ranking chiefship for Mwogozi was thanking him for his ability to mobilize labor to build for the king, but it was also drawing Mwogozi's productive capacity further into the king's domain. He also attempted to remove from power people who did not support him: that Kyaddondo was diminished in the process of creating Bulemeezi expressed the kabaka's displeasure at indications of rebellion in that area.[80] Mawanda made a further, powerful innovation in the pattern of prestige in the capital by intensifying the conceptual links between a particular territory, chiefship of that territory, and a place in the center of the kingdom. Chiefs who had held autonomous power and linked that power to the kabaka through a vocabulary of reciprocal obligation now came to be understood as chiefs of particular ssazas, who also had distinctive authority.[81] Mawanda also established headquarters for the chiefships of Kyaddondo, Kyaggwe, Ssingo, and Bulemeezi, and people built broad, straight roads linking those ssaza headquarters with the capital.[82]

People eventually came to think of Buganda in the way that Mawanda had shaped it: the order of ssaza chiefships that Mawanda had created defined the kingdom. However, in the early eighteenth century, in the fulminating chaos of princes and lineages competing for control of the kingdom, these innovations had little immediate effect. Two kings of the generation of Mawanda's grandfather had died in office, all three kabakas of Mawanda's generation were murdered, and of the following four kings, only one was not murdered—a king who abdicated in favor of a brother who wished to kill him.

Expansion of the number of prominent chiefs and turmoil over chiefly prestige characterized the pattern of chiefship creation in the seventeenth and eighteenth centuries. The perception that clans lost power and kings gained it ignores the very short life span of kings of these generations. Kings were taking away many lineage privileges; however, lineages were killing many kings. In the maneuvering for relative advantage that expansion entailed, kings created new hereditary chiefships and also attempted to deprive some lineages of chiefships they had held. Dynastic traditions remarked on changes in ritual and in the order of chiefship, but it is more difficult to discern the subtle transformations caused by the wars of expansion. This period's disorder came not only from the challenge of incorporating the king's newly asserted power to allocate conquered land as chiefships, but also from the dilemma of nonfree people brought into Buganda as the booty of the wars.

The wars of expansion brought large numbers of captive people into Buganda. According to Kaggwa's description of the division of war booty, more war captives were women than men, but both men and women were taken.[83] Records of royal wives and concubines provide insight into the number of nonfree people coming into the kingdom. Kateregga, the kabaka who began the wars of expansion, had three hundred women who were not named wives; his predecessor, Kimbugwe, had only seven such women. Each subsequent king until Semakookiro in the late eighteenth century maintained between one hundred and seven hundred women attached to the palace who did not have the status of named wives. According to Kaggwa, these women were divided among the king's favorite wives and their subordinates so that "these might maintain their positions of dignity" and that the status of the captured women "was practically slavery."[84] Stolen women were distributed to the principal chiefs of the kingdom, chiefs who had led an expedition, and men who had participated in it; the supply of women captives is probably what allowed ordinary Baganda to begin to practice polygamy during the reign of Kateregga.[85] At the end of the eighteenth century, the numbers of captured women in Buganda rose dramatically: Semakookiro had eighty-five hundred nonfree women, and his successor, Kamanya, had over ten thousand. Explorer Richard Burton noted that Kabaka Ssuuna, who ruled in the mid-nineteenth century, had given two to three hundred women to one Arab trader; and Robert Felkin thought that the "constant influx of women into the country as prisoners of war" had led to a ratio of three and a half women to one man.[86] One Ganda chief remembered that in the mid-nineteenth century his father had possessed "twenty cattle and 100 wives."[87] Ganda women and the free followers of chiefs suffered a drastic reduction in their status as a result of the presence of nonfree people.[88]

Captive people brought into the kingdom as a result of wars of expansion allowed both the king and other powerful men to create units of productive labor unhooked from networks of reciprocal obligation. The new kind of chiefship created around the time of Mawanda, known as ekitongole, seems to have been to some degree a way of organizing nonfree labor. All the work performed by the people in an ekitongole belonged exclusively to the person who created that ekitongole. While the king had to reciprocate in some way for the labor and produce offered by other kinds of chiefs, the produce of an ekitongole entailed no obligation. This might have seemed to be a useful increase in the king's realm of action, but the incipient commodification of production in ebitongole had destabilizing consequences. Chiefs who captured

Figure 3.1 Ganda couple walking, 1906. The status of women declined when participants in the wars of expansion brought large numbers of captive women into the kingdom. (Vittorio Sella)

people in the wars of expansion created their own ebitongole, and the ebitongole of chiefs detached them from the network of redistribution centered in the kabaka's court. The possibility created by control over nonfree people redirected competition between chiefs: instead of competing with their peers to attract followers, chiefs began to compete to control the kabakaship in order to be able to control the supply of nonfree labor.

In contrast to chiefships named after important people or significant interactions in the past, ebitongole chiefships were usually named for what they were supposed to accomplish, and they carried the implication of directing resources toward a particular productive activity. Kabaka Namugala, who ruled in the mid-eighteenth century, established the ebitongole Ekigalagala ("for the purpose of spreading out") and Kitamanyang'amba ("for the purpose of knowing what is said"). A generation later, Kabaka Kamanya established the chiefship Ekikinakulya ("for the purpose of things to eat").[89] Consolidating military victories was the purpose of some of the original ebitongole chiefships, and for this reason they have been erroneously considered a form of military chiefship.[90] Settling an area to incorporate new territory into Buganda could be one purpose toward which the kabaka directed productive resources, but there were many others. An ekitongole on Buganga was called Ekibukula Mabira ("for the purpose of opening up of the forests") because the clan elder had asked the kabaka for hunters to drive away elephants and buffaloes that were attacking people, and the ekitongole was the land supplied to meet the food needs of the hunters. Other ebitongole in the same area were Kikwekwesi, the place where the head of all the kabaka's servants obtained labor and supplies, and Kisomose, the place where the makers of kabaka's drums and boards for the game *mweso* lived, grew their food, and carried out their work.[91]

Evidence that many or most of the people in ebitongole chiefships were war captives comes from descriptions of the history of particular ebitongole and also indirectly. The Ekisalosalo, one of the military regiment ebitongole, was formed "for a body of pages captured in war."[92] Kabaka Ssuuna assigned an ekitongole to captured Banyoro potters.[93] Less direct evidence comes from a recognition that large amounts of labor were required to begin cultivation of unopened land. Ebitongole were created on land without people until Kabaka Mwanga's final conflict with chiefs in the 1880s.[94] It seems logical to assume that ebitongole chiefships were initially created when captive people began to enter the kingdom, because the captives had to be attached to land in the kingdom in a new way. According to Kiwanuka, the kabaka created a special ekitongole to open up a resource poor or unhealthy area, such as the mbwa fly region of Kyaggwe, and "people would be obliged to go and settle there."[95] The nonfree status of some ebitongole chiefs can be inferred from the comment that a chief always had an officer to "keep his umbilical cord," but in the late nineteenth century some people became chiefs without having an umbilical cord to be looked after. Ebitongole were not entirely peopled by nonfree followers: Apolo Kaggwa observed that in the late nineteenth century, free people flocked to chiefs who had large numbers of slaves, because they were attracted by the wealth and prestige of those chiefships.[96]

Chiefs created their own ebitongole chiefships using nonfree people. Stanislaus Mugwanya created the ekitongole Kirima Ntungo, meaning "to

cultivate sesame seeds"; he may have had export to Bunyoro or to the caravan trade in mind.[97] In the late nineteenth century Mukwenda, chief of Ssingo,
created an ekitongole named Ekirumba, in memory of Ddumba, the previous
chief. The title of the chief was Mulumba, and the first holder of this post was
an enslaved Musoga man who had been captured in his childhood.[98] The chief
Omulwanyamuli created the ekitongole Ekirwanyamuli in Buganga as a place
where his people could obtain bananas when they visited the lake to fish. Since
the ekitongole had been allocated as uncultivated land, the chief had probably assigned captives to open the land and cultivate it.[99] Ebitongole consist-
ing of nonfree men with guns that powerful chiefs created in the late
nineteenth century led Buganda into civil war.

Ekitongole chiefship and stolen people undermined the practices of gift
exchange and service that connected the nodes of power in the Buganda polity. Eventually, the unobligated, nonfree labor turned the logic of prestige in
the capital upside down. Chiefs became able to command labor that allowed
them to build "handsome houses and neat fences" in the capital, which made
the king jealous, and kabakas had reason to fear the idle dependents of their
chiefs.[100] Kabakas who used nonfree ebitongole to accomplish their goals did
not need to satisfy their chiefs, and chiefs who controlled ebitongole became
less reliant on the "love" of the king. Chiefs who had slave wives and slave
workers had less need to prove by their behavior that they were more generous and just than neighboring chiefs in order to retain free followers. The
importation of masses of stolen people into Buganda led to an increase in
violence at every level. It contributed to six generations of royal killings, because chiefs tried to replace kings who did not value them or rely on them
appropriately. Also, coalitions of chiefs tried to put "their" prince on the throne
in order to benefit most fully from the flow of captives. It undermined the
security of chiefs in office, as kabakas tried to reward their allies and punish
those who aligned against them. Since nonfree people diminished the value
of free followers to their chiefs, nonfree ebitongole followers and stolen wives
profoundly undermined the status of ordinary people in Buganda.

Kabaka Semakookiro, who ruled at the end of the eighteenth century, attempted to solve the problem of unending conflict among rivals for the throne
by killing all the princes except a few potential heirs, who were imprisoned.
Clan elder Kalikuzinga told Michael Wright that this solution had been considered so abominable that the priest of Mukasa had insisted on making the
suggestion to the king with no one listening.[101] This drastic action did not end
competition for the throne, but it eliminated some of the constraints on kabakas'
actions. Nineteenth-century visitors to Buganda observed a kind of daily
coercive violence that suggests a disintegrating social order. Chiefs and the king
mutilated their followers as a form of punishment for seemingly trivial of-

Figure 3.2 An Ekitongole receives Stanley, 1875. An ekitongole with thousands of men greeted Stanley on Kabaka Muteesa's behalf in 1875. (Stanley, *Through the Dark Continent,* 148)

fenses.[102] The execution of people attending the kabaka's court appeared to be an almost casual occurrence. Kaggwa remembered the violence of the late nineteenth century like this: "On the whole this killing reached terrible excesses. Sometimes the king put to death his own children, brothers, and sisters. Sometimes it was the other way round, several of the children conspiring together to kill their father. The chiefs killed their servants for next to nothing. The death penalty became so ordinary that it often put the chiefs in a dilemma."[103] These conditions created the insuperable ideological dilemma that led Buganda toward the civil war of the late nineteenth century. In the Ganda discourse of power, the exchanges between followers and superiors that people called "love" became increasingly coercive, but when people spoke about love and intended force, the perception that love was important still mattered.

The social and political balance that people in Buganda had put together through assertions of reciprocal obligation became destabilized through the vast increase in territory and importation of masses of stolen people that followed Buganda's successful expansion in the seventeenth and eighteenth centuries. Kabakas and the priests of lubaale deities had attempted to negotiate their relative power (not always successfully) through carefully calibrated exchanges of gifts. Chiefs fought other chiefs for prestige and followers in displays of generosity and in well-argued cases. In the gathering of "all of Buganda," kabakas could dampen competition among chiefs for followers, but the wars of expansion exacerbated competition of every kind. In an unsuccessful attempt to halt the violent domestic turmoil brought about by the expansion, Kabaka Mawanda codified reciprocal obligation between territorial chiefs, royal wives, and the kabaka, defining Buganda as ten ssazas under named chiefs. Ganda kings were only able to counteract the danger of unobligated power by undermining a fundamental premise of the Ganda social order—that followers could withdraw support.

NOTES

1. Original sources that reinforce this point of view are Kaggwa's contribution to "Enquiry into Native Land Tenure," esp. p. 4, and his March 18, 1922, memorandum to Kabaka Daudi Chwa, which became part of the Butaka Land Commission records listing every victory of a Kabaka over a clan leader. "Commission," 561–564. The point of view that kabakas attempted to systematically take over the power of other controllers of territory can be found in Southwold, *Bureaucracy and Chiefship;* D. Anthony Low, *Buganda in Modern History* (Los Angeles: University of California Press, 1971), 30; D. Anthony Low, "The Northern Interior, 1840–1884," in *History of East Africa,* vol. 1, ed. Roland Oliver and Gervase Mathew (Oxford: Clarendon Press, 1963), 334; Fallers, "Social Stratification," 97; and Wrigley, *Kingship,* 65. Relying on oral histories recounted by clan elders, Michael Wright disputed the view that clans and kabakas had been in conflict or that Buganda had been despotic. Wright, *Buganda in the Heroic Age,* 2–4, 206. Other nonroyalist perspectives were published in *Ebifa* and *Munno,* by Gomotoka and others; these are explored in Kiwanuka, *History of Buganda,* 99–100; and Ray, *Myth, Ritual, and Kingship,* 96–13.

2. As Michael Twaddle has pointed out, Buganda scholarship has not adequately distinguished between slaves and free followers of a chief. Michael Twaddle, "Slaves and Peasants in Buganda," in *Slavery and Other Forms of Unfree Labour,* ed. Leonie J. Archer (London: Routledge, 1988), 121–122; Michael Twaddle, "The Ending of Slavery in Buganda," in *The End of Slavery in Africa,* ed. Suzanne Miers and Richard Roberts (Madison: University of Wisconsin Press, 1988), 144.

3. Ferdinand Walser, *Luganda Proverbs* (Kampala: Mill Hill Missionaries, 1984), proverbs 2938, 1034.

4. "Enquiry," Zachariah Kisingiri, 12; "Enquiry," Baziri Seboa Kauwa, 95–96, 98–99.

5. Fallers, "Social Stratification," 74.

6. Mair, *An African People,* 183; Mackay, *Pioneer Missionary,* 197; E. Frank Muhereza, *Land Tenure and Peasant Adaptations: Some Reflections on Agricultural Production in Luwero District,* Working Paper no. 27 (Kampala: Centre for Basic Research Publications, 1992), 41.

7. Roscoe, *The Baganda,* 471–472.

8. Kaggwa, *Kings,* 58.

9. Kaggwa, *Ekitabo ky Kika Kya Nsenene,* 17.

10. "Commission," Makobo Kalonde, 428.

11. Roscoe, *The Baganda,* 21.

12. Mair, *An African People,* 183; Sitefano Serwange to Apolo Kaggwa, August 1913, Kaggwa Papers, AR KA 43/52; Mackay, *Pioneer Missionary,* 208–209.

13. Roscoe, *The Baganda,* 44.

14. Ibid., 241; Martin Southwold, "Leadership, Authority, and the Village Community," in *The King's Men,* ed. Lloyd Fallers (New York: Oxford University Press, 1964), 214. Wright observed that "low tension" characterized Ganda political interactions: differences were not pursued to the point at which conflict would become necessary. Wright, *Buganda in the Heroic Age,* 51. This perception stands in contrast to that of Lloyd Fallers, articulated in "Despotism, Status Culture, and Social Mobility in an African Kingdom," *Comparative Studies in Society and History* 2 (1959): 4–32, 20, that the lack of clearly delineated functions of each of the multiple office holders would have increased the power of the kabaka.

15. "Enquiry," Rasito Kawaga, 24; Mair, *An African People,* 175.

16. "Enquiry," Tefiro Mulumba Kuluji, 33; "Enquiry," Baziri Seboa Kauwa, 95–96; Medard "Croissance," 404. Receiving tribute through chains of authority figures entitled to take a portion of what was given was a well-established pattern in Buganda: early in the twentieth century, Catholics and Protestants built their cathedrals and schools by collecting from followers using this technique. Budo Board of Governors File, 23/10/1924, Kabali Papers, AR KA 2/2, Makerere University Library Africana Collection.

17. "Commission," Erenesti Kakoza, 451.

18. Fallers, "Social Stratification," 96–97. The pattern continued into the twentieth century, when a British administrator complained, "shambas situated in the center of one division are not ruled by the chief of the division in which they are situated, but arbitrarily placed under the administration of the chief chosen by the owner of the land." D. W. Cooper to Provincial Commissioner, January 2, 1912, Entebbe Secretariat Archives Secretariat Minute Paper (SMP) 2349, cited in J. A. Atanda, "The *Bakopi* in the Kingdom of Buganda, 1900–1927: An Analysis of the Condition of the Peasant Class in Early Colonial Period," cyclostyled paper labeled "History Department, MSP/16," Northwestern University Africana Collection, 7.16.

19. As we shall see in Chapter 4, Kabaka Mwanga's own authority was called into question (and, by some accounts, entirely rejected) during the years in which control over the island was disputed, and the kabaka's own dubious position might have contributed to Bussi leaders' rejection of the overrule of the Gabunga. However, the logic of the Bussi witnesses, who proved their autonomy by referencing their actions in relation to the ssaza chief, suggests that autonomous authority within the territory of a ssaza chief was not unusual.

20. "Commission," Yosiya Sajabi Semugala, 385.

21. "Commission," Zedi Zirimenya, 359.

22. "Commission," Malaki Musajakawa, 345.

23. Mikael Karlstrom argues that public events in Uganda have one invited guest of honor because that guest functions like the kabaka as a mediator of conflict: "the power holder, the situational apex of the public event, is the guarantor of a level playing field and the regulator of competitive energies." Karlstrom, "Cultural Kingdom in Uganda," 380–382.

24. Kaggwa, *Customs,* 21.

25. "Enquiry," Rasito Kawaga, 27; "Enquiry," Apolo Kaggwa, 70. This is one of the

themes of the testimony of clan elders before the Butaka Land Commission in 1924; see, for example, "Commission," Daudi Basudde, 352.

26. The story of the rise and fall of the servant Kiyanzi, which carried on for several generations, is an example of this. Kaggwa, *Kings,* 146–149.

27. James Augustus Grant, *A Walk Across Africa, or Domestic Sceneries from My Nile Journal* (Edinburgh: Blackwood and Sons, 1864), 231.

28. Kaggwa, *Basekabaka,* trans. Musoke, 177; Wright, *Buganda in the Heroic Age,* 167–168.

29. Hattersley, *The Baganda at Home,* 20.

30. "Enquiry," Tefiro Mulumba Kuluji, 34.

31. Zimbe, *Buganda,* 71; Kaggwa, *Customs,* 88.

32. Kaggwa, *Customs,* 92; Fallers, "Social Stratification," 110; John Hanning Speke, *Journey of the Discovery of the Source of the Nile* (Edinburgh: Blackwood and Sons, 1863), 251.

33. Rowe, "Revolution," 8; E. Wamala, "The Socio-Political Philosophy of Traditional Buganda Society: Breaks and Continuity into the Present," in *The Foundations of Social Life: Ugandan Philosophical Studies,* ed. E. T. Alfovo et al., Cultural Heritage and Contemporary Change Series no 2, Africa, vol. 2 (Washington, D.C.: Council for Research in Values and Philosophy), 47.

34. Mackay, *Pioneer Missionary,* 187.

35. J. F. Faupel, *African Holocaust: The Story of the Uganda Martyrs* (1962; reprint, Kampala St. Paul Publications–Africa, 1984), 114–115.

36. Ezera Kabali Papers, AR KA 2/3, File E, Makerere University Library Africana Collection.

37. "Enquiry," Zakalo Naduli Kibare and Kamya Mesusala, 108; Fallers, "Social Stratification," 108.

38. Wrigley, *Kingship,* 87.

39. Roscoe, *The Baganda,* 519. Apolo Kaggwa drew detailed maps of the capital and palace in the time of Kabakas Suna (1825–1852) and Mutesa (1852–1879) consulting "the most intelligent of the old men who knew the place."

40. Gorju, *Entre le Victoria,* 136.

41. Roscoe, *The Baganda,* 203.

42. Ibid., 104–106, 156–157, 253; "Enquiry," Stanislaus Mugwanya, 3; "Enquiry," Joshua Mugema, 69, 101.

43. Kaggwa, *Customs,* 123.

44. Gorju, *Entre le Victoria,* 85; Wright, *Buganda in the Heroic Age,* 1–5, 204–205.

45. Roscoe, *The Baganda,* 273–276; Mair, *An African People,* 231–233; Kaggwa, *Customs,* 112–117; "Enquiry," Tefiro Mulumba Kuluji, 52.

46. Tantala, "Early History of Kitara," 320; John V. Taylor, *The Growth of the Church in Buganda* (London: SCM Press, 1958), 201.

47. Wrigley, *Kingship,* 167.

48. Kiwanuka sees kabakas as having gained unchecked power over other forces, including lubaale deities; and Wrigley also interprets the dynastic tradition as implying that kabakas checked the power of lubaale mediums. Kiwanuka, *History of Buganda,* 109; Wrigley, *Kingship,* 184.

49. Roscoe, *The Baganda,* 290, 298; Fallers, "Social Stratification," 103; "Enquiry," Tefiro Mulumba Kuluji, 58; Speke, *Journey,* 425–426.

50. Roscoe, *The Baganda,* 298–300, 303, 305, 309. Richard Reid and Henri Medard describe the relationship of kabakas and lubaale deities as that of "peers exchanging embassies." Richard Reid and Henri Medard, "Merchants, Missions, and the Remaking of the Urban Environment in Bugandam c.1840–90," in *Africa's Urban Past,* ed. David. M. Anderson and Richard Rathbone (Portsmouth, N.H.: Heinemann, 2000), 103.

51. M.S.M. Semakula Kiwanuka interprets this tradition as demonstrating "the growing powers of the monarchy." Kiwanuka, *History of Buganda,* 109.

52. Kaggwa, *Kings,* 59; Wrigley, *Kingship,* 182.

53. Roscoe, *The Baganda,* 319–320.

54. Kaggwa, *Kings,* 83–84; Roscoe, *The Baganda,* 224.

55. Ashe, *Chronicles,* 105; Medard, "Croissance," 555–557.

56. Mackay, *Pioneer Missionary,* 149–150, 155–156; Roscoe, *The Baganda,* 299.

57. Kaggwa, *Basekabaka,* trans. Musoke, 128.

58. Roscoe, *The Baganda,* 273, 301.

59. Gorju, *Entre le Victoria,* 118–119; Wrigley, *Kingship,* 172, 212, 215; Kiwanuka, *History of Buganda,* 99–100; Southwold, *Bureaucracy and Chiefship,* 9.

60. Kiwanuka, *History of Buganda,* 115, 117.

61. It is useful to consider that the kings-over-clans perception gained currency in the context of twentieth-century politics. Apolo Kaggwa provided this explanation while he was being questioned about his actions in allocating land five years earlier. Half a century later, as the British Protectorate of Uganda gave way to a British-styled independent Uganda, Martin Southwold wrote about Ganda chiefship as a modernizing bureaucracy. "Enquiry," Apolo Kaggwa, 4; Southwold, *Bureaucracy and Chiefship* 9, 13.

62. Kaggwa, *Customs,* 162; Fallers, "Social Stratification," 96.

63. Cohen, *Womunafu's Bunafu,* 159.

64. Kiwanuka, *History of Buganda,* 100; Southwold, *Bureaucracy and Chiefship,* 9.

65. Kaggwa, *Basekabaka,* trans. Musoke, 60; cf. Kaggwa, *Kings,* 59.

66. Gorju, *Entre le Victoria,* 135.

67. Wrigley, *Kingship,* 173; Kaggwa, *Customs,* 68–69, 166.

68. Kaggwa, *Customs,* 28; Kaggwa, *Kings,* 144.

69. Cosmas Gitta, "International Human Rights: An Imperial Imposition? (A Case Study of Buganda, 1856–1955)" (Ph.D. diss., Columbia University, 1998), 114.

70. "Enquiry," Zachariah Kisingiri, 10.

71. Ibid.

72. Kaggwa, *Kings,* 55, 58.

73. Kaggwa, *Customs,* 78.

74. Ibid., 15–16.

75. Ibid., 83.

76. Kaggwa, *Kings,* 62–68.

77. Kiwanuka questions the place of "the people" in these histories, suggesting that internecine struggle, rather than rebellion against oppression, characterized the period. He observes that nearly every king for the next ten reigns had to defend the throne against rivals. The dynastic tradition describes personal details of these battles and says less about the coalitions of chiefs and lineages that supported each rival chief, but it is important to recognize that princes who fought for the throne acted in conjunction with a set of lineages and figures of authority who chose to support them instead of the ruling kabaka. Kiwanuka, *History of Buganda,* 103.

78. Wrigley, *Kingship,* 117–118.

79. Roscoe, *The Baganda,* 252; Gorju, *Entre le Victoria,* 138.

80. Kiwanuka, *Kings,* 74.

81. "Enquiry," Kwega, 86–87.

82. Kiwanuka, *History of Buganda,* 114.

83. Kaggwa, *Customs,* 92.

84. Nakanyike B. Musisi, "Women, 'Elite Polygyny,' and Buganda State Formation," *Signs* 16:4 (1991): 757–786; Kaggwa, *Customs,* 67.

85. Kaggwa, *Customs,* 68; Gorju, *Entre le Victoria,* 120.

86. Richard Burton, quoted in John Tosh, "The Northern Interlacustrine Region," in *Pre-Colonial African Trade: Essays on Trade in Central and Eastern Africa Before 1900,* ed. Richard Gray and David Birmingham (London: Oxford University Press, 1970), 112; Robert Felkin, quoted in Twaddle "Ending of Slavery," 126.

87. "Enquiry," Nsimbi, 28.

88. Twaddle, "Ending of Slavery," 123–124, 144.

89. "Commission," Apolo Kaggwa, 563.

90. Kiwanuka, *History of Buganda,* 120.

91. "Commission," Mikairi Kidza and Stanislaus Mugwanya, 401.

92. Wright, *Buganda in the Heroic Age,* 26.

93. "Commission," Yosiya Sensalire, 472.

94. "Commission," Shem Spire Mukasa, 522; "Enquiry," Apolo Kaggwa, 4.

95. Kiwanuka, *History of Buganda,* 119.

96. "Enquiry," Tefiro Mulumba Kuluji, 55; Kaggwa, *Basekabaka,* trans. Musoke, 340; Twaddle, "Ending of Slavery," 122.

97. "Commission," Stanislaus Mugwanya, 395.

98. Faupel, *African Holocaust,* 29–30.

99. "Commission," Mikairi Kidza, 401.

100. Ashe, *Chronicles,* 94–95; Zimbe, *Buganda,* 82.

101. Wright, *Buganda in the Heroic Age,* 2.

102. Gitta, quoting Kaggwa, "International Human Rights," 123; Mackay, *Pioneer Missionary,* 199.

103. Kaggwa, *Customs,* 84.

4

CHIEFSHIP IN THE DISSOLUTION AND RESTORATION OF CIVIL ORDER, 1857–1899

Civil war and social disorder convulsed Buganda in the late nineteenth century. Four kabakas were installed in less than a decade, tens of thousands died from famine and disease, and the institutions of the polity appeared to fall apart. By the end of the war Ganda chiefs appeared to have temporarily ceded the kabaka's authority to allocate land—the ultimate demonstration of his authority—to British officers. The war has been perceived as a "religious revolution" in which modernizing Ganda Christians and Muslims toppled paganism and then fought each other to make Buganda Catholic, Protestant, or Muslim: contemporary Ganda chroniclers, missionary and colonial observers, and historians have interpreted the war in these sectarian terms.[1] New religious categories were only one dimension of the war in Buganda from 1888 to 1896, however. It was also, fundamentally, a Ganda expression of the collapse of social institutions that affected all of eastern Africa as a consequence of trade in ivory and slaves.[2] In Buganda, the exchange of cloth and guns for people both undermined the legitimacy of the kabaka and transformed the autonomous power of chiefs. The faction leaders in the civil war were chiefs who had new religious convictions, and also new wealth from independent trading with Arabs, new power from followers who attached to them instead of to the king, and an expanded set of potential foreign allies. The premise of reciprocal obligation that had knit together the polity was challenged on two fronts. Ekitongole chiefship and the dissolution of authority caused by enslavement challenged the connection between economic production and political power, and at the same time, the conversion of Ganda chiefs to

Christianity and Islam created new meanings and new obligations that had to be integrated into Ganda practices of power.

The overthrow of Mwanga in 1888 intensified a period of self-destruction in which armed Ganda factions raided and slaved against each other inside their own country. That these groups were known by the allegiance to new religions of their leaders, who became wealthy through plundering and the sale of people, challenges the perception that Buganda overthrew a pagan king in order to modernize through the influence of Christianity and Islam. The war caused unprecedented devastation because Ganda mechanisms for maintaining social order ceased to function: weak kabakas could not quell competition among chiefs below them, chiefs could not strategize together to pressure an oppressive kabaka when all alternative kabakas had been killed, and the moderating influences exercised by the kibaale, particular chiefs, and royal women all depended on the presence of a strong kabaka who would respond to their actions. The gap between people's perception that followers had choices and rulers cared for their followers and the reality of escalating violence and coercion now became increasingly complex with people's commitment to new sets of ideas in conflict with each other. In these difficult circumstances, Ganda chiefs forged a compromise by reimagining the central power of the kabaka as a coalition of chiefs, and by incorporating new religions into the relationships of reciprocal obligation that ordered control of land in the kingdom. In 1889, 1892, and 1893, a rearrangement of land controlled by the various factions sealed attempts to end the war. The failure of the first of these efforts, along with the further collapse of the kabaka's authority under Mwanga after he was reinstalled, appears to have motivated Ganda chiefs to resolve the conflict by giving Captain Lugard the kabaka's role of allocating chiefships. The assignment of Catholic, Protestant, and Muslim provinces by the Ganda chiefs with the support of various British substitute-kabakas resolved the political and social turmoil of the preceding decade by effectively integrating the new and potentially dangerous religious categories into the structure of the Buganda kingdom.

The first three sections of this chapter examine the unfolding violence of the late nineteenth century in East Africa: the destructive effects of the caravan trade on the power of the kabaka, the development of chiefs who wielded autonomous military power, and the integration of new forms of spiritual authority into the growing conflict. The fourth section demonstrates how Ganda chiefs used reciprocal obligation expressed in control of land to end the spiral of violence.

BUGANDA AND THE TRADE IN IVORY AND SLAVES

Trade goods that had come from the East African coast were first mentioned in Ganda epic tradition in the time of Kabaka Semakookiro in the late 1700s,

Figure 4.1   Kabaka Muteesa receives Speke and Grant, 1862. Kabaka Muteesa determined where his foreign guests stayed, what food and other gifts they received, and whether labor to allow them to travel further would be provided. (Speke, *Journal of the Discovery of the Source of the Nile,* 389)

and successive kabakas managed for half a century to incorporate these new things into the circulation of goods that expressed Ganda social hierarchies.[3] They accomplished this by making specific chiefs responsible for trade in various markets on the edges of the kingdom. At first, goods from the coast flowed exclusively to and from the kabaka. In 1861, after John Hanning Speke's visit, Kabaka Muteesa killed a chief—the mutongole of Karema— for acquiring cloth in Karagwe that he had not turned over to the king.[4] Foreign traders were met at the borders of the kingdom and escorted to the capital, and food was provided to them in order to prevent them for interacting with people or trading on their own. Through most of Kabaka Muteesa's reign, foreigners—both traders and missionaries—were the guests of the kabaka at the capital: they could only acquire food or labor when the kabaka supplied it, and were forced to offer their goods to the kabaka on his terms.[5] The absolute nature of the kabaka's control over foreign travel and trade was illustrated by Mwanga's killing of Bishop Hannington in 1885; he had aroused suspicion when he failed to enter from the correct direction and changed his travel route without informing the kabaka.[6]

Neither the authority of the kabaka nor Buganda's well-developed forms of hierarchical exchange could withstand the negative effects of the caravan trade that reached Buganda in search of sources of ivory, which had been depleted closer to the coast (see Map 4.1, on following page). Traders acquired slaves to carry ivory tusks to the coast, and the existence of a market for human

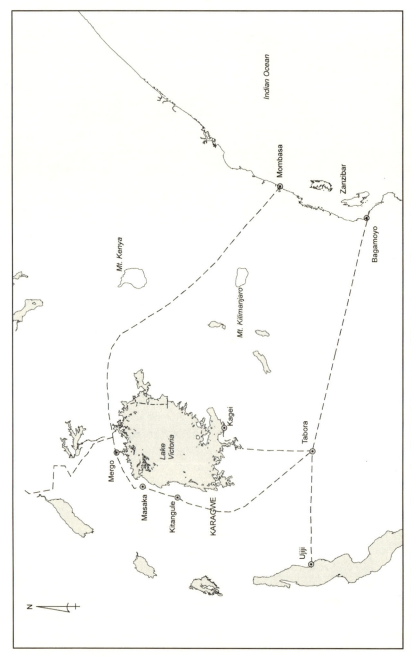

Map 4.1 Trade Routes to Buganda. (Derived from Arye Oded, *Islam in Uganda*, 24)

beings transformed the practice of utilizing the labor of war captives into more aggressive forms of slave raiding. Ivory harvesting easily merged into slave raiding, as guns were the tools of both trades, and sources of ivory were quickly depleted.[7] The argument that late-nineteenth-century enslavement was different in degree and character from earlier uses of war captives contradicts a tradition of scholarship on Buganda that views Ganda slavery as static or as a phenomenon that increased in scale without having serious social repercussions.[8] The view that accelerating enslavement is central to civil war in Buganda is based on recorded memories of the nature of enslavement, the documented increase in raiding and in captives taken into Buganda, evidence of slave buyers' participation in Ganda war making, and the ways that the kabaka's loss of authority over his chiefs was connected to slave raiding.

Baganda remember the time when people began to be sold to the coast. Selling people for cloth was entirely different than other kinds of nonfreedom (such as pawning) that people experienced in their lives. According to M.S.M. Kiwanuka, Kabaka Muteesa was the first to allow the selling of people. The impact of an Arab selling cloth in 1868 was recorded by Apolo Kaggwa: "[Muteesa] found an Arab by name Wamisi had arrived at the capital of Nakawa, bringing with him a lot of cloths and many other things. The Kabaka distributed cloths to princesses and ladies [to pages and specific chiefs]. . . . [L]ater on he gave cloths to all chiefs and ordered them to buy. Many people, boys and girls were sold to the Arabs in exchange for cloths."[9] In 1883 Philip O'Flaherty reported that he had had a conversation with Kabaka Muteesa about the effects of trading slaves to the coast. Muteesa said that two years earlier he had been trading ivory, but "such a thirst for cloth has caught hold of [the Baganda] that they will sell men and women for guns, powder, and shot, cloth, soap, etc." According to O'Flaherty, Muteesa regretted the trade, but felt he could not prevent it.[10] A son of one of the first Christian chiefs described the late nineteenth century as a time when "a piece of soap could buy a man, and a measure of bafuta [cotton cloth] could buy many slaves."[11]

One indication that raiding for slaves to sell to Arab traders was changing the nature of Buganda's wars is the intensification of conflict during the nineteenth century.[12] Kaggwa's history describes not only an increase in conflict, but also more conflicts that resulted in the death of the expeditions' leaders. He names "a lot of slaves," as well as women and cattle, as booty from battles in this period.[13] The huge increase in the number of royal wives also suggests that the nature of warfare was changing.[14] Alexander Mackay wrote in 1881: "One army has been sent east to murder and plunder. Not even the natives themselves can call it *war,* they all say it is for robbery and devastation."[15] He wrote to the *Times* in January of 1889 that Buganda and Bunyoro "have generally large armies in the field, in one direction or another, devastating whole regions of their inhabitants." Kabaka Muteesa attacked estates that had been protected from raiding "from time immemorial"; these included the estates of lubaale deities, and also estates of the nnamasole, his mother. Muteesa may have violated Ganda morality in this way because he had decided that the lubaale mediums were frauds, as John Rowe suggests, but it is also possible that the estates became vulnerable as social disorder and the need to supply traders increased.[16]

According to Mackay, Arabs supplied guns and powder for plundering expeditions, and then received "women, children, and ivory" procured in the raids as payment.[17] Traders sent agents into the field with the armies to select the slaves they wanted.[18] Kiwanuka observes that Ganda military success declined after 1880; this is perhaps because Buganda's neighbors were also participating in the exchange of cloth and guns for ivory and slaves. Richard Waller outlines the increasing importance of guns in Buganda: in 1875 there had been approximately five hundred; in 1882, Robert Felkin complained, "Mutesa's cry is always guns and gunpowder"; he calculated that there were two thousand guns in the country, and guns and powder had completely replaced all other trade items. Waller notes that in the 1880s Mackay described traders bringing nothing but guns, and O'Flaherty reported the arrival of a trader with six hundred rifles.[19]

Kabaka Muteesa brought the caravan trade closer to his court in order to maintain his supervision of the distribution of goods, but eventually was overcome by forces inherent in the trade that he could not control. Waller identifies three stages in Buganda's external trade: a first stage in which royal agents traded on behalf of the kabaka in Karagwe; a second stage, after the death of Kabaka Ssuuna, when trade shifted to the Ukerewe Islands and Kabaka Muteesa controlled access to Buganda by controlling canoe transport of traded goods across Lake Victoria; and a third stage, in the 1880s, when the focus of trade shifted to Muteesa's court. Waller argues that the kabaka had used the distribution of prestige goods, such as guns and slaves, to enhance his power and his followers' obligation to him: the huge increase in both trade goods and plunder unbalanced the system and the kabaka's place in the center of it.[20] Since mutual obligations and relationships in Buganda were expressed in the exchange of tribute and gifts, it makes sense that social relationships were fundamentally disrupted by massive increases in goods for exchange. The collapse of authority that characterized late-nineteenth-century Buganda was not merely the result of an enlarged market: it was also a consequence of the nature of a particular type of trade. The possibility of gaining wealth and power by selling slaves introduced a new kind of violence into the relationship of the kabaka to his chiefs, and of chiefs to their people. This is evident in the increasing autonomy of the chiefs, and in Kabaka Mwanga's ultimately ineffective attempts to reassert control over them.

THE EROSION OF CHIEFLY OBLIGATION TO THE KING

A new kind of authority figure emerged in East African societies with the expansion of trade in ivory and captured people. East African "rugaruga" were followers of a powerful "big man" who broke the rules of social interaction and exerted power over others through military force.[21] The way people lived in their environment changed in response to the emergence of this new figure: they grouped themselves into large defensive settlements, behind walls of stone and spiny cactus, whose ruined outlines are still sometimes visible in the rural landscape. In the well-developed bureaucracy of Buganda, the destabilizing potential of a new kind of trade was manifested in changes in the actions and role of chiefs, and in the total deterioration of the authority of the king, which began under Kabaka Muteesa and reached its culmination with the overthrow of Kabaka Mwanga in 1888. Most histories of the period explain the collapse of the kabaka's power in terms of Mwanga's personal qualities: his youth and insecurity; his excessive attachment to pages who were his lovers and his consequent inability to value the advice of senior chiefs; his pagan small-mindedness and fear of the followers of new religions.[22] While it is true that Mwanga did not lead Buganda effectively when he assumed the kabakaship in 1884, the turmoil of the 1880s must be considered a factor, in addition to Mwanga's personal capacity. This was a time when things were turned upside down, when young men obtained power they did not deserve, and strong government from the center of the kingdom became impossible. Ganda chiefs did not manifest the inversion of all socially appropriate behavior that characterized the rugaruga, but they amassed and deployed wealth and force in ways that were fundamentally destructive.

The ability to control people, arms, and cloth without receiving them through the kabaka gave chiefs autonomous power and prestige and the central importance of the kabaka began to deteriorate.[23] Chiefs of the border provinces who came into unsupervised contact with traders were the first ones able to trade on their own account: the ppookino and kaggo irritated Kabaka Muteesa by selling ivory and obtaining cloth without his permission, and this may have contributed to the redirection of trade first to Ukerewe and then to Rubaga. While the katikkiro, kimbugwe, and some royal women had in the past exercised a degree of autonomous power that somewhat curtailed that of the kabaka, Katikkiro Mukasa, who "even sold his relatives into slavery," amassed wealth and power on an unprecedented scale.[24] The katikkiro's customary control of the kingdom's ivory trade benefited him personally, but in addition he acquired two of the most important chiefships—becoming the ppookino of Buddu and then the ssekiboobo of Kyaggwe, which gave him a greater capacity to direct long-distance trade to his own benefit.[25] People attributed Kabaka Muteesa's obvious weakness in relation to his chiefs to his lingering venereal disease and drummed "he has taken too long to die."[26]

According to Zimbe, Kabaka Muteesa counteracted the discontent by publicly acknowledging the power of his katikkiro: he asked to make blood brotherhood with Mukasa, told the chiefs in the Lukiiko to obey the katikkiro, and
directed that Mukasa's sons should be given royal names and be carried like
princes.[27]

The productive possibilities of long-distance trade made ebitongole
chiefships more powerful, and more destabilizing, than they had been a century earlier, when they channeled war captives into labor in Buganda. An
ekitongole chief who had guns for hunting or defense could become wealthy
independently of the kabaka by raiding and disposing of slaves on his own.
Kabakas Ssuuna and Muteesa dramatically increased the number of ebitongole
chiefships, perhaps in an effort to regain authority they were losing to ssaza
chiefs who were using captive people to direct production to their own benefit. Kaggwa explained the remarkable wealth of batongole (the chiefs of
ebitongole) in terms of their success in war:

> Their areas carried great honour and people used to flock to them and they
> were therefore well cultivated. . . . When the Kabaka was at war, people in
> such areas (Bitongole) excelled in capturing the booty for they were always
> young men. From what they had captured their chief (Mutongole) would
> choose the best and consequently became a rich man. Such a chief would
> also act as the Kabaka's messenger and thus again become rich for he was
> given presents.[28]

The presents they gave to ebitongole chiefs may suggest that Muteesa and
Mwanga recognized the possibility that these chiefs might act outside of their
control and attempted to maintain their allegiance.

Michael Twaddle's richly detailed biography of Semei Kakungulu documents the potential independence of an ekitongole chief. Kakungulu obtained
an ekitongole for elephant hunting from Kabaka Muteesa in 1884. Kakungulu
had arrived in Buganda with experience in elephant hunting, and Muteesa gave
him "guns, gun caps, and bullets," and land in Buddu. This land had been
attached to a different chieftaincy, but was reallocated to the new ekitongole,
which was called "Ekirumba Njovu"—"for hunting elephants"—and
Kakungulu's title was "Omulumba Njovu"—"hunter of elephants."[29] Although
nominally under the control of Kabaka Muteesa and required to turn over all
the ivory he acquired, Kakungulu's control of one hundred guns enabled him
to build up an independent following through predation. According to Paulo
Kibi, at this time Kakungulu had a drumbeat:

> I eat what I choose:
> I eat what I find:
> I eat whatever does not belong to me.[30]

Kakungulu and his men raided Nkore on their own, without instructions from Muteesa, and disposed of the cattle and slaves they obtained in Kiziba. Even when Kakungulu and his men participated in a raid against Bunyoro initiated by the kabaka, Kakungulu's men were punished for looting inside Buganda. That his activities went beyond the pale of appropriate behavior for subordinate chiefs is evident in the story that Katikkiro Mukasa either placed Kakungulu in stocks or threatened him with death; he was only saved by the intervention of his blood brother the ppookino or, in another version of the story, by the kabaka himself.[31]

The power that men like Kakungulu created for themselves in the tumultuous circumstances of late-nineteenth-century East Africa was mercurial. Chiefs continued to compete for followers, but free allegiance or the distribution of war captives were no longer the only means of obtaining them. As the chief of an elephant-hunting ekitongole, located on a route along which guns were being brought into Buganda, Kakungulu raided people and cattle without passing them on to the kabaka, and collected followers of his own. Kakungulu was able to attract followers by offering to arm them, and also by trading ivory for enslaved people. He was not, however, able to maintain the following he created for himself. Kakungulu lost his chiefship, the Ekitongole of Ekirumba Njovu, when Mwanga was deposed. As soon as Kakungulu lost the chiefship, seventy of his followers deserted him for the new katikkiro, Honorat Nyonyintono. These men had "belonged" to Kakungulu, but they chose to align themselves with the strongest leader available.[32] An enslaved follower's ability to choose his chief may have been enhanced by the possession of a rifle, but in Buganda as in so many other regions, social order unraveled when big men controlled unfree men with guns.

The kabaka's control over chiefs deteriorated markedly as the amount of military hardware in the nation increased in the 1880s. Robert Ashe reported that the escort taking him to the capital made an "impromptu slave raid" during the journey.[33] In 1862, members of the party escorting James Grant to Buganda did not plunder in their own country, "for fear of the wrath of their king."[34] Waller also points out that Charles Pearson estimated that 75 percent of the slaves taken in a raid were not reported to the kabaka, "the rest having been secretly disposed of by the chiefs."[35] By the 1880s the kabaka received only ivory, and chiefs retained cattle, women, and slaves.[36] This represents a diminution in the kabaka's share, and may have been a recognition that chiefs would retain slaves and cattle on their own whether or not the kabaka gave them permission.

Mwanga's creation of new, armed ebitongole occurred in the context of increasing chiefly autonomy from the king. As chiefs became less dependent on the kabaka's gifts and signs of his favor, the king attempted to undermine their power. Mwanga took large areas from ssaza chiefs between 1886 and

1888 in order to create four new ebitongole, which he placed under the control of young men. These were the Ekitongole Ekiwuliriza, "the chiefship of listening carefully"; the Ekitongole Ekigwanika, "the chiefship of wealth"; the Ekitongole Ekijasi, "the chiefship of guns"; and the Ekitongole Ekiyinda, "the chiefship of menacing noise."[37] Not only did Mwanga take land that had been under the control of ssaza chiefs to make the new ebitongole chiefships, but he told the new batongole to establish their chiefships in every province—presumably by force. According to Martin Southwold, these ebitongole represented Mwanga's attempt to remove power from the established chiefs and give it to young chiefs he could control more easily.[38] However, in the highly disordered context of Buganda in the 1880s, it is difficult to assert that Mwanga was actually creating new chiefships in order to advance the structure of the state. As Kiwanuka points out, Buganda was in such turmoil at the time that chiefly authority over land was not readily discernible. A more accurate assessment is that in creating huge new ebitongole, Mwanga was merely naming as chiefs new power-holders who had emerged from circumstances of the violent exchange of ivory and people for guns, and attempting to assert authority over them.[39]

Participants in these events later described them in ways that highlighted the erosion of the actions and positive emotions that people expected to characterize reciprocal obligation. Bartolomayo Zimbe remembered that "he loved young men, this Mwanga. Very often he discussed affairs with Katikiro Mukasa alone without consulting any of the old chiefs." He compared Mwanga's relationships with the chiefs to a relationship with "images of long departed people," saying, "One does not care for these things and much in the same way Mwanga did not care for old chiefs." For Zimbe, a significant enactment of royal favor was the proof of this attitude: "the Kabaka always appointed young men to distribute what booty the old chiefs had brought back and he always gave them power to jeer them."[40]

Mwanga failed in his attempt to win control over the powerful young men with guns in order to counteract the growing autonomy of ssaza chiefs. People deserted other chiefs to become the followers of the batongole, and "by 1888 the four new Bitongole had nearly 100,000 men, all young and arrogant."[41] Apolo Kaggwa's account of this period describes the kabaka's lack of control: "the morals of the country became deteriorated as we young men adapted a bad habit of robbing people of their cattle and goats at random; and people found on the way were killed for no just cause. The Kabaka knew of this and he did not care for the well-being of his country at all. He liked the young men more than his chiefs."[42] Bartolomayo Zimbe described how people responded to the activities of his ekitongole, the Bainda:

> We were given a distinguishing mark by which everybody recognized and feared us: flags proceeded us and a fiddler played with the song "They never

came, these are other people" (Tibajanga nti bane balala). . . . Everybody ran away and into the jungle; he who did not was beaten to death. The people grumbled and said, "Kabaka Mwanga has killed his own country himself since his children have killed it," but we were happy.[43]

Mwanga may have intended to reaffirm his authority over the hierarchy of chiefs, but the batongole and their followers "became the rulers of the country"; they raided and took captives without any inhibitions.[44]

In 1888 Mwanga attempted to assert the kabaka's authority through a ritual upon which kings had relied to consolidate their power in the past. A royal journey to "show the kabaka" allowed people to demonstrate allegiance and to offer tribute, and for the king to bestow favor, give gifts, and investigate the depth of loyalty of his chiefs, who competed in the hospitality they offered. Mwanga—and the times—turned this ritual upside down. He required Mackay and Lourdel to accompany him, but he took no chiefs; "He was now surrounded by these young men and nobody else was his friend."[45] Instead of receiving and giving gifts that would have cemented his relationship with his subjects, "he ruthlessly robbed and raided his own people."[46] In Kyaggwe, Ssingo, and Buddu, he raided hundreds of cattle, and seized "vast numbers" of women and children. On his return to the capital, he distributed these people as gifts to his pages. People saw this as grossly unjust, not only because Mwanga had demanded too much, but also because the followers he enriched with human plunder had not been introduced in the palace by chiefs and therefore had no legitimate role in the kingdom's hierarchy.

Mwanga's final, unsuccessful attempt to consolidate his authority was his demand that his people dig a large artificial lake in the capital: requiring unnecessary work was a way of making people demonstrate their allegiance that had been deployed by other kabakas.[47] Everyone, of every status, was required to participate in this public work or face heavy fines. A royal drum "everybody must come with soil" was beaten calling people to work on the lake at three o'clock in the morning. Kaggwa wrote that anyone who did not arrive early in the morning was fined one woman and one head of cattle, and Ashe reported that insufficient labor at the lake resulted in fines of large numbers of women, expensive cloths, and guns.[48] According to Zimbe, people had to pay to leave the worksite, by placing five cowries in one of twelve huge baskets (one for each of the provinces, one for ebitongole, and one for princes and princesses). Zimbe's description of what was wrong with the project suggests how Mwanga used it to assert an upside-down order of power:

Chiefs, princesses, saza chiefs, commoners were all covered with dirt; the Kabaka made no distinction and it was only his favourite youths whom he called "children" who had respite. Further he gave every village and chieftainship, from the saza posts, villages of princesses or bataka to either

Bainda, Bawanika or Bawuliriza composed of these "children" so that they mistreated Buganda plundering cows and goats and fowls and barkcloth to a degree so disgraceful that all people, chiefs and common folk hated Sekabaka Mwanga who encouraged them, adding to the insult of making them wake up at 3 o'clock to dig his lake all through the day and be baked by the sun.[49]

Baganda remember not only the unreasonable fines, but also the horrifying humiliation forced on important, elderly chiefs who were made to sit in the mud if they arrived late.[50] Mwanga's bizarre behavior in the last months before he was overthrown can be understood as a desperate attempt to assert authority over subjects who were not expressing allegiance willingly, and also as a means to obtain wealth in goods and slaves both by fining his subjects heavily and by creating situations in which they would offer bribes to avoid humiliation.

Kabaka Mwanga was deposed because his chiefs withdrew the will to be governed by him: the firsthand accounts of the events in 1888 are reminiscent of the history of Kabaka Kagulu, a century and a half earlier, whose reign ended when his chiefs retreated to a hill overlooking the palace and jeered.[51] This moment came for Mwanga when the followers of new religions refused to embark in canoes for a journey on the lake that they suspected would lead to their deaths: Mwanga's katikkiro told him, "All Buganda refuses to take you to Sesse."[52] Mwanga, like Kagulu, was overthrown when people became fed up with entirely unreasonable demands. Long-distance trade in ivory and people had given Ganda chiefs some autonomy from the king, and his escalating efforts to reassert his authority led those chiefs to unite and withdraw their support.

NEW RELIGIONS AND SOCIAL DISORDER

Mwanga's fall was one moment in an unfolding crisis of authority in Buganda that was much larger than a palace coup. Fundamental terms of how to be a chief, how to express authority, and how and why to be productive had been altered by the possibilities and the violence of long-distance trade. This moment of political, social, and economic turmoil also entailed an ideological crisis, as Arab traders and European explorers had introduced new ways of thinking about the world in the form of Islam and Christianity. The conversion of large numbers of Baganda to these faiths in the nineteenth century was so unique, so attractive to observers, and so clearly genuine that it has tended to overshadow other aspects of the processes of change under way at the time.[53] Without denying the significance of conversion for individuals and for their communities, it is important to keep in mind that the people who became Muslims and Christians did not stop being Baganda. The late nineteenth century was an encompassingly difficult time for the Baganda, intellectually as well as on every other level. People expected the kabaka to act as an effective arbiter of conflict among chiefs, but no kabaka filled that expectation from Muteesa's reign onward. World religions became a principle for organizing relationships at a time when other means of organizing them were not functioning effectively.

Baganda embraced Islam and Christianity with ardent enthusiasm. Kabaka Muteesa instructed people in the court to fast, pray, and learn to read the Quran. One courtier remembered that women would be asked to read the most difficult passages, so that chiefs who could not read them could avoid embarrassment. Rowe notes that the king observed Ramadan for eight successive years, and fasting produced a Ganda song:

> Those who are fasting from water,
> and do not eat their day-time meal,
> They are waiting for the Muslim feast.[54]

Jean Brierley and Thomas Spear suggest that the social turmoil caused by "trade, arms, threats of conquest and new diseases" gave Baganda reason to seek solace in Christianity, an observation that would also be valid for the strong commitments Baganda made to Islam.[55] New religions were so closely identified with reading that converts were called "readers." George Pilkington wrote in 1892 that the mission needed "not thousands, but millions" of books and "if we don't supply the demand, the Roman Catholics will"; sales by the Church Missionary Society in 1898 amounted to ten tons of cowries. Thousands of people attended the Protestant and Catholic churches that were built in Mmengo at the end of the civil war.[56]

Reading and prayer gave young men access to spiritual power without the mediation of their elders. In the new religions, positions of spiritual leadership were open to young converts who had been pages at the lowest level of the Ganda chiefly hierarchy. The preponderance of younger people among converts may have occurred because they felt the challenges of the dissolution of authority more acutely; it is also possible that they felt more willing to explore new faiths because, at the bottom of the chiefly hierarchy, they had fewer responsibilities and less to lose.

Ganda Muslims, Protestants, and Catholics used their new sets of ideas to create social institutions that did the kinds of things that organizations of people had always done in Buganda. Michael Twaddle argues that this happened gradually. In his interpretation, the attempt to organize the kingdom as a Muslim state under Kalema was the real beginning of religious revolution, and "it was in reaction to this convergence between Islam and clientage that

Honorat Nyonyintono and Apolo Kaggwa attempted to build counter-clientages with markedly Catholic and Protestant characteristics."[57] As this transition took place, the new religions not only became spiritually effective practices and forms of identity, but also provided ways to organize economic activity and to wield political power. In the context of European imperial strategizing in East Africa, Protestants connected to the Imperial British East Africa Company sometimes thought of themselves as adherents to "English religion," while the Catholic missionaries' skepticism regarding British imperialist intentions caused the Catholics to be known for a while as followers of "French religion."[58] In the highly unstable context of the late nineteenth century, the center of people's allegiance was shifting from the kabaka, who no longer wielded overarching authority, to chiefs. Adherence to religion became an element of the authority of those chiefs. As Michael Wright points out, Ganda categories of clan and family continued to be salient, and throughout the war people defended and protected family and clan relatives of different faiths.[59]

Religions became alternative categories in which people could continue to make the social arrangements they had always made.[60] It has been said that the Baganda were fighting each other *for* religion, but this perspective ignores the larger East African context and the instabilities that would have led to armed conflict whether or not the protagonists had adopted new religions. A more accurate perception is that in the midst of the profound collapse of authority occasioned by enslavement and guns, people in Buganda came to fight each other *with* religion. Loyalty to the new faiths began to influence their alliances, their sources of supply, and their maneuvers to gain political power. Fighting with religion made ending the war particularly difficult, because no one could rely on the conflict-quelling consequences of the kabaka's absolute power, and because the ideological and economic dimensions of new religious communities facilitated a prolongation of hostilities.

Baganda practiced the new religions using the logic of reciprocal obligation. Christians and Muslims expected a co-religionist who was a chief to take them in and take care of them. The early missionaries took on the role of nurturing "their" Christians; Rowe states that "missionaries found themselves accepting applicants who wished to 'senga' them."[61] The leaders of the Protestant Church in the 1890s "addressed their missionary colleagues as *mwana watu,* literally 'my darling child.'"[62] When Katikkiro Honorat Nyonyintono was killed in a battle, his mostly Catholic followers found it impossible to continue fighting: "they were not cowardly but were distraught and did not see why they should fight just for Protestants."[63] The logical connection of personal and religious allegiance motivated a few people to switch religions in order to gain chiefships: Simioni Sebutta had been a Catholic in 1886, but became a Protestant when offered the position of Kiryagonja, after he did not get the chiefship he had wanted as a Catholic. Yosefu Sebowa was promised a chiefship if he converted to Catholicism, which he did, and became Kisalosalo.[64]

The new religious communities became arenas for competition over status in the same way that Ganda chiefs had competed with each other over relative status in other circumstances. Individuals chosen to lead Christian groups in any given engagement had authority over the division of spoils. Before one battle in 1890, a messenger had to be sent back to Mwanga to inquire whether it was acceptable for a Protestant, Kakungulu, to take over the leadership of a campaign whose original Catholic leader was indisposed. The group of Catholics and Protestants who retreated to Ankole clashed with the Christian group who had drawn back to islands in Lake Victoria over the issues of seniority and control of spoils: these groups were known as the "grain-eaters" and the "fish-eaters."[65] Entirely new forms of authority fostered further conflicts over relative status. For example, a conflict arose between the ppookino and the katikkiro because the ppookino was lower than the katikkiro in the chiefly hierarchy but higher than him in the church council hierarchy: he did not want to take orders from someone who had a lower position than his in the church council.[66]

After the kabaka lost the ability to direct all trade to the center of the kingdom, chiefs turned their capacities to organize production and trade to the advantage of their respective factions. Residents of the Ssese islands, who were either Catholic or pagan, held a monopoly on canoes at times during the war, so that lack of access to lake transport was a problem for Protestants, and one of the great weaknesses of Kabaka Kalema, who was aligned with the Muslim faction. The Catholic and Protestant coalition suffered because they needed food, and essential supplies of food were controlled by Ganda chiefs in Kyaggwe and Bulemeezi who were not readers (converts to new religions).[67] Each faction had sources of supply from the coast. Muslims obtained their guns through Arabs, and Christians through the former missionary Charles Stokes. Co-religionists who were not Baganda participated actively in the war through their efforts to provide supplies. James Miti states that Kipanda, an Arab trader at Magu at the south end of Lake Victoria, sent a dhow of guns and ammunition that he paid for himself, and told his people to attack and sink Stokes's boat if they found it.[68]

The destruction engendered by the civil war and the terrible calamity of people slaving inside their own society have been underemphasized by historians, who have focused on the religious identity of the combatants and described the war as a conflict between new and old ideas. Participants' written accounts of the war portray an effort to overthrow an unsatisfactory king that spun out of control in volatile conditions in which young men with guns had power. Part of the challenge of the war for Ganda Christians and Muslims was to find ways to integrate new and powerful ideas into their organization of Ganda society, but to frame this as a conflict between tradition and modernity avoids the issue of what was actually new. Literacy and world religions were new in nineteenth-century Buganda; the practice of capturing people and selling them was also new. Flags were new, and so was the experience of a complete collapse of the king's authority over chiefs.

The Muslim and Christian leaders of the ebitongole created by Muteesa and Mwanga had become wealthy and powerful through plundering, raiding, and enslaving inside as well as outside Buganda. Following the overthrow of Mwanga in September 1888, Ganda chiefs turned those violent mechanisms for creating wealth on each other. As the coalition of chiefs supporting Kabaka Kiwewa collapsed in October 12, 1888, Christians under Kaggwa fled with so much cloth that Kaggwa (who had given it to them) "had to hold us by the hand for we had such heaps on our heads that we could not see our way."[69] When Christians retook Mmengo a year later, in September 1889, the Christian army failed to capture Kalema because people stopped to plunder. Paulo Kibi, a combatant, explained, "What saved Kalema was our poverty. Just when our victory was almost complete, everybody went to the place of the coastal traders in order to plunder the cloth."[70] Kaggwa acknowledged that in an engagement he led in Mawokota, "the Mohamedans were defeated and their wives plundered," but he states that the wives were later returned.[71] Protestant missionary Ashe, who returned to Buganda during the war, wrote that probably not all the women had been returned after that engagement, and that loot was the main objective of the combatants.[72]

Miti, who followed his participation in the war with a distinguished career in the Uganda Protectorate government, stated clearly that enslavement was a goal of making war. He wrote that to "plunder and carry off of men and women from the vanquished side on every occasion was the order of the day at that time" and "it was each warrior's ambition to fight hard in order to be able to return home with plunder and captives."[73] He acknowledged that he himself had taken "not less than seventeen female captives and some six male prisoners of war" in the attack on the Buvuma Islands in which Major Macdonald had participated and forbidden any enslavement, and suggested that many hundreds of captives had been smuggled away into Buganda by other Ganda warriors.

Miti also described an incident indicating not only that people were being enslaved, but also that many of the captured people were being sold to Arabs. Kabarega, the king of Bunyoro, had sent an army to assist Kalema in 1890. This army became disoriented retreating from a battle, and accidentally went further into Buganda, where "they fell into a trap and many of them were captured and made prisoners or slaves." Miti describes how the captured people attempted to prove their value to the Ganda captors, pleading to remain with those who had captured them: "A Munyoro potter or blacksmith would plead his case by assuring his Baganda captors that his knowledge of pottery or of the manufacture of spears, as the case might be, would be found very useful if he were only kept under their service."[74] After the Muslims had been driven from Mmengo in 1889, according to Miti, they began plundering food and property all over Ssingo, and into Ggomba and Busujju: "Women, children and even old men fell victims to the Mohamedan's acts of cruelty, some of them being killed on the spot, others being carried away for sale to his Arab friend as slaves."[75] When Christian chiefs organized themselves to stop the raiding, they engaged in a battle in Lumanyo, where they surprised the Muslims and routed them, causing the retreating army to drop their plunder. Captured women and children were abandoned along the road. The Christian army returned them to their families, and the children whose families could not be found (because the children were too young to identify themselves) were adopted. A praise song devised for Kakungulu during the war, *"Kangabaana, eyawangula abensambya"*—"The scatterer of children, the one who conquered those of Nsambya," suggests the social consequences of the war.[76] Lucy Mair noted in 1934 that one consequence of the war was that many children who had been captured too young to know their family name had inadvertently married into their own clan, which led to a proverb stating that looking for a lost relative is inadvisable.[77]

Figure 4.2 Nnamasole Muganzirwazza receives Speke and Grant, 1862. Weak kings made later queen mothers less significant in the governance of the kingdom than Nnamasole Muganzirwazza had been. (Speke, *Journal of the Discovery of the Source of the Nile,* 390)

Baganda remembered the war as a time of unimaginable destruction. The population of Bunyoro is said to have increased because so many people fled from war and the danger of enslavement in Buganda. An image that recurs in descriptions of the war is of corpses rotting by the roadside because no one was available to bury them. People stopped cultivating out of fear, and in the ensuing famine people dug up the stumps of banana trees in order to eat the roots. Warriors with guns "used to assuage their hunger by force of arms, carrying guns with them wherever they went and threatening to shoot anyone who would not give them food."[78] An outbreak of bubonic plague followed the famine. Estimates of the death toll range from seven thousand to four hundred thousand.[79] After October 1889, Muslim armies moved into and then out of Kyaddondo and Busiro because they were empty of people and animals and there was nothing left to raid; the armies then proceeded to plunder all of Kyaggwe. German imperial entrepreneur Carl Peters passed through Kyaggwe early in 1890 and found "a desolation of destroyed banana groves, with vultures gorging on unburied corpses and the wind raising flurries of ashes in the burnt villages."[80]

The civil war fundamentally undermined the institution of the kabaka. Success for any of the factions in the civil war depended on having a prince of the drum—one entitled to become king because he was a direct descendant of a kabaka. Among the first actions of the Christian group upon its withdrawal to Ankole in 1888 was an attempt to acquire a prince of the drum. Bawmweyana, one of Muteesa's sons, bribed his guard to allow him to escape and join the Christians, but Kalema had sent people to search for him upon his escape, and he was captured. Kalema then decided to kill all the princes of the drum, and also all the princesses, because if his enemies had no potential kabaka in their camp, they would have no means of regaining power.[81] Princesses were killed as well as princes since the British were ruled by a woman; therefore, it seemed possible that Christians might make a princess kabaka. One generation earlier, Muteesa's mother, Nnamasole Muganzirwazza, had caused the deaths of eleven of Ssuuna's sons through starvation: only Mbogo, Mainja, and Kabaka Muteesa had been left alive.[82] The killing of two entire generations of princes (and one of princesses) was a disaster for Buganda because it created a dearth of potential legitimate leadership. Just as had happened in the previous century, social conditions deteriorated when people could no longer withdraw support from a ruler. When Kalema died of smallpox after his retreat from Mmengo, the only potential kabakas were Muslim leader Mbogo, two young sons of Kalema and Kiwewa who were out of the country with Catholic missionaries, and Mwanga, who had already been deposed once.

The Christians turned to Mwanga because they had no other means of maintaining a credible bid for control of the kingdom, but this choice irrevocably altered the practice of power in the kingdom. Since Mwanga had demonstrated his ineptness as a ruler and the chiefs had demonstrated their lack of respect for him the first time they overthrew him, his return to power inevitably entailed a further diminution of the authority of the kabaka. Since chiefs, royal women, spirit mediums, and other figures of authority all exercised power in relation to a strong kabaka, a weak kabaka who could not be replaced led to chaos. The wars also undermined the authority of some Ganda leaders: the nnamasole and lubuga lost their critical political role when chiefs ignored the king. The kimbugwe, the chief who was officially the keeper of the kabaka's "twin" (an elaborate charm that contained the kabaka's umbilical cord), had had a pivotal role in Ganda politics, but the kimbugwe chiefship was abolished in 1892 because "during the Christian reign, we could not honor the traditional twin-god."[83] The representatives of lubaale deities, who had served to safely focus legitimate criticism of the kabaka, also lost their influence with the spread of Christianity and Islam, and with the general disorder of the time. Kakungulu was said to have a new drumbeat when the Christians and their allies gathered on Bulingugwe Island:

I eat whatever I find:
I eat whatever belongs to *emmandwa* (deities' mediums).[84]

Kabaka Muteesa had been obliged to provide hospitality and gifts for the priest of the shrine of Mukasa, lubaale of Lake Victoria, and to make a show of accepting his advice. The son of that priest had lost his followers and his land was taken by the Gabunga, chief of the Ssese Islands, in the 1890s; the grandson claimed to be "an important mutaka in Sesse as well as in Buganda" but, when questioned, admitted that he had received land as a tenant of Gabunga and performed services as Gabunga's man.[85]

The crisis of newly strong chiefs and a thoroughly weak kabaka led to "wars that did not let go."[86] After the "year of three kings" (Mwanga, Kiwewa, and Kalema), a coalition of the forces of Christian chiefs and the forces of avowedly pagan chiefs brought Mwanga back to Mmengo, after battles that had left fields where "skulls are as numerous . . . as mushrooms."[87] Groups who considered themselves supporters of the Muslim Kabaka Kalema, and after his death the Muslim Kabaka Mbogo, fought against the reestablishment of Mwanga all over Buganda. In 1892, fighting broke out in Mmengo between people who identified themselves as Protestant and people who identified themselves as Catholic. In 1893, negotiations for territory (see text that follows) ended conflict among the new religious factions, and in 1897, Baganda participated in fighting against the rebelling Sudanese troops. From 1897 to 1899, Mwanga and a coalition of chiefs fought against Baganda who allied themselves with "the Kampala European." Reporting on the volatile situation in Mmengo in 1890, Captain Macdonald noted that the "proud, sensitive, and suspicious" chiefs acted in their own interest, and the kabaka "had but little hold over powerful, intriguing chiefs . . . ripe for any contingency that promised a chance of plunder."[88] The "religious revolution" framework explains these continuing conflicts in terms of which religious group held Mmengo or wanted to control it: but the triggers for each outburst of hostilities were so trivial that conflict seems to have been prolonged for its own sake. More war meant further opportunities to acquire the wealth that came from raiding.

INCORPORATING RELIGION IN THE ORDER OF THE KINGDOM TO END THE WAR

At each shift in the control of the kingdom, the victorious group reallocated important chiefships. Naming the people who would control the ssazas and the important functions of the kingdom was a way of stating the order of the nation. In the oral traditions of Buganda recorded by Apolo Kaggwa, the stories of each kabaka concluded with a list of the important chiefs during that reign; the named chiefs, in their named chiefships, constituted Buganda. During the civil war period, naming the chiefs was also a way of identifying how those who had taken control of the capital intended to manage the complicated problem of competing claims for authority among factions of chiefs. The problem faced by the groups of chiefs who came to power was to find a way to map the increasingly salient new categories of allegiance to Islam, and to "English" and "French" Christianity, onto the structures of ssaza and subsidiary chiefships. Over and over again, these efforts failed. The order of Buganda, defined in chiefships of territories and chiefships of important functions, could not hold together at a time when organizing raiding had become the dominant occupation of chiefs. Furthermore, attempting to integrate new religious categories into the structure of chiefships in a logical way created even more instability, because the new categories always provided reasons for rationalizing renewed conflict. Various factions of chiefs attempted successively more radical techniques for combining religion and chiefly control of the provinces as the war continued.

In 1888 the Muslims and their Catholic and Protestant blood brothers assigned the office of katikkiro to Christians, gave more than half the ssaza chiefships to Muslims, and gave two heavily armed ebitongole to both Christians and Muslims; but this division fell apart within six weeks because an assertive Christian chief agitated for the post of Kauta, a chiefship that included the function of cooking for the palace and also land in the central provinces. His claim upset the precarious balance of power that had been negotiated and led to an armed skirmish that caused Christians to leave for Ankole.[89] Those remaining in Mmengo then had to carry out the action of renaming the chiefs of the nation in order to replace the Christian chiefs who had left. However, this exercise in naming authority exacerbated tensions between Kabaka Kiwewa and the Muslim chiefs who had brought him to power, resulting in a violent episode that ended in the departure of Kiwewa, the installation of Kabaka Kalema, and a further naming of chiefships to replace those who had just been killed. Both the Christian faction and the Muslim faction appointed chiefs for all the significant chiefships, even when they did not control the ssazas to which they were naming chiefs. Wright points out that the Muslims twice reappointed a chief for Buddu when the intended Muslim chief was killed, even though the Muslim faction never held that area after they abandoned Mmengo.[90]

When the coalition of factions who identified themselves as Christian regained control of part of the mainland near Mmengo in October 1889, they named chiefs for all the ssazas of the country. Two aspects of the chiefs' action reveal the intensifying crisis of authority in Buganda: the chiefs created an order of chiefship for the kingdom that attempted to thoroughly balance the power of Protestant and Catholic factions, and they made these allocations entirely without the participation of Kabaka Mwanga. According to an eyewitness, Mwanga "had no power" in the allocation; the chiefs made their decisions and informed him afterward.[91] This is the clearest possible evidence that the central place of authority in Buganda was empty. The structure of exchange that required everything to flow into and out of the center no longer functioned, and the figure who held the central position in this structure no longer had real power.

The group of chiefs who had beaten Kalema named chiefs in a way that defined Buganda as a balance of "English religion" adherents and "French religion" adherents at every level. The elaborate system they devised of alternating Protestant and Catholic chiefs appears to be an attempt to use the structure of chiefly control over territory and over subordinate chiefs to diffuse potential conflict. This system is described in detail in the report of Captain Macdonald in 1892:

> The estates, chieftainships and posts of honour and importance were divided equally between the two parties on a system which aimed at absolute fairness and justice, but which was so complicated as in itself to contribute a great and ever present source of danger.
>
> The principle adopted seems simple enough—every holder of a post was to be under a superior of the opposite party. Thus the owner of a Catholic *shamba* (estate) was under a Protestant sub-chief, who in turn was subordinate to a Roman Catholic chief and so on and vice versa. This may have been instituted as a safeguard against injustice and to prevent the parties concentrating and becoming dangerous to each other. Be this as it may,

events proved that no more certain method of breeding disorder and injustice could well have been devised.[92]

The alternation of Protestant and Catholic authorities permeated Ganda structures of power: even the estates of the nnamasole, the lubuga, and those of the katikkiro and kimbugwe in every province were supposed to have subchiefs of the other religious persuasion under chiefs who held the same faith as the controllers of the estates.[93]

The orderly and logical plan imposed by the chiefs could not function in the actual conditions in Buganda at that time. In the imagined Buganda of the named chiefships, networks of chiefs expressed their relationship to each other by passing tribute up the hierarchy and receiving gifts down it, but actually the ssazas were devastated by raiding and decimated by famine and disease. The authority of chiefs should have derived from their submission to the kabaka and the kabaka's recognition of their role. Actually, there was no authority, only intense competition among powerful, armed chiefs, which they hoped to keep in check through their willful intention to share power.

The ordering of the nation under layers of Protestant and Catholic chiefs implied that all people in authority were to be Christian. Since not all Baganda were Christian, this decision indicates the connection people made between political and spiritual authority—people of the appropriate religion would have to be found to rule in each particular locality, and the people below that chief would follow his religious lead. It is possible that the coterie of chiefs who initiated this plan believed that commitment to Christian faith implied a capacity to live peacefully. It is also possible that they chose complete power-sharing in every direction as a means to prevent any accusation of unfairness. Some members of the coalition that had defeated Kalema were denied a leading role with the rationalization "bhang is not religion."[94] Since bhang smoking was identified with elephant hunting (and had been forbidden by kabakas in the past), the exclusion of bhang-smokers may have represented an attempt to eliminate the instabilities associated with new wealth and new military power.

Whatever the intentions and aspirations of the group of chiefs who devised the ordering of Buganda in alternating layers of Catholic and Protestant chiefs, the system did not work. The Baganda were accustomed to changes in chiefship being ordinary, fluid, and easily accomplished; this system required the order of chiefship to stay exactly as it was at the moment the system had been initiated. Any change of chief, or any chief's change in religion, became a source of conflict between the "English" and "French" factions. When a chief changed his religious allegiance, he lost control of that chiefship. This was logical since the chiefs had linked the political authority inherent in control over land to prescribed religious allegiances, but it was impossible to carry out in the context of the Ganda practice of constantly reordering chiefships. Irresolvable problems arose when royal women, controllers of substantial amounts of land, became Christians. The chief Yoswa Wasekere changed from Protestant to Catholic, provoking another confrontation. Catholic missionaries asserted that the principle of religious freedom required that people be allowed to retain land, even if they changed religions. In the volatile atmosphere of 1890, disagreements over who should control land quickly escalated into armed confrontation between Catholics and Protestants. When a minor chief in Kyaggwe who held what was supposed to be a Protestant chiefship became a Catholic, Protestants tried to evict the chief and Catholics agitated for him to remain. Semei Kakungulu, who was at that time the chief's superior, traveled to Kyaggwe to resolve the problem, thirteen people were killed on the disputed estate, and shots were fired in Mmengo.[95]

Mwanga was entirely incapable of asserting the kabaka's authority over land that might have resolved the disputes. The chiefs considered Mwanga to be someone who could be "herded like an ox" and they manipulated him to get the decisions they wanted.[96] In 1891 a dispute arose because Mwanga had secretly given a village on Bussi Island to a Catholic, although this area should have been under the control of Gabunga, a chief in the Ssese Islands, which had been designated a Protestant chiefship. Two Catholics had been killed when they went to take possession of the land, because Gabunga's men had refused to give it up, saying it was impossible that the land could have been transferred if the katikkiro's representative was not there to "show the land" and make the transfer. When Mwanga attempted to decide against Gabunga, a Protestant chief stood up in the Lukiiko and shouted, "No, sir Kabaka! You are wrong! Do not adjudge so! Where were the Katikiro's representatives? You are wrong!" Less than a generation earlier, people had been executed for sneezing in the presence of the kabaka, but on this occasion Mwanga withdrew from the room, and the accusing chief was never punished.[97]

Captain Lugard of the Imperial British East Africa Company arrived in Buganda at this time of fulminating tension, and immediately became embroiled in the conflict over land and political authority. He was sent to set up his camp on land associated with Catholics; when the Catholics discovered that he was not a "Mufaransa" (follower of "French" religion), they demanded that he be moved. Mwanga told him to relocate as a guest of Protestants, but he refused to obey the king's orders. "The people were badly impressed by the white visitor's boldness and positive defiance," wrote one contemporary, and the name of Kampala hill was lengthened to "Kampala Alizala Bigwe," meaning "the white man's selection of Kampala as his headquarters will result in strife."[98] The leading chiefs who were struggling to manage constant conflict over land allocation in a climate of armed suspicion began to use Lugard in the way that they had been using Mwanga and also Kalema: he became the voice of authority that justified the chiefship allocations they were seeking. Catholics as well as Protestants sought the resolution of land disputes with Lugard instead of Mwanga.[99] Lugard wrote that he

> tried to form a court of arbitration [for the land and eviction disputes] in which I could hear the circumstances from representatives of each side and would act as arbitrator. I found however that no one would agree that this court should consist of less than some four on each side. This number led to violent and heated argument, either side telling a completely different story, both undoubtedly lying. In addition, the circumstances were so involved and intricate that I felt myself in despair of arriving at any solution.[100]

The situation described by Lugard sounds similar to the Lukiiko, the Buganda council of chiefs, which met before the kabaka. The issues—cases related to chiefship and authority over land—were those discussed in the Lukiiko, and the atmosphere of complex and passionate debate was likewise that of the Lukiiko. However, Lugard had taken the place of the kabaka, and the Ganda chiefs had allowed him to do it.

Why did the Ganda chiefs allow a newly arrived British agent, with a reputation for bad manners, to take on the kabaka's centrally significant function of naming those who had authority over land? We cannot assume that the Baganda deferred to Lugard because they thought he had a competence or insight that they themselves lacked: a dozen years later, when the British presence was more firmly established, Baganda were adamant in protecting their control over land issues from any British meddling. Rather, Ganda chiefs gave Lugard and later British agents kabaka-like powers in the 1890s because Ganda forms of authority had been undermined first by the destabilizing cycle of long-distance trade in cloth, guns, ivory, and people and then by civil war. In 1890, Ganda chiefs were trying to re-create legitimate authority that had been undermined by enslavement and to integrate potentially dangerous new religions into the familiar, formerly stable order of chiefs controlling land. They were failing, and constantly renewing the possibility of war, because the order of chiefships they wanted to re-create required a powerful authority at the center. Mwanga was not able to serve as that figure, and without doing so intentionally, the Christian chiefs gave the role to "the Kampala European."[101]

It is important to pay attention to the significant difference between Ganda intentions in their relationship with Lugard and Lugard's intentions in his relationship with them. Lugard had told the gathering of "all of Buganda" that his mission was to create friendship and amity between his nation and Buganda; this was manifestly sensible to the Baganda. What both sides understood by this friendship, and how it would be demonstrated, became clear to all the protagonists only gradually. In his account, written decades later, James Miti emphasized British justice—Lugard paid compensation when his goats damaged someone's property, and he introduced "justice along entirely new lines." Kaggwa's account elides the period in time in which Catholics relied on Lugard as an arbitrator and emphasizes the Catholic complaint that "the Baganda Protestants had as their kabaka, the Kampala European."[102] In 1890, Baganda did not consider the sovereignty of their nation to be threatened by friendship with England.

The attempt to weave Protestant and Catholic allegiance into the entire structure of Ganda chiefship in every province fell apart completely with the outbreak of armed conflict in January 1892. Catholics took Mwanga and fled from Mmengo. Protestants pursued them and "plundered a lot of cattle."[103] Two months later, Kaggwa reallocated the chiefships, giving them to Protestants. Kaggwa avoided the accusation that he was assuming the role of kabaka by resurrecting the title of Sebwana, the chief who had taken care of the kingdom between the departure of Kabaka Cwa and the arrival of Kabaka Kimera in the distant past. At this time, people discussed whether the ambitious Protestant leader Apolo Kaggwa should become kabaka. Kaggwa refused, saying it would be wrong for a peasant to become kabaka, and that as a nonroyal person he would not have the capacity to judge impartially. According to Kalikuzinga, Kaggwa said, "as a Kabaka, I could not sleep well."[104] Instead, Kaggwa continued to forge a relationship with "the Kampala European" in which each acted to legitimize the other's power. Kaggwa (and, initially, other chiefs as well) used Lugard and successive British agents to consolidate the emerging chiefly hegemony within Buganda, and the British used Kaggwa and the Baganda to conquer the rest of Uganda.

The Catholics stopped fighting and came back to Mmengo through a reconceptualization of the structure of the kingdom: territory was now assigned to different religious groups. Catholic missionaries, who wanted their followers to be able to develop a Catholic society, may have contributed to this plan, which represented a fundamentally different approach to dealing with the unending potential for conflict inherent in the categories of the new religions.[105] Miti reports a rumor that the Catholic missionaries had appealed to Lugard for a province for their people, and that Lugard refused, saying that "as he was a white man like themselves and as such only a stranger in the country, he did not consider it within his power to settle the matter of splitting up the country. It was the duty of the people themselves, although he had a voice in the matter."[106] Kaggwa wrote about the decision as though it was made by Lugard, and most historians have followed his lead. However, Lugard himself claimed, some thirty years later, that the decision had been made by the Baganda: "There was never any such thing [as a 'Lugard settlement']. After the fighting in 1892 the Baganda Chiefs urged that the two parties could not live together without a recurrence of murders etc. and they urged that each should take different provinces. This they did."[107] The Baganda had used land allocation to define relationships between people for generations, and associating provinces with religious groups was a logical next step after the attempt to associate religion with specific chiefships had failed. Since Ganda chiefs had been making decisions about land and chiefship before Lugard's arrival, and since the new allocation followed a thoroughly Ganda idiom regarding the meaning of land, it seems likely that Ganda chiefs made this decision also. It only became associated with Lugard when people looked back from a point in time when Ganda autonomy had been diminished.

Ganda chiefs mapped religious categories onto Ganda ssazas with attention to Ganda forms of meaning that might have been neglected if the reallocation of land had been a British decision. A new drum with the beat "Reliance on the side of the Lake" was created to identify Buddu as a Catholic area. Stanislaus Mugwanya, the leader of the Catholics at that time, moved "all the Catholic chiefs who were in Bulemeezi, Kyaggwe, Kyaddondo and those of Kimbugwe and Kaima, Mujasi and Lubuga together with all their people" and allocated a place for them to live in Buddu. The allocations were made by Mugwanya in person.[108] Bataka (clan elders) on butaka land in Buddu who were Protestant were replaced as bataka by members of their families who were Catholic, but clan members did not have to leave butaka land.[109] All the Protestant chiefs in Buddu received chiefships in other ssazas; all the Catholic chiefs from other ssazas received some amount of territory in Buddu. The Ganda chiefs who planned these complicated movements of people intended to create peace by separating the factions whose disagreements had seemed uncontrollable. At the same time, the movement of chiefs and people to newly allocated land was a reassertion, after the chaos of the war, of the productive and orderly purposes that chiefs and their followers were supposed to fulfill.

The initial 1892 allocations of Buddu to Catholics and of the three small provinces of Ggomba, Butambala, and Busujju to Muslims did not create peace because the territories given to non-Protestants were too small. Muslim chiefs who had held important posts were forced to occupy minor chiefships that did not entail much land or many followers. Mugwanya later said that he could not give any chief, no matter what his status, more than four estates, "for had I done so I should not have been able to put all the Catholic Chiefs in one single County."[110] Catholics and Muslims felt that the disproportionate allocation of land to Protestants violated the moral logic of the kingdom, and so withheld the labor they were obligated to supply to the center of the kingdom. Refusing to provide people to work for the kabaka was the first stage of rebellion, and tension escalated. Songs objecting to work circulated among Muslims: "The Kasujju (chief of the Moslem province Busujju) said that to work for Mwanga was to eat pigs"; and neither the Catholics nor the Muslim chiefs were able to muster respectably sized forces for work at Mmengo.[111] Conflict over working for the kabaka caused the Muslims to withdraw and fight again, and as result they lost all but Butambala province in 1893. Muslims had no alternative but to scatter and live on the lands of Christian chiefs who would accept them: this marked the end of Muslim political power in Buganda.[112] The potential that Catholics' unwillingness to work might also lead to war caused a further negotiation of titles and territory in 1893. This gave the Catholic faction chiefship titles equivalent to the major titles held by Protestants, land between Buddu and Mmengo, land in Mmengo, and also the provinces of Mawokota, Buwekula, Ssese, and Busujju.[113] Each of these actions defined the nation in symbolically significant ways as both Protestant and Catholic. The newly created Catholic Katikkiro and other titles affirmed the equivalence of the two factions in the structure of the country, additional Mmengo land gave the Catholics a place in the center of the kingdom, and the reallocation of land gave the Catholic faction rich and densely populated areas on the shore of the lake.

This symbolic and practical reconstitution of the kingdom effectively ended the civil war in Buganda. This is how people remembered it thirty years later, that "there had been many Civil wars in Buganda and that what had put a stop to these wars was the division of the country."[114] The violent ambition of armed Ganda chiefs was channeled into collaboration with the British in the conquest of the neighboring polities. Mwanga's inability to rule with authority was finally resolved when he refused to cooperate with chiefs and British agents attempting to control him. He withdrew from the capital, led a rebellion of "bitter nostalgia," and was replaced as kabaka by his infant son.[115]

In the 1890s, Ganda chiefs assumed themselves to be the hosts of the British presence in the region. They had chosen to create a relationship with a distant power that would involve them in obligations and yield advantages. Baganda clearly considered their kingdom to be sovereign in the 1890s, the presence of British commissioners, subcommissioners, and fort commanders not withstanding. This is particularly evident if we keep in mind that for the Baganda, control of land signified political power. Acting Commissioner Ternan wrote to Sir Clement Hill in 1899 that "we have a mile square at Kampala and a similar bit at Port Alice and are much cramped." They could not get land for a rifle range, and the prison had to be in the garden of the Buganda subcommissioner. "You would be surprised," he wrote, "at the way we have hitherto been jammed up." He noted that "the chiefs are very niggardly as regards Govt. though generous to the Missions about land"—the missions owned between thirty-five and fifty square miles, which they had received as gifts. Considering the inability of the British authorities to get even unoccupied lands, he concluded, "one rather wonders where the British Govt. comes in."[116]

Without a doubt, Ganda chiefs assumed that courtesy, respect, and a deliberate assertion of the dignity of all authority figures on both sides would characterize their relationship with the British. In this they were immediately disappointed. A group of chiefs wrote to the Imperial British East Africa Company asking that a "God-fearing man" be sent to replace Lugard.[117] People called Colonel Colville, the acting commissioner in 1894, "Mmandwa," that is, a man who is possessed and therefore behaves in an irresponsible and illogical manner. Ansorge, temporarily the British authority in Buganda in 1895, was known as "Njota Vvu"—a man so antisocial that no one would bring him firewood and he had to live in the dark.[118] In a few months in office in 1895, Ansorge had dismissed chiefs on what the Baganda thought were trivial charges, placed Ssekiboobo, a high-ranking chief, in a chain gang, and imprisoned a wife of Kabaka Mwanga.[119] His superior wrote that he had "made a perfect old ass of himself, and did a lot of harm all round both with the King, Chiefs and people."[120]

In the 1890s, Ganda chiefs and British officials evoked each other's authority to effectively wield power. The leading chiefs in Buganda claimed that some of their decisions had been made by "the Kampala European" and George Wilson described his role as "running the show with the two Katikkiros and Kago."[121] Two Lukiikos—the "King's Lukiiko" and the "Lukiiko of the Kampala European"—required the presence of chiefs for deliberations.[122] Chiefs were admonished that they were not to call the newly created council "the Lukiiko of the Kampala European" but instead call it "the Baraza of the Representative of His Majesty the King of England at Fort Kampala," but later instructions reminded chiefs of their obligation to attend "the Lukiiko of the Kampala European." Acting Commissioner Colville wrote to the Foreign Office that he had created the new council because he recognized that the existing Lukiiko posed a problem for British authority. Although he criticized what he considered to be the inefficiency and disorderliness of Lukiiko proceedings, he explained that the "sound" decisions he observed it make on a land question "led me to consider what scheme would provide the necessary controlling power over the Council without creating jealous apprehension that we were aiming at relieving the Chiefs of their legitimate responsibilities." The acting commissioner's response to his observations of the effectiveness of the Lukiiko was to create a parallel institution. Colville's replica of the Lukiiko became "popular beyond anticipation," and "after a time the scheme grew and all questions of any gravity were voluntarily brought to the Baraza after their passage through the Lukiiko."[123] The enthusiastic participation of Ganda chiefs in the "Lukiiko of the Kampala European" as well as the "King's Lukiiko" may suggest that people were still striving, in the 1890s, to re-create the pinnacle of authority that had been the kabaka's place at the center of the kingdom.

CONCLUSION

The familiar story of Buganda's civil war explains how the uniquely enlightened Baganda created their modern nation. Versions of this narrative usually highlight the confrontation of Christians and Muslims with Kabaka Mwanga on the shore of Lake Victoria, emphasizing the inevitability of new ideas replacing old ones; the moment when Mwanga invited the Imperial British East Africa Company to help him win back his country, explaining British and Ganda cooperation; and Lugard handing out guns during the battle of Mmengo, underlining British power and later Protestant hegemony. It is also possible to see the civil war as something not so unique, a time when Baganda were caught up in the vortex of change that transformed East African societies in the late nineteenth century and responded in ways that have to do not only with their new religions, but also with the cultural resources of a people who had established an ordered kingdom based on relationships of reciprocal obligation marked with permanently cultivated land. Placing Buganda in a larger context, the first critical moment of the civil war was the raiding in 1888 by armed, uncontrollable ebitongole chiefs and their followers, and Mwanga's royal tour in which he raided and enslaved people across the nation: the patterns of exchange that linked people and leaders had been replaced by violence. A second significant moment in the civil war was the allocation of chiefships by a group of Christian chiefs, who decided on the order of the country themselves, and informed Kabaka Mwanga afterward: the center of Buganda's hierarchy was functionally vacant. A protracted but essential element of the story was the failure of the system of interweaving Catholic and Protestant chiefships at every rank: leading chiefs had recognized the need to mold new religions into the nation, but had not found a workable method. Finally, the resolution of the civil war, from this point of view, was not the arrival of powerful British administrators who took sides and took control, but the creative, innovative actions of Ganda chiefs, who reconceptualized the nation as a balance of Catholic and Protestant power, and expressed that new vision in drumbeats, symbolic space in the capital, and the allocation of chiefships and land.

NOTES

1. Kaggwa recounts the plundering undertaken by the kabaka and chiefs, and also the provocations of "unnatural vice," but identifies the onerous burden of digging the lake as the cause of the revolt against Mwanga. Kaggwa, *Basekabaka,* trans. Musoke, 96/141-100/143 (N.B. typescript double pagination). The conflict is cast in religious categories by Wright, *Buganda in the Heroic Age,* 34, 40, 164–165; Kiwanuka, *History of Buganda,* 192–193; John Milner Gray, "The Year of the Three Kings of Buganda," *Uganda Journal* 14 (1949): 15–52; Christopher C. Wrigley, "The Christian Revolution in Buganda,"

Comparative Studies in Society and History 2 (1959): 33–48; and D. Anthony Low, "Religion and Society in Buganda 1874–1900," *East African Studies* (Kampala) no. 8 (1957). John Rowe interpreted the overthrow of Mwanga as a result of Muteesa's innovations. Rowe, "Revolution," 142, 188. According to Michael Twaddle, it was less a religious revolution than a palace coup, and the revolutionary implications of regime change emerged in the attempt to make Buganda a Muslim state. Michael Twaddle, *Kakungulu and the Creation of Uganda 1868–1928* (Athens: Ohio University Press, 1993), 35; Twaddle, "Muslim Revolution in Buganda," 54–72.

2. This analysis relies on Richard Waller's unpublished essay "The Traditional Economy of Buganda," John Tosh's description of the Ganda contribution to precolonial trade in "The Northern Interlacustrine Region," and Steven Feierman's analysis of the consequences of long distance trade for a kingdom with a tribute-based economy in *The Shambaa Kingdom: A History* (Madison: University of Wisconsin Press, 1974).

3. Items traded from the coast have been found in archaeological sites in Uganda dated at several centuries before Kabaka Semakookiro. David Schoenbrun, personal communication. It is possible that Ganda traditions associate trade with Kabaka Semakookiro because long-distance trading expeditions began to reach Buganda during his reign.

4. Kaggwa, *Basekabaka,* trans. Musoke, 103, 64/123.

5. Mackay, *Pioneer Missionary,* 216–217; Waller, "Traditional Economy," 22, 30.

6. Ashe, *Chronicles,* 72–73.

7. Steven Feierman, "A Century of Ironies in East Africa (c.1780–1890)," in Philip Curtin, Steven Feierman, Leonard Thompson, and Jan Vansina, *African History: From Earliest Times to Independence* (New York: Longman, 1995), 354.

8. Fallers, "Social Stratification," 111–112; Christopher C. Wrigley, "The Changing Economic Structure of Buganda," in *The King's Men,* ed. Lloyd Fallers (New York: Oxford University Press, 1964), 19, 21, 25. Kiwanuka argues that there was no slave trade until after 1860. Kiwanuka, *History of Buganda,* 167. Rowe states that while convicted criminals and foreign captives had been removed from Buganda in the past, enslavement of Baganda by their fellows began at this time. Rowe, "Revolution," 152.

9. Kaggwa, *Basekabaka,* trans. Musoke, 66/124.

10. Philip O'Flaherty, quoted in Waller, "Traditional Economy," 31.

11. E.M.K. Mulira, *Sir Apolo Kaggwa, CKCMG, MBE* (Kampala: Buganda Bookshop, 1949), manuscript translation seen courtesy of John Rowe.

12. Waller, "Traditional Economy," 31. Twaddle argues that patterns of plundering became formalized. Twaddle, *Kakungulu,* 13. Kiwanuka states that the power of the monarchy increased. Kiwanuka, *History of Buganda,* 108.

13. Kaggwa, *Basekabaka,* trans. Musoke, 63/122.

14. Musisi, "Elite Polygyny," 769.

15. Mackay, *Pioneer Missionary,* 180–181.

16. For example, his raid on Batombogwe hill; Kaggwa, *Basekabaka,* trans. Musoke, 82/133, 65/123; Rowe, "Revolution," 70.

17. Mackay, *Pioneer Missionary,* 435.

18. Waller, "Traditional Economy," 32.

19. Ibid., 29.

20. Ibid., 28, 32.

21. John Iliffe, *A Modern History of Tanganyika* (Cambridge: Cambridge University Press, 1979), 75; Medard, "Croissance," 470–471.

22. Gorju, *Entre le Victoria,* 120; Gray, "Year of the Three Kings," 15; Wright, *Buganda in the Heroic Age,* 28; Kiwanuka, *History of Buganda,* 194. I see the growing power of chiefs as a descent into chaos fueled by slaving, and not as a potentially competent emerging bureaucracy. Cf. Fallers, "Social Stratification," 111; Wrigley, "Changing Economic Structure," 25–26; Low, "The Northern Interior," 334; and D. Anthony Low, "The Making and Implementation of the Uganda Agreement of 1900," in D. Anthony Low and R. Cranford Pratt, *Buganda and British Overrule: 1900–1955, Two Studies* (London: Oxford University Press, 1960), 4. Michael Twaddle critiques the lack of attention to slavery by Buganda scholars in "The Ending of Slavery," 144.

23. John Rowe draws attention to the destabilizing consequences of chiefs not obligated to the king in "Revolution," 153, 166, 182.

24. Kiwanuka notes in Kaggwa, *Kings,* 184. John Rowe details Katikkiro Mukasa's relationship with Kabaka Muteesa in "Revolution," 139–143, 148–152.

25. Kaggwa, *Kings,* 183; Ashe, *Chronicles,* 116.

26. Zimbe, *Buganda,* 82–83.

27. Kaggwa, *Basekabaka,* trans. Musoke, 85/135.

28. Ibid., 340/277.

29. Twaddle, *Kakungulu,* 37.

30. Ibid., 21.

31. Ibid., 22–23.

32. Ibid., 37, 28.

33. Waller, "Traditional Economy," 32.

34. Grant, *A Walk Across Africa,* 202.

35. Waller, "Traditional Economy," 32.

36. Twaddle, *Kakungulu,* 14; Kaggwa, *Customs,* 92.

37. Kiwanuka, *History of Buganda,* 198–199; Kaggwa, *Basekabaka,* trans. Musoke, 99/143.

38. Southwold, "Bureaucracy and Chiefship," 15–17.

39. Kiwanuka, *History of Buganda,* 199. According to Twaddle, the purpose of these new ebitongole chieftaincies was to guard Mwanga, but the information available about them suggests the ebitongole acted in their own interest. Twaddle, *Kakungulu,* 59.

40. Zimbe, *Buganda,* 174, 176.

41. Kiwanuka, *History of Buganda,* 199.

42. Kaggwa, *Basekabaka,* trans. Musoke, 98/142.

43. Zimbe, *Buganda,* 162.

44. Kiwanuka, *History of Buganda,* 199.

45. Zimbe, *Buganda,* 157; Faupel, *African Holocaust,* 82.

46. Ashe, *Chronicles,* 90; James S. Miti, "A History of Buganda," n.d., typescript translation in Makerere University Library Africana Collection (N.B. problematic pagination), 252–297.

47. For example, Kabaka Mutesa had required the Kaima to build a hill inside his palace in 1871; Kaggwa, *Basekabaka,* trans. Musoke, 78/139.

48. Kaggwa, *Basekabaka,* trans. Musoke, 100/143; Ashe, *Chronicles,* 93.

49. Zimbe, *Buganda,* 151–153.

50. Kaggwa, *Basekabaka,* trans. Musoke, 100/143; Zimbe, *Buganda,* 154.

51. Kaggwa, *Kings,* 63.

52. Ashe, *Chronicles,* 102.

53. See endnote 1.

54. Rowe, "Revolution," 63–94 passim, song, 76.

55. Jean Brierley and Thomas Spear, "Mutesa, the Missionaries, and Christian Conversion in Buganda," *International Journal of African Historical Studies* 21:4 (1988): 617.

56. Charles F. Harford-Battersby, *Pilkington of Uganda,* 2nd ed. (London: Marshall Brothers, 1898), 199, 201; Taylor, *Growth of the Church,* 93.

57. Michael Twaddle, "The Emergence of Politico-Religious Groupings in Late Nineteenth Century Buganda," *Journal of African History* 29 (1988): 86–87.

58. Twaddle, "Politico-Religious Groupings," 99. Twaddle demonstrates in this essay that followers of the world religions did not begin to fight each other at the instigation of missionaries, and that spiritual, political, and material motives were intertwined.

59. Wright, *Buganda in the Heroic Age,* 114–115.

60. According to Bakale Mukasa, "They did not fight for religion but for chieftainship." Quoted in Twaddle, *Kakungulu,* 40–41.

61. Rowe, "Revolution," 180.

62. R. H. Walker, quoted in Taylor, *Growth of the Church,* 84.

63. Wamala, quoted in Twaddle, *Kakungulu,* 44.

64. Wright, *Buganda in the Heroic Age,* 116.

65. Twaddle, 51.

66. Ashe, *Chronicles,* 141.

67. Ibid., 41; Hamu Mukasa, quoted in Twaddle, *Kakungulu,* 47.

68. Miti, "A History," 349.

69. Zimbe, *Buganda,* 204.

70. Twaddle, *Kakungulu,* 55.

71. Kaggwa, *Basekabaka,* trans. Musoke, 116/153.

72. Ashe, *Chronicles,* 137, 139.

73. Miti, "A History," 409.

74. Ibid., 359.

75. Ibid., 368.

76. Twaddle, *Kakungulu,*78.

77. Mair, *African People,* 79.

78. Miti, "A History," 361.

79. The lower estimate is from Ashe, *Chronicles,* 144; the higher estimate is from Kaggwa, *Basekabaka,* trans. Musoke, 119/155.

80. Wright, *Buganda in the Heroic Age,* 101.

81. Miti, "A History," 337; Kaggwa, *Basekabaka,* trans. Musoke, 114; Medard, "Croissance," 346–350.

82. Kaggwa, *Kings,* 168.

83. Kaggwa, *Basekabaka,* trans. Musoke, 104/146.

84. Twaddle, *Kakungulu,* 50.

85. "Commission," Guggu, Yosiya Ajabi Sumugala, and Gabunga, 384–387; Medard, "Croissance," 495.

86. Mulira, "Sir Apolo Kaggwa," 2.

87. Twaddle, 52.

88. J.R.L. Macdonald, "Report on Uganda Disturbances in Spring, 1892" (1893) Public Records Office (PRO) Foreign Office (FO) Series FO s (African) F02/60, 106b.

89. Twaddle, *Kakungulu,* 38.

90. Wright, *Buganda in the Heroic Age,* 64.

91. Ibid., 117, 95.

92. Macdonald, "Report on Uganda Disturbances," 107b.

93. Ibid., 108b–109a.

94. Wright, *Buganda in the Heroic Age,* 95–96.

95. Medard, "Croissance," 555; Twaddle, *Kakungulu,* 77.

96. Wright, *Buganda in the Heroic Age,* 99.

97. Kalikuzinga, quoted in Wright, *Buganda in the Heroic Age,* 118.

98. Miti, "A History," 369.

99. Wright, *Buganda in the Heroic Age,* 117.

100. L. L. Kato, "Government Land Policy in Uganda: 1889 to 1900," *Uganda Journal* 35:2 (1971): 154.

101. Kaggwa, *Basekabaka,* trans. Musoke, 124/158.

102. Miti, "A History," 375; Kaggwa, *Basekabaka,* trans. Musoke, 124/158.

103. Kaggwa, *Basekabaka,* trans. Musoke, 128.

104. Ibid., 129/161; Wright, *Buganda in the Heroic Age,* 119–120.

105. Henri Medard, personal communication.

106. Miti, 391; Kaggwa, *Basekabaka,* trans. Musoke,130/162.

107. Entebbe Archives, Secretariat Minute Paper (SMP) 6902, document identified as 221D.

108. "Commission," Stanislaus Mugwanya, 394.

109. "Commission," Matayo Serubuzi, 422; "Commission," Erenesti Kakoza, 450.

110. "Commission," Stanislaus Mugwanya, 399.

111. Wright, *Buganda in the Heroic Age,* 144, 147; Kaggwa, *Basekabaka,* trans. Musoke, 136/166; Medard, "Croissance," 526–531.

112. Kaggwa attributes these decisions to "the Kampala European" (Major Macdonald). Kaggwa, *Basekabaka,* trans. Musoke, 140/168, 146/172. Miti claims that Mwanga made them after a long and inconclusive discussion by the Lukiiko and Macdonald approved. Miti, "A History," 424.

113. Kaggwa reports this as a decision made by Portal. Kaggwa, *Basekabaka,* trans. Musoke, 135/165. Miti reports it as a discussion in which Portal urged Mwanga and the Lukiiko to take the action. Miti, "A History," 410–411.

114. "Commission," Apolo Kaggwa et al. to the "Chairman of the Commission of Inquiry," 603.

115. Wright, *Buganda in the Heroic Age,* 162.

116. Ternan to Hill, PRO FO 2/202, 261.

117. Wright, *Buganda in the Heroic Age,* 128.

118. Ibid., 169; Twaddle, *Kakungulu* 107.

119. H. A. FoxBourne, Secretary, Aborigine Protection Society, to Earl of Kimberly, April 10, 1895, uncataloged papers of Archdeacon John Henry Walker, in Royal Commonwealth Society Papers at Cambridge University; W. J. Ansorge, *Under the African Sun: A Description of Native Races in Uganda, Sporting Adventures, and Other Experiences* (New York, Longmans, Green, 1899), 129.

120. Jackson to Clement Hill, April 20, 1895, PRO FO 2. It is interesting to note that Ansorge "summed up" his accomplishment "as upholding British prestige and authority, and maintaining friendly relations with King Mwanga and all the great Waganda chiefs, Protestant and Roman Catholic." Ansorge, *Under the African Sun,* 121.

121. Kaggwa, *Basekabaka,* trans. Musoke, 135/165, 140/168, 146/172; George Wilson, quoted in Low, "Agreement," 46.

122. East Africa Confidential, May 7, 1897, "Africa from Commissioners and Consuls General in Uganda, January to October 1897," PRO FO 2/13320-23.

123. February 6, 1906, to the Foreign Office, PRO CO 536/ 5, "Uganda 1906, Vol. 1: Commissioner January and February," no. 26.

5

WHEN THE MILES CAME: ASSERTING SOVEREIGNTY WITH LAND

Miles came to Buganda in 1900, when the boundaries of vast tracts of individually owned land were measured out in square miles on top of the webs of overlapping allegiances that divided up the ridges and hills of the country. No inherent, compelling logic motivated the innovation of a new form of land tenure; as we have seen, Ganda chiefs had successfully used the language of land allocation to demonstrate their assumption of authority that had been the kabaka's, and to reimpose stability after the civil wars. Private property in land was in a way a misunderstanding—one consequence of an agreement between Ganda and British negotiators that could not go according to plan, because the ruling Ganda chiefs planned to use land and their alliance with the British to consolidate their hold on power, and the British envoy planned to rationalize the alienation of land in order to attract settlers and make the colony pay. Most turn-of-the-century treaties between African rulers and potential colonial powers involved a high degree of mutual misunderstanding: the Uganda Agreement of 1900 was perhaps unique in that both parties invested considerable resources and effort in its implementation, because both anticipated they would benefit. It is ironic that none of their expectations was met. The Baganda chose their land first, and the British Crown land turned out to be mostly rocky hill tops and useless swamps. Gaining title did not give Ganda chiefs the lock on power they anticipated, because the social relationships that the Baganda defined through exchanges on the land were fundamentally transformed by colonial overrule and a cash economy. Mailo, the form of land tenure that developed from the land clauses of the agreement, embodied its creators' contradictory intentions and assumptions about land.

One of the enduring myths of mailo land is that the regents who negotiated the 1900 Agreement were land-grabbers, who offered Buganda to the

British in order to secure the largest possible amounts of land for themselves. The huge estates amassed by Apolo Kaggwa, the prime minister; Stanislaus Mugwanya, the chief justice; and a few others give weight to this point of view, as does the most available documentary evidence, which dates from the 1920s. The imperious, self-justifying manner in which Kaggwa rebuffed clan elders who had lost all their clan lands and were unable to bury their relatives and the proof that Kaggwa had allotted miles to all of his sons, including one who was unborn at the time, make it easy to support the view that mailo did not work from the beginning because the "big men" were selfish. What actually happened in 1900 is more complicated and more interesting.

The creation of mailo land is a story of intense intellectual and social creativity; of meaningful things that stay the same in a new context, of things that have to stretch and change, and of fundamentally important things that become no longer possible. In allocating mailo land, the ruling Ganda chiefs carried out a complex and extensive act of cultural translation. They inscribed the new order of power in Buganda, with themselves at the top, into the spaces of square miles on the land, and they created ways for ideas that were important in Buganda—such as the importance of remembered places relevant to deceased kings—to continue to have meaning in a landscape of private land ownership. Since Baganda used control of land to express relationships of power, their success at allocating valuable land to themselves and worthless land to their British "protectors" must be understood as an eloquent statement of Ganda intentions regarding sovereignty.

The Baganda who received land and those who did not at first understood private land ownership as a slight variation on familiar terms and patterns; the forms of marking control over land, of attaching a person to land and a chief, and of being sent away from land, were all applied to mailo land. One disjuncture between mailo and Ganda land use in the past was immediately obvious: What happened to the authority of ancestors buried in land to claim it for their descendants and influence the living if land could be owned by people who were not descendants of the ancestors buried there? The elimination of the authority of dead ancestors over people on the land was emblematic of the ways that private land ownership narrowed and flattened the social relationships that land had represented in Buganda.

The Ganda chiefs who became land owners attempted to use their new property in the ways that land had been used in Buganda in the past: to define relationships, create sustenance, and achieve security and status. Achieving these familiar goals became more difficult because the Uganda Agreement of 1900 entailed challenges to the Ganda order of things. British Protectorate authorities competed with Ganda authorities. The chiefs' roles as intermediaries in calling out labor and collecting tax and their inability to protect people from fines and harsh treatment undermined the logic of reciprocal obligation.

The authority of chiefs-turned-landowners was also threatened by the introduction of a new vocabulary of status in European commodities and behaviors, and by the possibility that followers could abandon chiefs and maintain themselves through wages or the production of cotton for cash.

MAILO ALLOCATION AND AUTHORITY IN BUGANDA IN 1900

In negotiating the Uganda Agreement, Ganda chiefs used their well-developed skills of getting what they wanted from a figure of authority who considered himself to be utterly powerful. Sir Harry Johnston, appointed special commissioner at a salary Foreign Office functionaries thought ridiculously exorbitant, was charged with setting up an administration that would give the Uganda Protectorate "the advantages enjoyed by the inhabitants of other portions of the tropical possessions or protectorates of her Majesty."[1] Development and trade, and the salaries of administrators to supervise those processes, would be paid for through taxation. His instructions noted that as Uganda was "under the nominal dominion of the King of Uganda," revenue in that portion of the territory "would be collected in the name of the king." Johnston sent a draft of his plans to the Foreign Office from Naivasha (in what is now Kenya), before he had even arrived in Uganda. He planned to institute a hut tax and a gun tax, and make the largest chiefs responsible for tax collection. The Crown would retain "waste and uncultivated" land, peasant cultivators would keep their plots under the supervision of a board of Europeans, and the king and a few leading chiefs would receive small land grants. He had received a dispatch regarding land based on investigations by his predecessor, Colonel Ternan, but he was not really interested in anyone else's ideas. "Upon reaching Uganda," he wrote, "I shall endeavour as quickly as due regard for local conditions permit, to acquire complete control over the disposal of the land."[2]

Ganda regents and their missionary allies immediately recognized that Johnston's plan deprived Ganda rulers of any real power, and the Agreement that emerged from two months of negotiations was substantially different from his original proposal.[3] Johnston's hut tax, gun tax, and provision that chiefs would collect taxes remained. However, the final version contained clauses ensuring Ganda control over affairs in the kingdom that gave Buganda an enduring and powerful autonomy within the Protectorate. Johnston gave up his claim of the Crown's right to uncultivated land, a substantial and extraordinary concession for a proponent of British Empire in 1900. Instead, Ganda chiefs were to receive the lands they currently occupied—estimated to be nine thousand square miles—and the Crown would receive the rest. The Agreement confirmed and completed the process begun in 1894, through which neighboring polities lost land to Buganda.[4] After the commissioner's welcome to Kampala, Miss Furley of the Church Missionary Society had observed, "it is a little pity that he starts by thinking the Chief's children who do not know how to take care of themselves and must be taken care of, but he will find out he is not dealing with children."[5]

The ruling Ganda chiefs and Sir Harry Johnston negotiated with each other using profoundly different concepts of the nature of power and how it should be displayed. The chiefs (Apolo Kaggwa, Stanislaus Mugwanya, and Zakaria Kizito) demonstrated their strength and the British Crown's obligation to them through gifts of service and statements of allegiance that involved the labor of thousands of followers. Johnston was welcomed in the hall the chiefs had built for the Kampala Lukiiko, "a fine mud building, large and lofty, with whitewashed walls, the posts and ceiling being reeded" that held two thousand people.[6] As he arrived, orderly crowds of Baganda lined his route, "the roads for a considerable distance were most beautifully decorated by day and illuminated by night with torches, the torch-bearers numbering many thousands."[7] This visible proof of the chiefs' commitment to British authority was matched in their written communication, which claimed a humble longing to learn from Johnston:

> For it is the rules of the Queen which we seek to put into force in Buganda. Failure on our part to carry out any request is due to the immaturity of our country which is not yet used to carrying out the orders of the Queen. Because of that inexperience we shall proceed slowly in all spheres until we are able to proceed on our own. This indeed is the reason for our begging you to leave us to rule so that we may under your tutelage rule wisely.[8]

All these actions and statements invoked reciprocal obligation. "It is not good for us to be poor and people to laugh at us saying 'look at those who call themselves friends of the Queen being short of money.'" The Baganda had shown how much they loved and cared for the queen, and therefore her representatives would have to respond with equivalent appreciation and generosity for the Baganda, or risk damage to the queen's reputation: "For our country, you should remember, Sir, is unique in Central Africa. For years we have been friends of the Queen, and even you yourself said so. . . . We who are called friends of the Queen are afraid of losing respect for this will make some people laugh at us."[9] The Ganda chiefs sought to retain control over their land and their government by asserting their desire to be obedient.

Sir Harry Johnston understood power in a more linear fashion. He confidently asserted the superiority of British rule, British institutions, and British ideas, especially his own.[10] He thought Africans could not "advance much above the status of savagery" except through labor for wages that would lead them along the path of progress blazed by Britain.[11] He expected all Europeans to model civilization for all Africans. At his welcoming reception, he entered the Lukiiko hall alone, and then all the European men in the country were introduced, one at a time, according to rank. After the lowliest foreign resident came the regents, Prince Mbogo, and all the ssaza chiefs. Miss Furley and the eight other British and French women in the country "were not introduced, but smuggled into the room beforehand, and placed in a long row along the wall."[12] He wrote to the chiefs that "the Baganda are at present very nearly at the bottom of the scale." When Ganda negotiators pointed out that Johnston's system would eliminate the positions of 793 lower-level chiefs, he responded:

> I am asked how they are to continue to exist after these changes. Are they to go on as before plundering the people, or what are they to do? [The former holder of a chiefship] can continue to live on the produce of his estate if he chooses to live an idle life. If he prefers a more active existence he can no doubt find employment under the Government, or he can trade, or he can pursue any honest livelihood.[13]

Johnston met with the ruling Ganda chiefs once, and then left Kampala for Entebbe: he did not anticipate a need for face to face negotiations, because he had told the chiefs what was good for them and he expected them to agree.

A number of factors probably contributed to the Ganda ruling chiefs' success in shaping the Agreement in a way that preserved, at least to some extent, the order of the kingdom. Some missionaries warned Johnston that his plan might lead to a Ganda rebellion; he may have felt that he had to accommodate them in order to preserve the Protectorate, which depended on Ganda military support. Glenn McKnight argues that "Baganda chiefs held the upper hand" because they had demonstrated military superiority in their victory over rebellious Sudanese mercenaries and Kabaka Mwanga.[14] While records of negotiations contain no hint of a threat from the Ganda leaders, the regents did invoke the backing they had given the British in their letters to Johnston. Regarding a gun tax, they wrote that "we are serving the Queen with those guns and we are not entirely serving ourselves." Referring to the Ganda chief Kakungulu, then engaged in pacifying the Bakedi, they wrote, "What about the guns he has? They have not yet stopped serving the Queen." They reminded Johnston that they had fought with and captured Kabaka Mwanga.[15] Ganda military strength clearly mattered to Johnston: he explained that he planned to place all the Protectorate troops in the Ganda capital because they have "warlike tendencies," "possess 10,000 to 12,000 guns," and "are the only people for a long time to come who can deal a serious blow at British rule."[16]

Missionary interlocutors also made a difference. Their commitment to a civilizing mission involved an appreciation of Ganda society developed in decades of close interaction, and they were anxious about the damage Johnston might cause. Archdeacon Walker of the Church Missionary Society wrote to his brother: "Sir Harry is not 'Almighty' though he speaks as if he thought himself so, and the Waganda are not of less consequence than sparrows, though Sir Harry seems to think they need not be considered. I wish he had made a study of the people before he made up his mind as to what he would do. We have had so many disasters here that we cannot stand many more."[17] The Church Missionary Society, White Fathers, and the Mill Hill Fathers (English Catholics who had recently arrived in Uganda) all made efforts to convince Johnston to accommodate the concerns of the Ganda chiefs. The translations and explanations provided by Archdeacon Walker ensured that the Ganda participants understood Johnston's intentions. Anthony Low argues that Archdeacon Walker's intervention with Johnston led to the extra grants of land (twenty miles to Kaggwa, fifteen to Mugwanya, and ten to Kizito) that some interpreters have considered to be a buy-off of the regents.[18] If the Banyoro and others had had missionary friends as the Baganda did, perhaps they would not have lost territory to the enlarged Buganda that came out of the Agreement.

The subtle and strategic negotiating of the Ganda ruling chiefs must also have been a factor. They agreed to a hut tax, but suggested a reduction for the first year and requested that the chiefs receive one-third. They agreed to a gun tax, but asked that guns used for defense be exempted. They requested tax exemptions for invalids and old people and on buildings that were not houses. Reminding Johnston continuously of their friendship with the queen, they questioned the erasure of each essential aspect of Ganda governance. "We would further enquire if our king is no longer so and what is the reason for his removal?" "We also would ask if our Council is abolished." They described the work performed by 783 Bakungu chiefs below the ssaza chiefs and asked, "What then will become of these chiefs? Will they rank as Bakopi? If our fellow chiefs are to be so degraded, how will our contentment exist?" They questioned what would happen to the capital: "What will make a Saza Chief attend at the capital in future? There will no longer be a Kabaka or Council which made him come up in the past." "We would also enquire what will maintain the Queen-Mother who has had so many estates?"[19] The final Agreement recognized the structures of authority—from subsidiary chiefs to the Lukiiko and the kabaka—that Ganda chiefs insisted were important.

Johnston had told the Buganda subcommissioner, "I cannot trust the chiefs and people of this country to deal with the waste land in an honest and sensible fashion," but the chiefs won the battle over uncultivated land.[20] They asked where the two thousand youths who married every year would settle. They asked where they would find pasture, land for annual crops, and sources of clay. They asked about all the products of forests—firewood, wood for building, for canoe construction, and for making charcoal—and how people who lived far from a forest would obtain them. What would become of the coffee forests planted by their forefathers? They asked:

> Are we going to live as strangers in our country? Formerly there used to be very little waste land in Buganda, but the wars which went on for 11 years have depopulated the country. We would ask therefore that we be allowed to utilize waste lands for agricultural and pastoral purposes, and that you will only sell to non-natives such places as will be unoccupied for these purposes, the revenue accruing from such transactions going to the government.[21]

The Agreement recognized these concerns by granting the Ganda chiefs the right to choose their nine thousand square miles of land before the Crown would choose its share.

The Foreign Office officials who frowned at Sir Harry Johnston's expenses might have thought the Uganda Agreement overpriced. Uganda did become profitable, but not through the white settlers Johnston had hoped to secure, and the Agreement had enduring unintended consequences. It gave the leaders of a colonized Buganda a powerful tool that they used against the Protectorate, Foreign Office, and Colonial Office authorities for more than half a century, and the involuntary surrender of territory to Buganda by neighboring polities haunted Uganda politics.

Abstract allotments matching political status with an amount of land were therefore the beginning of private land ownership in Buganda. According the agreement, 350 square miles were reserved for the kabaka and 150 for the queen mother, the princes, and princesses; each of the three regents was to receive 32 square miles, and each chief of a ssaza was to receive 16. Mbogo, an uncle of the kabaka's who had been a potential contender for the throne, received 24 miles for himself and his fellow Muslims.[22] The lower chiefs were to divide the remaining 8,000 square miles that the negotiators of the Agreement determined to be the Ganda share of the nation. In order to implement this miniature scramble for African land, the regents and senior chiefs drew up a list of several thousand chiefs whose status entitled them to become land owners, and the number of square miles that each one deserved. The most important of these chiefs chose their "miles" first, and the less important had to find pieces of land for themselves after the senior chiefs had chosen.

Although granting mailo land title was a new form of land allocation, the Ganda principle that land delineated relationships remained in effect. The shift in power, evident during the civil war, from the clans and king to the ruling chiefs, was intensified.[23] The regents and the chiefs in the Lukiiko, rather than the kabaka, now made land allocation decisions. Authority to allocate land

Figure 5.1   Katikkiro Apolo Kaggwa in a governess car, ca. 1908. Apolo Kaggwa received more land than any other nonroyal individual in the mailo allocation; followers pulling him in a cart also demonstrated his status. (Royal Commonwealth Society Archives, Cambridge University)

flowed down from higher chiefs to lower chiefs: those who wanted land brought a paper from their ssaza chiefs to the Lukiiko stating that they deserved to be allotted miles.[24] Claimants' relative status was the criterion by which decisions were made; therefore, the regents and Prince Mbogo won disputes about land whenever anyone attempted to challenge their claims.[25]

The members of the Lukiiko had given themselves the king's authority to grant land to others, and they expected their authority over land to be absolute. They successfully challenged encroachments on that authority. In July 1905 the ssaza chief of Mawokota, the *kaima,* tried to implement orders from Martin, the Buganda district officer, regarding the preservation of forest land. The Lukiiko secretary noted, "The Lukiko was very displeased over the Kaima's behaviour, because he had only paid attention to the European's orders without caring for what the Lukiko said." They countermanded the kaima's decision, and made sure their interpretation of mailo procedures prevailed.[26] The Lukiiko refused to involve itself in land questions involving a *kibanja* (the plot assigned by the chief or owner to a follower), even though it was wanted for the worthy purpose of building a school. "Then we of the Lukiko told them that we had no power over a kibanja which had an occupant. . . . Go and come to an understanding with Tela Sebugulu, the kibanja owner, whereby you give him another kibanja while he sells this one to you."[27]

The ruling chiefs gave themselves more land than chiefs had controlled in the past. They rationalized their selfishness by saying they needed more land than chiefs had ever controlled because they had more power than chiefs had ever had in the past; it made sense.[28] The creation of new chiefly offices meant other important chiefs had to lose land so that the greater importance of the new chieftainships would be evident. For example, Zakaria Kisingiri moved up from being the *kangaawo,* one of the most important ssaza chiefs, to become the *omuwanika,* a new position created in the aftermath of the civil wars, "and he had therefore to look for another place where to make his headquarters of his new Chieftainship, to which he had now been appointed i.e. that of Treasurer; and he had also to look for some other estates in which he would mark out his private miles. . . . So Kisingiri selected Bombo where he made his private headquarters, and Chief Kibale was the Lukiko's representative who handed over these estates to Kisingiri. Again Kisingiri went down to Luwalo and made his official headquarters there, where he had to turn out Chief Musitala from the estate in question."[29]

The sense that mailo allocation inscribed the new chiefly hierarchy onto the land is evident in the testimony of a clan leader a quarter of a century later, at the Protectorate Commission of Inquiry into Butaka Clan Lands. Abuta Lusekera, a mutaka of the Otter clan on Buganga in Mawokota ssaza, had gone to cut poles to build a church, when he was met on the road by a man who had come to tell him that he had been turned out of his estate. "I left the poles on the road and went straight to the capital and went and asked Mugwanya whether it was really true that he had turned me out of my estate, and he replied that it was true."[30] Lusekera was told that he had been allotted eight miles of land, but he would have to find them some other place, because Mugwanya had taken his land. He got a certificate for two miles of land, went to the katikkiro to complain, went back to Mugwanya and begged, and ended up with nothing but the land around his forefathers' graves. The forty-seven estates he lost were part of the valuable fishing area that twenty years earlier had been claimed by the Catholics, and before that had been ebitongole of various chiefs and the kabaka.[31] Responding to this accusation, Mugwanya was unrepentant. If he had taken the best estates in Mawokota, it was because his new position—one that had never existed before—required the best estates. He said the Lukiiko had sent representatives to take away the land of Lusekera and his fellow clan leaders because "the question of miles in Buganda is a very important one."[32] He explained that they had to alter the original distribution of 1893 because a physical place, in the form of estates, had to be created for the new position of second katikkiro. "As I had been appointed the Second

Katikiro I was given more miles than the other Saza Chiefs, which miles I marked out on my old estates as well as on the other estates which were given to me by the Lukiko, and which had been pointed out to me by the Lukiko Representatives."[33] This involved batongole moving to other places, and "even the Saza Chief Matayo Kisule had to evacuate his own estate which I took up." His prior position as the kimbugwe had involved a certain amount of status, but his new position entailed greater status, so he had to take other people's land. In this way a handful of the most powerful chiefs came to control tens of square miles of densely populated land: thousands of people who had held authority as lesser chiefs regretted the absence of a strong kabaka at the center.

GANDA MEANINGS FOR LAND APPLIED TO MAILO

The procedure for becoming a mailo estate owner combined Ganda forms of land allocation with European ones. The person who received a piece of land was given "a typewritten slip of paper on which was written the estate."[34] These papers had great import; a request by the Mugerere in 1905 to exchange miles with someone else whose land "was more appropriate for a chief" was turned down "because these places were already shared out and type-written copies of the certificates are already complete in which names of the places appear."[35] Once the typewritten paper was produced, the recipient went to the chief of the ssaza where his estate was located, and the ssaza chief designated a representative to hand the estate over to him.[36] Alternatively, a representative of the Lukiiko was sent to resolve land allocation disputes; these representatives had to be properly introduced to the ssaza chief by the Lukiiko. The representative who had shown the land was always mentioned anytime the recipient of the land or the person who had been driven off of it referred to the transaction.[37] For several years, mailo allocation had the same kind of flexibility that Baganda were familiar with in land transactions: people traded estates without any reference to written documents, went to the people who had the land they wanted in order to get it back, and tried to convince the Lukiiko to give them a better allocation.[38]

When a new land owner "took up" a mailo estate, the person who had been the controller of that area left, taking his followers with him to the new land that he had been assigned.[39] Alternatively, his followers might choose to remain, and the incoming landowner would assume authority over the people on the land. In this situation, a clearly understood code of conduct governed how the new lord would treat his people, and failure to comply would lead to complaints against him.[40] Bishop Alfred Tucker, a keen observer and defender of Ganda rights to private land in his interaction with the Protectorate officials, later wrote for British public consumption about the transition to mailo: "The man in occupation had to be turned out, and he in his turn sought his portion of land . . . the occupant of these had to be turned out, and so on. Thus the game of 'general post' went on merrily until the whole population was in movement. Streams of men, women and children going east with all their household goods, cattle, sheep, goats, and fowls, met similar streams going west."[41] In Buganda people had always moved, searching for a more amenable chief or location or following bakungu and batongole chiefs to their new posts. One of the few commoners who spoke before the 1924 Bataka Land Commission explained, "the bakopi were very anxious to become wealthy so they went and became private tenants of the wealthy and generous chiefs"; bakopi did not have graves that were remembered, because they died on the land of their chiefs and their descendants expected that at some time they would move to another place.[42] The ordinariness of this movement is apparent in Mugwanya's description of evicting Jemusi Miti from Mawokota in 1892: "When I was distributing these estates I came upon this witness's butaka estate, but I found that he had already packed up all his things and was only waiting to greet me before leaving since he was a friend of mine."[43]

One reason that chiefs were willing to be turned out of their land was that people did not realize, in the first years after the imposition of mailo, that the reallocation would be permanent. Mikairi Kidza, one of the leaders of the case against mailo land in 1924, used the Ganda proverb "When an acquaintance robs you, you do not at once throw away the pad on which you have been carrying your load which has been robbed" to explain that those who lost land to more important chiefs assumed it would come back to them.[44] Those who brought the case against mailo also reminded the commission, *"Omutaka nyenje tefa muka"*—"The mutaka is a cockroach which does not die in the smoke."[45] In the past, if one kabaka had taken away land from a chief or a clan, another kabaka returned them to favor.

In choosing their mailo, people sought estates on fertile land in order to attract many followers, whose presence would give the landowner prestige. Estates near Lake Victoria, where people could fish as well as grow bananas and other crops, were the most sought after. People who were allocated less fertile land complained bitterly, because no one would live on their land. Writing to Apolo Kaggwa, the katikkiro, in 1905 Isake Kajane, "a man of Kaima," asked for different miles because the seven he had been allocated were in a place where *matooke*, the staple food, did not grow, and no people would go there.[46] Other people complained of being allocated land "in the desert," "in a district full of elephants," or in a place where leopards ate the goats. Wild places with many animals did not have enough people; there was no point to owning such land.[47] Some families tell stories of great-grandfathers or other relatives who were frustrated in their efforts to select their miles, because all the good land with people had already been taken by bigger chiefs, until some missionary friend explained that in the future, land without people would also be valuable, and that is how these families came to own their land.

Some evidence suggests that Protectorate officials encouraged the most powerful chiefs to take land with people. The kaggo, the ssaza chief of Kyaddondo, justified a request to the Lukiiko for populated land by referring to a statement by Bwana Tomkins: "I have only 10 square mailo in my Saza, six mailos are situated in Bulumezi. When we heard 'Bwana's' advice that if a person got land in a place where there are no people, if he found unclaimed land he could exchange his land. I am also in the same situation."[48] Apolo Kaggwa also succeeding in getting the governor to intervene on his behalf when the Lukiiko refused to grant him land he wanted (in this case, it was butaka land). A letter to the ssaza chief reports the instructions of "Bwana Balozi" (the governor): "So this man is defeated. This important man we promoted and is your leader; such an important man who has done a lot of honourable things for Buganda! No, go and give him that land he wants."[49] Protectorate officials' support for the leading chiefs combined with the chiefs' desire for populated land to shape who received fertile land in the mailo allocation.

People living on mailo land were the critical element in two land disputes heard by the Lukiiko in 1905. Samusoni of Bulemeezi and another man, Daudi Kaitakusa, had been turned off their land when another man marked out his miles in the place where they lived. Samusoni thought the man had taken more than the four miles to which he was entitled, and was willing to put up ten shillings to have the land surveyed. When it was discovered that the man actually had taken more than four miles, the extra miles were given to Samusoni and Daudi, but when Daudi returned from being away in Bunyoro, he had been given the whole land, even though he had a mile somewhere else. When Samusoni complained, the property was divided into two parts according to how many followers each would control: Samusoni was assigned thirteen kibanja (thirteen families of tenants) and Daudi received seven kibanja. Samusoni was allocated more because he had paid for the survey. In Senga, a man named Musajawaza had been given the butaka (land with ancestral graves) of Bude as his mailo, so Bude wanted to trade. The Lukiiko determined that in order to reclaim his land from Musajawaza, he should compensate him with six gardens, that is, the space for six families of followers.[50]

The immigration of Banyoro onto land beside the lake caused conflict between Enoka Mutalabwa and Yonasani Waswa, who had been given either the same land or adjoining lands by chief Kimbugwe in Bulemeezi. Mutalabwa had received it first, but had left only one man there, and the Kimbugwe later gave land in almost the same area to Waswa, who immediately began to build. He also put one of his men there. When thirty Banyoro settled by the lake, both Mutalabwa and Waswa wanted the place with these people to be theirs. Mugwanya, the chief judge of the Lukiiko, told Mutalabwa that Waswa deserved it because Mutalabwa had not built a house on the land, and "anyone who occupies empty land is not a thief." Mutalabwa objected that the land was his if it had been assigned to him, whether or not he had done anything with it. The Lukiiko tried to judge the case on the basis of documents, but neither man had any papers at all, so the Lukiiko "gave the whole place to Yona Waswa who had done building on the land."[51]

The calculus of kusenga, the relationship of a land-allocator and land-receiver, was clearly motivating people who obtained mailo land. Even as people positioned themselves to use mailo to develop successful relationships, alternative sources of status and security posed an even stronger threat to reciprocal obligation than during the civil war years.

The mapping of the Ganda hierarchy of chiefs onto estates of appropriate sizes was an assertion of Ganda ideas about the meaning of land that coexisted relatively smoothly with the forms of private property. Ganda uses of land that connected the living and dead were not so easy to reshape, and Ganda chiefs worked to maintain the important meanings of land in a new form. The most important problem was Busiro—literally, the place of shrines, where all the former kabakas were buried. The deceased kabakas expressed their concerns about the nation through mediums residing by their graves who embodied their spirits. The continued importance of former kings was demonstrated by followers, who also resided by the graves, who inherited the roles of each deceased kabaka's wives and ministers. The capital of the country faced Busiro, and the reigning kabaka visited his forefathers' shrines every month at the new moon.[52]

The first Lukiiko decision was that title to the land with the shrines would be in the names of the kabakas. "It was in this way: every dead Kabaka had his katikiro as well as his other chiefs at the place of his burial. Our intention was therefore that each dead Kabaka should be allotted one square mile which should be marked out in his name. This would have been in conformity with the old native custom for the deceased Kabaka to possess estates and their chiefs."[53] If the deceased kabakas had owned the land, the people living on it, maintaining the graves, and sustaining themselves from the banana gardens planted around would have been the kabakas' followers, and it was appropriate for deceased kings to continue to have followers. According to Kaggwa, however, "when we represented the matter to the British Government we were told that this proposal was impossible since a dead person cannot possess property."[54] The solution that made perfect sense in Ganda terms—the place where dead kings are buried and remembered belongs to the dead kings—was impossible in British terms, which stated that only living people could own land.

The eventual solution devised by the chiefs was an innovation that partially protected the kings from the disgrace of having the land of their graves owned by someone else, but it involved dilemmas of its own. The katikkiro called Mbogo, the head of the princes, Nalinya, the head of the princesses, and others to discuss how to solve the problem of Busiro:

> We put the matter which we had brought from the Commissioner before them, and we asked them to consider it carefully. . . . [T]hey decided to give up their original Mituba estates in the various counties, and each prince agreed to return to Busiro to the place of his ancestors. A prince marked out one square mile and a princess one square mile on the place of the graves of their ancestors.[55]

The neatness of this solution—"when the Lukiko gave the princes and princesses land containing the graves of their grandfather they were giving them their own butaka land of their ancestors"—was not wholly satisfactory, not only because the kabakas were no longer independent, but also because in Buganda princesses and princes had always been kept far from the king.[56] Princesses held large amounts of land and administered it using a hierarchy of chiefs that paralleled that of the kabaka; kabakas kept princes far from themselves, confined under the close guard of a relative of the kabakas' mothers, if they were allowed to live.[57] "We the Princes are not entitled to settle in Busiro where they had now taken us for from time immemorial Busiro has always been owned by the Kabaka alone."[58] Kabakas had a natural antipathy to princes, who might want to usurp the throne; it did not make sense to have princes accept the land that made them the kabakas' caretakers.

The intricate, complex ways in which control over land had reflected the order of reciprocal obligation in the kingdom were eliminated in the effort to assign more square miles to the king than to any other person. The regents, following British advice, assigned land that had intrinsic value in Ganda history to the living kabaka. One such land was Mangira, which was remembered as the first capital of Kabaka Kintu. The head of the Leopard clan, who had always lived there and carried on the work of remembering the importance of the place, wanted title to the land, but the regents had given it to the kabaka. "This estate was Kabaka Kintu's capital, and that is why it was marked out with the Kabaka's miles." A place that was said to be the burial place of Kintu was also assigned to the kabaka.[59] These allocations erased the capacity of people on the land to retain the prestige and purpose that had come from the work for an earlier kabaka that they commemorated through living on that land.

The intractable problem of mailo land was the conflict between the rights of a landowner and the undisputed rights of deceased clan leaders over the

land on which they were buried. Living descendants of clan and lineage leaders were obliged to maintain butaka, the banana gardens that held the graves
of important remembered ancestors. Actions critical to social reproduction
took place in butaka. These included ceremonies securing the health of children, marking the passing of generations, and defining the descent groups of
people responsible for taking care of each other. Butaka existed in every part
of the kingdom, although the most important ones were concentrated in the
central, oldest ssazas. People told Lucy Mair in the late 1920s that ceremonies related to childhood were held less commonly than they had been before that time, but butaka remained essential for identifying lineages and
defining lineage relationships.[60] The authority of ancestors in relation to their
descendants reached across time and space, but the places where they were
buried were unquestionably theirs.

Baganda did, in particular circumstances, intervene in the authority of dead
ancestors by removing their bones from the land, and burying them in another
place. A kabaka exhumed any bodies on land he intended to use as his capital, and ssaza chiefs forced the removal of graves when they feared that people
might be using the graves to establish rights to stay on that land.[61] "Clansmen who know about burials and disinterring, whether the latter is good or
bad," made these decisions with great deliberation. Apolo Kaggwa outraged
his clan members and the Lukiiko by removing five graves from Grasshopper
clan butaka that he received as mailo.[62] Among the immediate complaints was
a letter asking, "Did the dead ancestors give permission to have their bones
dug up at Senge?" Kaggwa justified his actions by claiming that unburying
bodies was not an abomination, because kabakas had done it in the past.[63] A
packed Lukiiko session, with large crowds listening outside the windows,
heard the case. Minutes of the meeting claim that Kaggwa told the Lukiiko
and Buganda District Officer Tomkins that he did not want to rebury the bodies
because it would prevent him from selling the land to white traders. The
Lukiiko, backed by Bwana Tomkins insisted that the bodies be reburied on
the butaka land. Masembe, a mutaka of the Grasshopper clan, wrote that in
unburying the bodies Kaggwa had *"yamaala kunyooma kika"*—"expressed
the uttermost contempt for the clan"—and that he had done it because he
thought there was no one who could challenge him on this or anything else.[64]
The incident threatened to divide the Grasshopper clan and an elder admonished Kaggwa, "In digging up those bones you also dug up your grandparents.
But they are now reburied and the ill feeling must come to an end."[65] Kaggwa
had attempted to extend his rights as a landowner into control of the bones
in a butaka: the response from his peers demonstrated that a landowner's authority did not extend to butaka graves on his land.

Although it eventually proved impossible, the Ganda chiefs attempted to
reconcile clans' and the subbranches of clans' maintenance of control of

hundreds of banana gardens containing significant graves with private land ownership in square miles. Mailo land was to be given to people who were chiefs, and the most senior bataka were all allotted a number of miles, often six or eight, because they were the heads of the clans. Lower-level bataka, however, those who were the heads of the secondary or tertiary levels of clans, were not all considered chiefs. The Lukiiko attempted to find someone who belonged to the appropriate clan branch and was on the mailo allotment list, and to assign the butaka to that member of the clan. This effort did not satisfy the clan leaders who had lost control of the butaka, because the people who received mailo for butaka land were often not members of the line of descent who were supposed to be in charge of the butaka.[66] The Lukiiko members argued that they had preserved butaka by allocating it to a member of the correct clan; the bataka maintained that only the correct descendant could control the land.[67]

The Lukiiko also made efforts to return butaka when it had been allocated to the wrong person, and defended the right of clans to hold on to butaka when chiefs asked for it. Blasito Kiwanuka described how the Hippopotamus clan had lost a *kasolya* (principal) butaka in Mbazi. When the leaders of the clan realized that their butaka had been allotted to someone else, they called a meeting, and then together visited the prime minister to ask for the return of their butaka. "He told them that if that was our actual Kasolya butaka land he would give us one square mile, and the Katikiro asked them to give him a member of our clan to whom he would give this square mile which should be taken to the head Mutaka of our clan."[68] In 1905 the ssaza chief Ssekiboobo asked for one of the miles belonging to Misusera Kibude, because some of Ssekiboobo's own mailos were empty, and "it is not very becoming of a Sekibobo to have mailo without inhabitants." The Lukiiko refused to allow him to have the land, however. "That land was given to Mesusera Kibude. It is his butaka on which there are his graves, we cannot take away that land from Kibude."[69] Negotiations to preserve some kind of clan control of butaka are a recurrent theme in the early records of the Lukiiko.

The attempts that the Lukiiko made to preserve clan control of butaka were considered by the 1920s to have been unsuccessful. One reason for this is the degree to which lost butaka had come to symbolize every possible social ill (see Chapter 7); another reason is that loss of butaka became the one legitimate complaint one could make against a mailo holder, and people who had other legitimate claims to land began to express those claims in terms of butaka. Looking past the highly charged discourse of the 1920s, however, it is possible to discern that the allocation of butaka land to people who were not the appropriate descendants caused real distress. People were prevented from burying clan elders on the appropriate butaka and had to bury "in the jungle."[70] Others described being unable to hold the *kwabya olumbe*, the

postfuneral rites that marked succession, "and up to the present day the funeral rites in connection with the burial of this Mutaka have not yet been performed, as his children have no place where they can gather together and
perform them, since they have now become just like slaves and outcasts."[71]
Some clan elders who had been allotted a number of miles, refused to take
their miles and instead became tenants in order to remain on the land with
the graves for which they were responsible.[72] People also immediately began
to buy the land that held their butaka.[73]

The implication in private land ownership, that all the rights and powers
related to that land are held by the owner, was fundamentally incompatible
with butaka, which affirmed the authority of dead ancestors over living people,
especially the people on the land around their graves. White marker stones
kept disappearing from the surveyed land in Bussi; people explained that
misambwa, the territorial nature spirits associated with those who had first
occupied the land, were taking them because they refused to allow their land
to be surveyed.[74] While some mailo owners allowed bataka to continue to live
on their land in order to accommodate the challenge to their authority posed
by ancestors buried in the ground, others responded to that challenge by driv-
ing off all the bataka.[75] Chiefs were clearly less comfortable with the alternative authority of butaka than the kabaka had been: the possibilities for bataka
to exercise authority over clan lands diminished dramatically when a coterie
of chiefs with foreign allies took the place of the utterly powerful kabaka. A
specific example of this is the butaka of the Hippopotamus clan on Mmengo
hill. Blasito Kiwanuka explained that the clan had controlled Mmengo hill
when Kabaka Muteesa moved his capital there in the mid-nineteenth century.
The kabaka took the part of the hill where the palace was then built, but left
the clan's butaka intact. When Apolo Kaggwa took the land as his mailo in
1900, however, he drove the clan off of the land entirely. After describing how
Kaggwa had been willing to give some of the land to others but not to the
clan elders who deserved it, Kiwanuka observed *"kisala munyazi"*: "a stolen
thing is missed most by the thief—when it is stolen again from him."[76]

MAILO ALLOCATION AND THE LOCATIONS OF POWER IN BUGANDA

Mailo land narrowed the locations of power in Ganda society. This subtle
but profound transition was in part inherent in tenure change—Ganda ways
of using land facilitated the maintenance of many layers of relationships of
superiors and followers in the same small geographic area, while mailo supported the authority of only one owner. This difference in the use of land,
however, reflected an important characteristic of the sets of tools for creating social order that were available to the Baganda and to their British colonial contemporaries. In Buganda, the centralizing control exerted by the

absolute power of the kabaka coexisted with a tendency to avoid conflict by creating multiple avenues of power. The layering effect of this strategy was inscribed on the landscape, as we have seen. Clans, lubaale spirits, royal women, the chiefs of ebitongole dedicated to specific purposes, and the chiefs appointed to administer areas might all exercise claims to the labor and produce of people in the same area, or nearly the same area.[77] For example, answering the question "To whom did the estate Namutamba belong?" Aligizande Mude explained, "Some of the estates at Namutamba were occupied by the Kabaka's cooks, and others were in possession of princes and princesses, and others belonged to the Bataka. There was also an Ekitongole called 'Ekikuta' at Lwogelo."[78] In contrast, the tendency of British colonials in Buganda was to consolidate power in one location, and to check alternatives with force. When the range of social relationships expressed through the medium of land declined dramatically with the creation of mailo, this was only partly a consequence of the characteristics of private property in land. It was also a manifestation of the colonial process of dismissing multiple sources of power, and the inability of Ganda leaders to effectively maintain alternatives to the singular form of power promoted by British officials.

The contrast between the Ganda inclination to diffuse power and the British inclination to consolidate it is evident in some of the early entries in the written records of the Lukiiko. Three men were fighting over the minor office of Bulala Mutuba. The Lukiiko gave it to one of them, created another office for the second, and told the third to remain in the position he had.[79] Two years later, the position of head of the clan of the princes was challenged by Mbogo, the prince who had been the Muslim contender for the throne. Mbogo asked, "Who will be the head of our clan between me and I. Ssabalangira?" The Lukiiko resolved "to let I. Ssabalangira continue to be the head of the members of the blood royal, while Mbogo should be the judge to hear all disputes between the princes."[80] In 1909 the provincial commissioner for Buganda had requested a list of chiefs who had been approved to collect taxes. The Lukiiko sent a list of all the chiefs, and of all their carefully selected assistants. The provincial commissioner sent this list back, saying that he did not want to know the names of the assistants, that all the names of the assistants should be removed, and that the list should be returned with only the names of chiefs.[81]

Lands controlled by lubaale spirits through their *bandwa,* mediums, were entirely eliminated in the mailo allocation, completing a process that had begun during the civil wars. Mediums had been one of the main sources of criticism of the kabakas and restraint on their power; the loss of their position and voice diminished the possibility for disagreement with the central authority of the state. Apolo Kaggwa partially acknowledged the lubaale deities' role in curbing the power of the kabaka in his explanation that lubaale land had been eliminated because it was a "bad custom" instead of a "good custom":

> [M]ost of the Bataka were of "Lubale" and the Kabaka used to turn out these bataka completely. . . . The good native customs were followed; that is those good customs of the bataka which are calculated to keep up the dignity of the Kabaka were observed, such as that of Mulumba—the Kabaka's Chief Gatekeeper, the Musolosa—the Keeper of the Kabaka's fire; the Nakatanza and Kibale who guard the Kabaka, and others of a like nature.[82]

Spirit mediums continued to exist in Buganda, but they lost authority when they lost their lands and their followers.

While the nnamasole and other royal women were given amounts of land that approximated their control of land in earlier times, their particular place outside normal categories no longer had validity. The nnamasole and the princesses had been people who did things other people did not do: they were women who did not get pregnant, who had lovers instead of husbands, who ruled like men, and who had power separate from the kabaka.[83] Queen mothers had exerted a direct influence on kabakas; princesses were critical to successful rebellions. Their political role of providing a counterbalance to the power of the kabaka lost meaning when the kabaka lost power in the civil wars. The hierarchy of administrative chiefs established by the regents and the British chiefs ignored royal women. After 1900, royal women had large amounts of land, but they could not do with it what they had done in the past. Legal battles that lasted for decades were the result of the continued existence of the forms of royal women's authority, even though they no longer had power.[84] What royal women did continue to do was to behave beyond the bounds of other people's rules: "[T]hese princesses are also very cheeky. When they come visiting they stay a whole month or a full week all the time drinking beer and without any thought of returning to their homes."[85] One origin of a land market in Buganda was the result of royal women selling land to support their dissolute lifestyles, which was all that remained of their role as the focus of political dissent.

Ebitongole, the lands that had been designated for a particular activity, lost that named purposefulness in the allocation of mailo. People continued to carry out the activity for which the ekitongole had been named—the kabaka's mweso board makers continued to carve, and the kabaka's cooks prepared food, but the statement of the importance of their activity inherent in the ekitongole was no longer present. The mweso board carvers stayed in the same location, but it was designated kabaka's land. When Mugema chose the ekitongole of the cooks as part of his mailo, the *kauta,* the chief of the cooks, took land in a different place as a chief entitled to mailo, while the cooks themselves moved to a different place.[86] The ekitongole of the barkcloth makers was marked out as kabaka's land; the barkcloth makers stayed there, but ceased to be the men of their chief, the *kasumba*.[87] The disaggregation of people from their work, from the person who was named the leader in charge of their work, and from the place that was dedicated to the importance of their work represented a loss of ability to deploy symbolic capital. People who lived on the kabaka's land and carved mweso boards and furniture were less significant, in a subtle way, than what they had been before—the people of the Ekitongole of Mweso.

Much of the obligation commemorated through occupation of land was erased in the allocation of mailo. People were not obliged to consider the ways that a particular land was used to remember past social relationships when they chose their miles. Some of the land that was meaningful to clans remained under their control, but obwesengeze land, which had been given to commemorate a connection between the kabaka and a particular individual, was almost entirely eliminated by mailo. An example of this was the estate Sai, which Kabaka Muteesa gave to Nsukusa, the man who cleaned his courtyard, and whose descendants were known as Mulimyambuga: "He who cleans the courtyard." The family had struggled to maintain the obwesengeze land over several decades—they lost it to the katikkiro but Kabaka Mwanga returned it, and its status during the Protestant-Catholic land divide was also disputed. Zakayo Nkuwe, the grandson of the original cleaner of the courtyard, continued to carry out that work, and tried to obtain the land as mailo. His claim was the kind that had little validity when the miles came, because it was based on marking a relationship to the kabaka. While service to the kabaka had meaning as a claim to land before miles, the role of cleaning the mbuga was not a chiefship, and the estate was taken by the katikkiro.[88] The security of widows also deteriorated as remembering the past became a less important use for land: one of the main duties of widows was to maintain the graves of their husbands and remember them. In later years, when this role became less important, judges noted with disgust the willingness of families to drive widows off the land.[89]

CHALLENGES TO THE SOCIAL LOGIC OF OBLIGATION: LAND, POWER, AND LABOR BEFORE COTTON CULTIVATION

The allocations of land by the Lukiiko ended the use of land for sustaining people who remembered important things, and the use of land for claiming the importance of specific activities and for supporting diffuse forms of authority. Yet in the narrowed forms of the emerging colonial order, land continued to be a means of defining who was powerful, and of binding followers to leaders. Logically, reciprocal obligation tied tenants to land owners in the same way that it had tied men and women to their chiefs—the existence of land title did not affect the relationship.

The implementation of other parts of the 1900 Uganda Agreement undermined reciprocal obligation in ways that were not immediately apparent. The authority that the British assumed for themselves eventually undercut the power of people who controlled land. When chiefs collected taxes and called out the labor required by the British at Entebbe, they behaved in ways that were unchiefly, and their followers abandoned them in droves. The contract implicit in relationships anchored on the land was that chiefs provided protection, followers provided status, and clanspeople sustained each other. As the social bonds of chiefs to their followers deteriorated under the stress of excessive demands, alternatives emerged in the form of cash wages and commodities purchased with cash: money began to be a means of acquiring status, protection, and sustenance. Tensions involving power, obligations, and money that originated in the initial years of the implementation of the 1900 Agreement grew in intensity in the following decade.

In 1900, the pinnacle of the Ganda hierarchy of power was, in theory, Kabaka Daudi Cwa, who as a child still held the respect of the Baganda but did not exercise any authority. Real authority over other people flowed from chiefs, from the assertively present regents, especially Apolo Kaggwa, and from the distant *balozi* (governor). Kaggwa reported a meeting in 1905 in which Bwana (Tomkins, the district commissioner) told three ssaza chiefs, "I have dismissed you." The second chief, the *mugerere,* asked why he was dismissed. Kaggwa reported that Bwana said, "Don't you know that you are a drunkard? And don't you know that you are lazy? Do you do anything? And you even do not carry out the instructions of the Lukiko and you simply sit in your house and drink beer."[90] The Lukiiko went on to discuss Tomkins's complaints and listen to the responses of chiefs who had been criticized, but did not challenge the dismissals themselves: abrupt dismissal of chiefs had been part of the kabaka's power, and it apparently made sense that the governor assumed it also. The chiefs also offered to Protectorate authorities the kinds of public displays of allegiance that had been fundamental to the expression of political power in Buganda in the past. When the governor came to visit, he was received by Daudi Chwa. "Balozi was coming to see the Kabaka at 10:00 a.m. The Regents went to wait for him at the Kabaka's house. When Balozi came they greeted him. Afterwards he saw the Kabaka and then went away."[91] In September 1905 the Lukiiko apologized for not properly respecting a visit of the governor: "[W]e, Lukiiko members, were very wrong for not sending chiefs in the county to meet Mr. Balozi. We understand our guilt, next time we shall send them to greet Balozi."[92] However, the governor did not have a kabaka's authority over the life of every person and could not act toward people as a kabaka had acted: partly because the Baganda did not grant him that authority, and partly because Protectorate modes of expressing authority were less direct. Ambiguity at the top was new for Buganda, and the regents and chiefs innovated in creating their relationship with the Protectorate.

In the first years of the twentieth century, Baganda interacted with British Protectorate officials on the basis of a calculation of equivalent ranks. The regents and the most powerful chiefs met with, dined with, and sometimes prayed with the Protectorate officers for Buganda; ssaza chiefs were expected to take care of those officers when they toured. Nonofficial Europeans did not get the same treatment. An engineer who demanded food from a lower-level chief was told that the chief "did not know what type of European he was— in any case he was not a Balozi."[93] Foreigners did not always have the same understanding of their status in relation to Baganda; Prime Minister Apolo Kaggwa reported that a European had complained when Kaggwa did not greet him at the Kampala fort, but, as Kaggwa explained to Leakey and to the Lukiiko, he had not greeted the man because he did not know him.[94]

Baganda slotted European strangers into Ganda notions of social hierarchy, and most foreigners conformed to some degree to the expectations made upon them as controllers of people and therefore pseudo-chiefs. Even British Protectorate officials initially interacted with Ganda chiefs in ways that emphasized their common position as rulers over others, and de-emphasized differences based on nationality, which later became paramount. A foot race

Figure 5.2 Bringing presents for Count Filippi, 1906. Gifts for the visiting Italian Count Filippi in 1906 demonstrated not only the courtesy and generosity of the presenting chief, but also his ability to command the labor that produced the gifts. (Vittorio Sella)

from Entebbe to Kampala, held in 1908 to mark King Edward's birthday, hints at the contrast between power relations in those early years, and the forms and faultlines of colonial authority later. The runners were the subordinants of Ganda chiefs, of the other kingdoms in the Protectorate, and of British officials—the list of winners gives their names, "their lords," and their ssazas (unfortunately, the names and statuses of the foreign competitors were not listed because they all lost). These runners "arrived here when it was still daylight before the celebrations were over. They beat all the foreigners none of whom dared come near us."[95] In 1908, foreigners could compete in races with Baganda in which it was certain they would lose. The military and political indebtedness of the British to the Baganda to some degree accounts for British officials' respect of Ganda authority, but Ganda understandings of their own power also shaped the relationship.[96]

In the years immediately after the signing of the Uganda Agreement, Ganda chiefs expected the British to comply with Ganda standards of social relations, and intervened when they felt British officials were not treating Baganda in an acceptable way. In 1902 the regents complained to George Wilson, the deputy commissioner for Buganda, about the treatment of laborers in Entebbe. They told him that workers could not get food, that they were beaten, and that they had to work for too many hours, especially because they were not given a break in the middle of the day. Those who were left in the camp because they were too ill to work had no one to care for them and were not even given water. The regents believed that people had died on returning to their homes because of the bad treatment they received while laboring in Entebbe.[97] Their complaints led to an investigation and some apparently ineffective attempts at reform. In 1908 the Lukiiko sent to a British official in Buganda two men who had been tied to a telegraph post and lashed by a "European engineer" when they stopped his laborers from taking food without permission. The Lukiiko wrote, "We too have seen the marks left on the two men's bodies as a result of the lashes. Some of the marks have of course disappeared, but the bruises can be clearly seen."[98] They expected the commissioner for Buganda to see the bruises and punish the European who had obviously acted inappropriately.

The Lukiiko initially maintained a clear sense of its obligations in relation to Europeans, and of the British Protectorate's responsibilities to the chiefs. In 1905 the Lukiiko refused to pay workmen who had carried bricks to build the house of a European called Sitalaka. "The Lukiko told Luzinda to take the four men to Borup and tell Borup that the Lukiiko was not prepared to pay the men. The instructions to move the bricks had originated with Borup not with the Lukiiko and he was therefore responsible to see that the men were paid."[99] When Stanley Tomkins, the provincial commissioner, disbanded the ssaza police, the Lukiiko replied, "We shall write now letters to saza chiefs to bring all policemen here quickly when they will be discharged, and that they should come quickly here to our office. Allow us by your kindness to do so."[100] However, a short time later they asked Tomkins to transfer the salaries of the police to the ssaza chiefs, who were then doing the work that the police had done previously.[101] A careful examination of the Ganda chiefs' interaction with British Protectorate officials shows much more than compliance and collaboration. The chiefs made public displays of respect and submitted to overt assertions of authority, but they also asked British officials to conform to Ganda notions of rank and to abide by Ganda notions of social obligation.

The real loss in Ganda power did not come from the existence of district and provincial officers, to whom the Lukiiko spoke with a voice of courteous authority. Instead, cash wages, taxes in rupees, and labor demands slowly began to undermine the economic and social logic of chiefly authority. Rupees were fundamentally strange in Buganda: a man named Sabakaki succeeded for a while in 1905 in selling small pieces of marble to people who needed the new currency; he had made six hundred cowries at least by the time the market keeper arrested him.[102] Rupees were different from cowries in what they could do. Rupees linked the productive relationships of Baganda with British expectations of colonial productivity, but this unfamiliar money also had consequences inside of Ganda social forms. Cash became an alternative to loyal service in the calculus of power: with wages people could acquire things that had previously only been obtainable through attachment to a chief. When the imposition of hut tax made rupees essential, everyone needed something that chiefs could not supply. Cash and labor demands did to people's relationships with chiefs what long-distance trade had done to chiefs' relationships with the kabaka several decades earlier: new possibilities challenged old allegiances.

Rupees and the things they could buy at first fit awkwardly in Ganda patterns of exchange. The tendency of chiefs to mark their status with unusual possessions continued as Baganda with money distinguished themselves with watches, bicycles, and consumer items such as gramophones. However, it is clear that people were adding new items into forms of exchange that had already existed: their use of new things represented innovation with Ganda categories of meaning, not a wholesale embrace of modernity from abroad.[103] For example, at a celebration by the Protestant community for the Gayaza girls school in 1907, girls received prizes including watches, Bibles, suitcases, and "a beautiful box with a greenish tint." The chiefs at the celebration all presented cows and goats to the kabaka, and goats to the nnamasole, and Yosefu Kago, the host of the event, also gave a cow to the katikkiro and goats to the other two regents. The kaggo cooked three cows, one goat, and 481 miwumbo (basket-sized amounts) of food for the guests. His carefully compiled list included, among other items, twenty-eight bottles of soda, 130 gourds of juice, one tin of biscuits, one tin of sugar, and one bottle of curry powder. In celebrating their girls school at Gayaza, and their strength as leaders of the nation, the Protestant chiefs used the language of exchange of cattle and food, and added into that familiar experience Bibles as awards for cleanliness and character, and bottles of soda.[104]

The beginning of a cusp of the dilemma posed by cash is apparent in Jemusi Miti's correspondence with the Lukiiko in the summer of 1900. Miti was a rising Ganda chief, a servant, in theory, of the kabaka. He had been instrumental in the British conquest of Bunyoro, and was installed by George Wilson (Bwana Tayali—"Mr. Ready") as the katikkiro of Bunyoro. Miti was acting in the best interests of Buganda, which he was supposed to do as a chief, but he also needed material support. The defeated Banyoro were not providing food. In the new forms of expressing power, Miti needed a salary, not the cattle and tribute of the conquered. Where would his salary come from? Wilson suggested that the British government might be motivated to annex Bunyoro to Buganda if the Lukiiko paid his salary. The Baganda wanted Miti in Bunyoro, and the Lukiiko members acknowledged the appropriateness of a salary, but they wanted him to kusenga, to work for Buganda out of a sense of responsibility for the nation: "Our friend, merely concentrate in doing that task which you were set for our sake and for the sake of your mother country, without pay for these four months. . . . If any good fruits shall come out of your present work we shall certainly remember your present sacrifices and you will be repaid in full. You shall be remembered. . . . We beg you very much to do your duty with fortitude."[105] That Miti stayed in Bunyoro, without the salary that ought to have indicated his status as a chief, demonstrates that the sense of obligation to one's superiors which the Lukiiko evoked was still very real.

Cash wages created an alternative motivation for working, and the developing expectation that work ought to be compensated with wages deprived chiefs of an important symbol of their people's allegiance. In November 1905 the Lukiiko discussed what work peasants were obliged to do for chiefs. Someone reported that the ssaza chief Mugerere was not allowing people to cultivate for chiefs unless they were paid. The Buganda district officer redefined reciprocal obligation as a commodified exchange, suggesting that peasants ought to weed the compounds of chiefs because that was where they went to have their disputes settled.[106] This functional reciprocity fell far short of the assertions of mutual bonds that had characterized exchanges between followers and chiefs in the past. The conflict is apparent in the ssaza chief Kiimba's explanation of his disagreement with the district commissioner in 1905. Kiimba had chosen a man named Bikaye to accompany an unnamed British official, but Bikaye refused to walk with him without wages. Kiimba told him to go anyway, but

Bikaye refused and instead went to the fort in Kampala, and complained that he was being asked to work with no wages. Then the chief Kiimba was called into the fort: "Mr. Munala called me and reprimanded me for ordering somebody to go when he had no wages. He told me to go and tell another person to go. I asked him (Mr. Munala) whether the other person I may select shall not refuse just as this one had done. I had chosen this person to go and I was not going to select another. Then we quarrelled violently with Mr. Munala."[107] Kiimba returned home and forced Bikaye to do the work he had been told to do. If his people did not follow his orders, how could he be a chief? And if one person refused to work without wages, why would the next one work? An indication that this threat to chiefly power was not yet generally perceived is that the Lukiiko criticized Kiimba for failing to uphold Ganda standards of politeness toward the district commissioner. It concluded, "After listening to all this we found Kiimba guilty because he had caused this quarrel by his insistence that a man, whom 'bwana' said shall not go, should go on this journey."[108] In 1905 the chiefs in the Lukiiko did not, as a group, doubt their capacity to command obedience from their followers.

Cash wages destabilized the bonds of people to chiefs, not only by giving people new expectations about the possible consequences of their labor, but also by providing an alternative means to acquire status that had come from having followers. After working in Entebbe, the ssaza chief Kiimba had a drum of praise, Kabalakoma, played along his route as he returned home. The purpose of the drum was to inform people that the government was pleased with his work; the Lukiiko agreed because Kiimba had funds (presumably from being paid in Entebbe) to pay the drummers.[109]

Men who had earned salaries as mission teachers or as translators or clerks for the Protectorate received mailo land in the original allocation: their wealth in rupees gave them power that translated into chiefly status as land holders.[110] These people were not buying land with their wealth in money; they were being given land because they had wealth in money. A notorious case of this was Bazade, a Munyoro who was a servant of the chief Mugema, who probably had arrived in Buganda as a slave. He became a treasurer for Mugema, the ssaza chief of Busiro, the county where all the kabaka's graves were located. Bazade was a clerk and interpreter for the British in 1900, and he received a square miles of land in Busiro and later obtained two miles in Bunyoro. Twenty years later, when the appalling story of an enslaved Munyoro becoming the owner of a square mile was raised before the Butaka Lands Commission, Bazade justified himself saying he was "a naturalized Muganda" and "had acquired all the native customs of the Baganda." He had received the mile in Busiro when it was discovered that someone else's estate was larger than the amount allotted to him. When asked specifically if he had been a chief at the time of the allocation, he replied, "I was a chief by virtue of being chief

Mugema's Treasurer; and I was also Interpreter here at Kampala; and when Mr. Sturrock came to Buganda he found me Interpreter here at Kampala."[111] As holding an office for a ssaza chief did not signify chiefly status for others, Bazade's ability to convince the Lukiiko to allocate him land must have been his status as interpreter. Perhaps Bazade had obtained the land by subterfuge because he was a clerk, but that was not the accusation made in the 1920s. Instead, witnesses were outraged that the Lukiiko had overlooked the man's questionable foreign origins in assigning him land. In 1900, before wage labor had become routine and even before chiefs began to receive salaries, the anomaly of Bazade's wealth that came from Europeans gave him status that made him the appropriate recipient of a mailo. Ganda mission teachers and wage earners obtained mailo the same way; the objection to Bazade was not that wealth in money should not have translated into control of land, but that Bazade was a foreigner.

Before 1910, rupees had become an essential part of the vocabulary of social relationships in Buganda. This happened when salaries were added to control of land as markers of chiefly status, and when rupees, rather than produce and labor, became a form of tribute that followers were obligated to present to chiefs. Salaries paid to chiefs in rupees had the long-term effect of reorienting those chiefs away from their followers and toward the Protectorate. While this may have been the goal intended by the Protectorate authorities, the salaries had different meanings for the Baganda and the British, especially at the beginning. The British conceived of salaries as payment to chiefs for their work, and withheld salaries when work was not accomplished, but the chiefs in the Lukiiko seem to have viewed salaries in rupees as a marker of status.[112] In an argument about fines, Kaggwa criticized his fellow regent Stanislaus Mugwanya, "If poor people are fined Rs. 100 for such offenses what will happen to Regents who receive salaries?"[113] The Lukiiko asked for salaries for people with high social status, whether or not they were doing work. "Greetings. We are informing you that the Princes Glamanzane Ndaula and Yusufu Kiwewa have no official salary. We beg the Government to consider their situation sympathetically."[114] Ndaula and Kiwewa had high status in terms of land, part of the thirty-two miles assigned to princes, but once the ssaza chiefs were receiving salaries, the position implied by their control of land was no longer enough. Rupees became part of the tribute that people on the land gave to those who had allocated it in 1908, when the Lukiiko recorded that it had decided "that for every produce from the land he (the landowner) shall be entitled to a share of 1/10th, that is Rs 1 from every Rs 10 proceeds from the sale of whatever the produce from the land."[115] This began the transition of tribute into rent, and rent into an economically valueless symbol of a social relationship (because of inflation) that would characterize relationships on the land for the rest of the twentieth century.

While British assumptions regarding their power in Buganda posed a challenge that was as yet unrecognized by the Ganda chiefs, and the insertion of money into social relationships was beginning to have subtle effects on the relationship of chiefs and followers, the imposition of tax in rupees had immediate, powerful, and dramatic consequences. Taxation undermined chiefship: first, because chiefs could not protect people as they were supposed to do, and second, because when people fled taxation there was no one left over whom chiefs could rule.

Baganda responded immediately to the imposition in 1900 of a three rupee hut tax, which could also be paid as one month's labor. Exactions by political authorities made sense in Buganda, and people treated the tax as a form of tribute. The stations of collectors overflowed with matooke flour, sesame, sisal, sheep, and cowries which were accepted in lieu of rupees.[116] The strong response caused the government to change the rules in 1901 to accept rupees only. (In 1901, the hundreds of thousands of cowries that had been taken in 1900 were burnt.)[117] The Entebbe officials had difficulty finding enough work for the labor that became available, and the poor organization of labor caused great hardship. Payment of taxes became more difficult after the first year, as people had already given the rupees that had been in circulation, and in-kind payments were not accepted.[118] At first, Ganda notions of who should not be obliged to work, because of age, illness, or other incapacity, were upheld, even though the district commissioner insisted on checking the exemptions.[119]

Hut tax was different from tributes that had been collected in the past, however, because people had to go outside of their productive activities to produce rupees, and the wealth that was collected went further away. The secretary of the Lukiiko articulated this in 1900: "Ever since the European made the Buganda Government a well which he drains at its spring—I mean the collection of taxes—what water do you expect to find in the well?"[120] The essence of the problem was that hut tax required rupees, which people did not have. Some people pawned their children in order to pay tax, and others were said to have committed suicide because they could not find the money.[121] The hut tax drained Ganda productivity by requiring cash that could only be obtained by offering labor outside the realm of Ganda productive activities. Not only did this movement to work for rupees take people away from hand manufacturing and activities that would otherwise have occupied them, but people suffered great material hardship traveling to work in an economy in which the provision of food was not commodified (see Chapter 6). People paid hut tax for several years before the spread of cotton cultivation gave them a source of rupees close to home, and the search for rupees in those years had enduring effects on Ganda social relationships. A common response to the difficulty posed by taxes was the Ganda response to a chief who made onerous demands: migration.

Leaving to avoid labor was ordinary and logical; in 1904, Lumondakua-matoke explained that his suspicious departure from the village soon after a fire had destroyed his wife's lover's house was not incriminating. He had left, he said, because he "wanted to go and live on another village where they do not work."[122] By 1901, there was a colony of Baganda across Lake Victoria in Kisumu, people who had left Buganda in order to avoid taxes.[123] In 1902, touring British officials noted that people had left for German territory or for Toro in order to avoid paying tax or doing labor. Describing Mawokota, Spire wrote, "In passing through the county my course led me from one deserted village to another. The place is fast becoming a wilderness."[124] According to the reports of district officers, eight hundred families left Buyaga in 1904, and two thousand men left Kakumiro.[125] Even chiefs moved to avoid taxation: Kaima, one of the ssaza chiefs, wrote to the Lukiiko demanding that it send home his subchiefs who were hiding from tax by staying in the capital.[126] British officials' perception of population loss are confirmed by reports from the ssaza chiefs of famine and marauding animals, which came into settled areas when the population declined. Samwiri Mukasa, the ssaza chief of Bulemeezi, wrote that wild pigs, bush bucks, monkeys, and buffaloes were eating food, and even intercepting people on the roads, and there was famine in the area in 1907.[127]

Conflicts over labor created an impossible contradiction for people who saw themselves as wielding authority within the logic of reciprocal obligation. Providing what one's superior asked for was essential to being a chief; taking care of followers was also essential to being a chief. In the same years that the powerful chiefs of Buganda were assigning to themselves huge mailo estates, they were attempting to satisfy their superiors and retain the allegiance of the people below them. By the time cotton cultivation reversed the flow of people out of Buganda, the character of chiefship had shifted perceptibly.

Chiefs in the Lukiiko did not seem to question their ability to supply the labor asked for by the Protectorate and that which was required for the "good of the kingdom." When chiefs experienced difficulty meeting excessive labor demands, they blamed each other for defective techniques in calling out labor. While the Ganda chiefs' willingness to provide labor has been seen as evidence of their eagerness to collaborate with British overrule, their concern for meeting labor demands can also be understood as an assertion of their capacity as rulers of people. The Lukiiko's response to Tomkins's request for five hundred laborers in September 1905 is typical: "We have seen it [your letter] very well. We shall immediately send messages to the counties where drums shall be sounded. That is how men shall be gathered quickly. As soon

Figure 5.3 Caravan with head loads, 1906. Baganda earned rupees to pay tax through work as porters. (Vittorio Sella)

as they arrive we shall send them to you. Goodbye our friend."[128] They immediately wrote to the ssaza chiefs: "Mr. S. Tomkins very much wants labourers to the number of 500 on this very day. Go through the people and beat drums and send all those who respond to the drum. Everybody shall find work, even those who have already paid their poll tax should come and work for more rupees to make them rich."[129] The Lukiiko's cheerful request for five hundred workers immediately indicates the chiefs' perception, in 1905, that people would be available to work when they were asked to do it. Labor demands made that year were listed by Stanley Tomkins following his tour to investigate the massive outmigration of Ganda peasants: the people who spoke to him said they had to work one month for their three-shilling tax to the Protectorate government, work one month for the chief, cultivate government land, and do "Bulungi Bwa Nsi," the work of bridging swamps, building the houses and fences of chiefs, and maintaining roads, which Ganda men had previously done.[130]

Whatever the chiefs expected, Ganda commoners were not able to meet the multiplying demands on their labor. Bickering about which chiefs were and were not doing their share to provide labor became common in the Lukiiko. Tomkins suspected, probably correctly, that the largest landowners were able to direct calls for labor away from their own tenants and he threatened to stop chiefs "who are actually avoiding making their people work, to induce crowds to settle on their lands."[131] When the ssaza chief Kasujju complained that "now when we call them [people asked to come

out to work] they won't come," he was told to call people only for important business, not small occasions.[132] Mbogo, the uncle of the kabaka, complained that Mamba clansmen should have helped to rebuild the shrine of
deceased Kabaka Ssuuna, but "I am the only one working on the
building . . . with the people on my estate. The Mamba clansmen should not
lie to you by saying that they work under their leader. Because Wapore could
not find men and he consequently returned here."[133] Chiefs accused each
other of forcing other people's tenants to work, and leaving their own undisturbed. A landowner with one mailo and three tenants, for example, might
be asked to provide all three for a communal project, and when his superior asked for more people and he had none to provide, the landowner would
be fined. Kaggwa lectured the chiefs in the Lukiiko that this problem was
"due to you chiefs who tend to choose men other that your own tenants or
if you do choose them then you do not know how to choose men."[134] The
expectation that people would leave home to work "for rupees to make them
rich" was coming directly into conflict with the expectation that people pro-
ducing on the land would make chiefs powerful.

Trying to determine why it had been unable to find the one thousand workers who had been asked for early in 1907, the Lukiiko investigated how many
workers had been supplied by each ssaza chief. It punished the chiefs who
had not sent a large number of men with fines of five, seven, or fifteen rupees, and those who had not sent any with fines of fifty rupees.[135] This action led to an angry discussion in which the chiefs accused each other of
imposing fines improperly. The ssaza chief Kitunzi said that in order to find
laborers, "the Kabaka should empower us to fine any of the people we govern. That is how they will grow to respect us and summon people quickly to
respond when we call." But Lubebe responded, "Is he saying so because he
has never fined any of us since he became Saza chief? When he always fines
people, does he come to you first to ask permission?" Kitunzi, shamed, sat
down without saying a word. This prompted the powerful ssaza chief Kasujju
to point out that the regents were constantly fining the ssaza chiefs, but "the
Kampala people" never imposed fines. The minutes of the Lukiiko record,
"We saw that his was a question that might incite others to disobey. So we
told him that although we were not fined by the Kampala powers we would
continue fining others including himself."[136] The chiefs in the Lukiiko con-
fronted a problem of authority that arose from labor requests by "the Kampala
people," which were beyond the capacity of Buganda to meet. But in order
to demonstrate their capacity and effectiveness as chiefs, to themselves and
to Kampala, the Ganda chiefs struggled to make laborers available. The pressure that was exerted, from regents to ssaza chiefs, from ssaza chiefs to lower
chiefs, and from lower chiefs to people, altered expectations of the interactions of chiefs and followers.

When people responded to the intensifying tax and labor demands by migrating, efforts to obtain tax and labor became more coercive. The Lukiiko eliminated the exemption for people living on Protestant and Catholic missionary estates, because "we have many tasks nowadays, what with being asked to provide labourers for Kampala we are conferring very hard and that is why saza chiefs were called upon to get labourers from estates belonging to the churches."[137] In December 1908, Kaggwa proposed a draconian plan under which any person who had not worked at construction, bridge building, or employment for Europeans would be fined ten rupees: three for tax, three for not working, and four as rent to their landlords. Kaggwa reported to the Lukiiko a discussion he had had with the governor, which, whether he intended it or not, graphically described the effects of cash on Ganda productive relationships:

> If we do not go into this matter, how shall all the people have to be employed? Europeans have been able to make so much cotton cloth which all the people now wear and this means no employment for our workers who used to make barkcloth. We do not even have a smithy for the making of iron sheets. There is only one occupation and that is to be employed on manual jobs.[138]

In September 1909, Kaggwa told the Lukiiko that people would not be allowed to move away from their bibanja (plots of allocated land) until they had paid their tax. Also, anyone who had not paid their tax by the end of March would be fined an extra two rupees.[139] The conundrum of chiefs' and Protectorate officials' asking for more from people who had the option of withdrawing their labor and moving away was resolved with the rapid spread of cotton cultivation for cash. Cash income from cotton production eased some of the tensions that taxation had introduced into Ganda social relationships, but at the same time it exacerbated challenges to the social logic of reciprocal obligation and the social network of clans.

CONCLUSION

The allocations of private land made by the Lukiiko demonstrated the continuing validity of Ganda perceptions of land, but also the limitations of those meanings in a new context. The ruling chiefs, who had absorbed much of the power of the kabaka, used mailo to solidify their power through control of land. The mailo allocation, which gave property rights over the fertile land to Baganda and over swamps to the British Crown, was a huge victory for the most powerful Ganda chiefs and the prestige of the kingdom, but smaller chiefs lost the valuable land they had previously controlled. The authority of the Lukiiko to allocate all land immediately came into conflict with the authority of deceased ancestors over land perceived to be theirs. Ganda intentions with mailo were the goals of reciprocal obligation; chiefs who were allocated land without people complained and tried to obtain different land; and remembered histories emphasize the apparent worthlessness of land without people. However, the logic of kusenga was profoundly challenged by implementation of the hut tax component of the 1900 Agreement. The "draining of the spring" of Ganda productivity through taxes and labor demands created tensions in the relationships of superiors to their people at the same time that cash wages began to provide alternative sources of both status and sustenance. The allocation of mailo land contributed to a narrowing of the locations of power in Buganda, while cash wages, taxes, and labor demands strained Ganda social relationships.

NOTES

1. Foreign Office to Sir H. Johnston, July 1, 1899, Foreign Office (FO) 2/200, no. 1. On Johnston's salary, see, among others, FO 2/203, July 28, 1899, and FO 2/203, no. 216.

2. H. Johnston to Foreign Office, Note on Ternan's Despatch no. 234, Uganda, 1899, FO 2/204.

3. D. Anthony Low provides the most comprehensive description and analysis of the negotiations in "The Making and Implementation of the Uganda Agreement of 1900" in D. A. Low and R. C. Pratt, *Buganda and British Overrule* (London: Oxford University Press, 1960). The Entebbe Secretariat Archives/Uganda National Archives sources cited by Low had been viewed by scholars in the 1980s but could not be located there in the 1990s.

4. D. A. Low, ed., *The Mind of Buganda: Documents of the Modern History of an African Kingdom* (Los Angeles: University of California Press, 1971), 37–41; Low, "Uganda Agreement," 68, 77; Medard, "Croissance," 247, 280; Wrigley, "Changing Economic Structure," 29–31.

5. E. M. Furley, Church Missionary Society Papers, University of Birmingham, G3 A7/0 1900, 52.

6. Ibid.

7. Johnston to Salisbury, December 24, 1899, FO 2/204, no. 26.

8. Regents of Buganda to Sir Harry Johnston, January 3, 1900, in Low, *Mind of Buganda*, 32–33.

9. Ibid.

10. "He is so wise in his own eyes that he will not take any advice readily." Church Missionary Society, Roscoe to Baylis, June 9, 1900, G3 A7/0 1900, 130.

11. Quoted in Glenn H. McKnight, "A Moral Economy of Development: Transforming the Discourse of Development in Uganda, 1895–1930" (Ph.D. diss., Queen's University, 1996), 14.

12. E. M. Furley, Church Missionary Society Papers, University of Birmingham, G3 A7/0 1900, 52.

13. Low, "Uganda Agreement," 57, 59.

14. McKnight, "Discourse of Development," 45–46, 54.

15. Regents of Buganda to Sir Harry Johnston, January 3, 1900, in Low, *Mind of Buganda*, 32–33.

16. Johnston, FO 2/297, quoted in Low, "Uganda Agreement," 94.

17. Walker, quoted in Low, "Uganda Agreement," 41.

18. Low, "Uganda Agreement," 80.

19. Regents of Buganda to Sir Harry Johnston, January 3, 1900, in Low, *Mind of Buganda,* 32–33.

20. Johnston, quoted in Low, "Uganda Agreement," 44.

21. Regents of Buganda to Sir Harry Johnston, January 3, 1900, in Low, *Mind of Buganda,* 32–33.

22. Uganda Protectorate, *Laws of Uganda 1951,* vol. 6 (Entebbe: Government Printer, 1951), 20–24.

23. "Commission," Stanislaus Mugwanya, 530.

24. "Commission," Apolo Kaggwa, 514.

25. "Commission," Semei Sebagala Kyadondo, 440–441; "Buganda Lukiiko Archives, 1894–1918," July 10, 1905, 24. Records translated into English at the East African Institute of Social Research, seen courtesy of John Rowe (cited hereafter as "Buganda Lukiiko" with date and page). The Makerere Institute of Social and Economic Research Library and the Makerere University Library Africana Collection received copies of this document in 2003.

26. "Buganda Lukiiko," July 14, 1905, 27.

27. "Buganda Lukiiko," April 4, 1907, 78.

28. "Commission," Apolo Kaggwa, 511.

29. "Commission," Stanislaus Mugwanya, 516.

30. "Commission," Abuta Lusekera, 404–405.

31. Ibid., 400–401, 406.

32. "Commission," Stanislaus Mugwanya, 528.

33. Ibid., 529.

34. "Commission," Alikisi Kasolobugundu, 413.

35. "Buganda Lukiiko," July 24, 1905, 49.

36. Commission," Samwiri Mukasa, 493.

37. "Buganda Lukiiko," June 26, 1905, 21.

38. "Commission," Aligizanda Mude, 338; "Commission," Masiyale Batanude, 364; "Buganda Lukiiko," July 24, 1905, 49.

39. "Commission," Stanislaus Mugwanya, 517.

40. "Buganda Lukiiko," July 10, 1905, 27.

41. Alfred R. Tucker, *Eighteen Years in Uganda and East Africa,* vol. 2 (London: Edward Arnold, 1908), 260–261.

42. "Commission," Danieri Serugabi, 540.

43. "Commission," Stanislaus Mugwanya, 502.

44. "Commission," Mikairi Kidza, 520.

45. "Commission," Daudi Basudde, 352.

46. Kajane to Kaggwa, August 29, 1905, CA 17, Box 1, Kaggwa Papers.

47. "Commission," Auguste Senfuma, 408; Yakaobo Mbugaereamura to Kaggwa, April 3, 1905, CA 15, Box 1, Kaggwa Papers.

48. "Buganda Lukiiko," May 22, 1905, 5.

49. S. Lumbuye and Amuli Manyamusenga to Samwili Mukasa Kangawo, October 2, 1904, CA 12, Kaggwa Papers.

50. "Buganda Lukiiko," August 28, 1905, 55.

51. Ibid., June 12, 1905, 15–16.

52. Roscoe, *The Baganda,* 283.

53. "Commission," Apolo Kaggwa, 517.

54. Ibid.

55. Ibid., 518.

56. "Commission," Apolo Kaggwa, Lewo Nsobya on behalf of Walusimbi, 466.

57. Roscoe, *The Baganda,* 237, 190.

58. "Commission," Paulo Kaliro, 419.

59. "Commission," Apolo Kaggwa, 416.

60. Mair, *An African People,* 54.

61. Kaggwa, *Kings,* 117, cf. Kaggwa, *Basekabaka,* trans. Musoke, chap. 13, p. 5; "Enquiry," Apolo Kaggwa, 3.

62. Samwili Mukasa Kangawo to Apolo Kaggwa, February 10, 1906, CA 26, Kaggwa Papers.

63. Kaggwa to Kangao, January 29, 1906, CA 25, Box 1, Kaggwa Papers.

64. Minutes signed S. Mukasa and M. Kangao, February 6, 1906, Uganda National Archives (UNA) Secretariat Minute Paper (SMP) 6902. I am grateful to Mikael Karlstrom for this reference.

65. Kajubi Muzibe Sebantindira to Kaggwa, October 4, 1906, CA 54, Box 1, Kaggwa Papers; Samwiri Mukasa on behalf of Mutaka Masembe to Kabaka, October 9, 1923, transmitting minutes of Lukiiko meeting of February 6, 1906, UNA A46 2212/SMP 6902.

66. "Commission," Malaki Musajakawa, 347.

67. "Commission," Blasito Kiwanuka, 456; Algizanda Ndugwa, 396.

68. "Commission," Blasito Kiwanuka, 453.

69. "Buganda Lukiiko," June 26, 1905, 22.

70. "Commission," Saulo Lugwisa on behalf of Namuguzi, 448; Zedi Zirimenya, 358.

71. "Commission," Lazalo Byuma Seryenvu, 486–487; Antwani Kaikuzi, 425.

72. "Commission," Ezera Kivebulaya, 423–424.

73. "Commission," Jemusi Miti, 501.

74. F. B. Welbourn, "Some Aspects of Kiganda Religion," *Uganda Journal* 26:2 (1962): 175. I am grateful to David Schoenbrun for this reference.

75. "Commission," Paulo Bakunga, 539.

76. "Commission," Blasito Kiwanuka, 454–455.

77. "Enquiry," Apolo Kaggwa, 3.

78. "Commission," Aligizande Mude, 337.

79. "Buganda Lukiiko," September 4, 1905, 58.

80. Ibid., April 23, 1906, 66.

81. Ibid., July 12, 1909, 109.

82. "Commission," Apolo Kaggwa, 513.

83. Hanson, "Queen Mothers"; Nakanyike B. Musisi, "Transformations of Baganda Women: From the Earliest Times to the Demise of the Kingdom in 1966" (Ph.D. diss., University of Toronto, 1991), 82–83.

84. "Buganda Lukiiko," October 10, 1914, 131–132; Kingdom of Buganda, *Customary Law Reports, 1940–1955: Being a Digest of Decisions on Customary Law Made by the Principal Court of His Highness the Kabaka of Buganda During the Years 1941–1951,* comp. E. S. Haydon, and I. S. Lule (Nairobi: E. A. Printers, 1956), 115–118.

85. "Buganda Lukiiko," January 24, 1907, 74.

86. "Commission," Apolo Kaggwa, 521.

87. "Commission," Stanislaus Mugwanya, 505.

88. "Commission," Zakayo Nkuwe, 388–392.

89. Kingdom of Buganda, *Customary Law Reports, 1940–1955,* Civil Case no. 38/46, 41–44.

90. "Buganda Lukiiko," April 29, 1905, 6–7.

91. Ibid., June 23, 1905, 21.

92. Ibid., October 2, 1905, 59.

93. Ibid., June 12, 1905, 13.

94. Ibid., August 17, 1907, 85.

95. Ibid., November 9, 1908, 106.

96. Low, *Buganda in Modern History,* 88, 96.

97. George Wilson to Commissioner Entebbe, August 22, 1902, ESA A8/2, quoted in J. A. Atanda, "The *Bakopi* in the Kingdom of Buganda, 1900–1927: An Analysis of the Condition of the Peasant Class in Early Colonial Period," cyclostyled paper labeled "History Department, MSP/16," Northwestern University Africana Collection, 7.

98. "Buganda Lukiiko," February 24, 1909, 99.

99. Ibid., July 10, 1905, 27.

100. Ibid., November 20, 1905, 63.

101. Ibid., April 17, 1907, 79.

102. Ibid., July 3, 1905, 24.

103. Sir Frederick Treves, *Uganda for a Holiday* (London: Smith, Elder, 1910), 223; Kaggwa, *Ekitabo kya Kika kya Nsenene,* 16. Although young chiefs represented themselves as "fiercely committed to a highly linear notion of 'progress,'" as Karlstrom suggests, their actions showed them to be deeply committed to building prestige through attracting and maintaining followers. Karlstrom, "Cultural Kingdom in Uganda," 105–107, 138.

104. "Buganda Lukiiko," March 25, 1907, 27.

105. Lukiko to Jemusi Miti, "Buganda Lukiiko," August 1, 1900, 69.

106. "Buganda Lukiiko," November 20, 1905, 62.

107. Ibid., May 29, 1905, 7–8.

108. Ibid.

109. Ibid., June 19, 1905, 17.

110. "Commission," Pasikale Bambaga, 459.

111. "Commission," Hezekiya Bazade, 483.

112. "Buganda Lukiiko," April 29, 1905, 7.

113. Ibid., June 12, 1905, 13.

114. Ibid., April 17, 1907, 79.

115. Ibid., March 24, 1908, 100.

116. Samwiri Mukasa, "The Record of My Service to the Kingdom of Buganda," quoted in Low, *Mind of Buganda,* 59–60.

117. Cyril Ehrlich, "The Economy of Buganda, 1893–1903," *Uganda Journal* 20:1 (1956): 20.

118. Tomkins to Sadler, April 16, 1902, ESA A8/2, quoted in Low, *Mind of Buganda,* 101.

119. Samwiri Mukasa, quoted in Low, *Mind of Buganda,* 60.

120. Lukiiko to Jemusi Miti Kibuka, "Buganda Lukiiko," July 30, 1900, 68.

121. *Mengo Notes,* December 1900, quoted in Low, *Mind of Buganda,* 100.

122. "Buganda Lukiiko," August 12, 1904, 4.

123. Her Majesty's Commissioner to Collector Kampala, July 17, 1901, ESA 19/1, quoted in Atanda, "Bakopi," 4.

124. Tomkins to Commissioner, April 16, 1902, ESA A8/1; Spire to Commissioner, October 24, 1902, ESA A8/2; quoted in Atanda, "Bakopi," 10–11.

125. Enclosures in Tomkins to Commissioner, March 3, 1904, and February 17, 1904, in ESA A8/4, quoted in Atanda, "Bakopi," 13.

126. "Buganda Lukiiko," December 18, 1905, 64.

127. Ibid., August 12, 1907, 85.

128. Lukiiko to S. Tomkins, "Buganda Lukiiko," September 4, 1907, 56.

129. Lukiiko to Ssaza Chiefs, "Buganda Lukiiko," September 4, 1905, 56.

130. Stanley Tomkins, *Report of a Tour Through Mawokota, Busuju, Gomba, Buddu, Kabula, Singo,* November 12, 1903, Enclosure in Tomkins to Commissioner, Entebe, November 13, 1903, ESA A8/3, quoted in Atanda, "Bakopi," 12.

131. Tomkins to Sadler, November 18, 1903, ESA A8/4, quoted in Atanda, "Bakopi," 13.

132. "Buganda Lukiiko," May 29, 1905, 9.

133. Ibid., April 22, 1907, 80.

134. Ibid., April 17, 1907, 12.

135. Ibid., June 10, 1907, 81.

136. Ibid., June 10, 1907, 82.

137. Ibid., April 17, 1907, 79.

138. Ibid., December 14, 1908, 106.

139. Ibid., September 27, 1909, 112.

6

THE EROSION OF RECIPROCAL OBLIGATION, 1906–1920

In the years immediately following the consolidation of power by elite Protestant chiefs through the allocation of mailo, Ganda social institutions underwent subtle but profound transformations. After the upheaval of the late nineteenth century, people had attempted to resume familiar, effective habits of interaction that had protected and sustained them and maintained Buganda from generation to generation. With the abolition of ekitongole chiefship and other forms of authority represented in control of land, productive labor no longer defined particular groups of people in the way it had in the past. However, work and gifts of the fruits of work still linked all the parts of the Ganda polity. Mailo landowners, like chiefs, secured followers through reciprocal obligation: the assignment of a plot of land implied an exchange of protection from the land-giver, and loyalty and service from the land-receiver. In 1900, clan elders still maintained links between people in gatherings at the burial sites of ancestors, and lineage networks and less formal groups of neighbors continued to provide each other assistance in house building, loaned food, and hospitality to strangers that enabled people to ensure their well-being. Half a generation later, in about 1920, the institutions of chief, clan, and lineage network still existed, but people's strategies for sustenance had changed. Networks of support and expectations of reciprocity operated on a smaller scale.

Many explanations for the transformation of Ganda social relationships do not actually hold up under close examination. British colonial authorities did not inspire them: whatever social engineering they might have intended, Ganda men and women met the challenges of the moment with confidence in their own social institutions. Nor is it accurate to assume that rupees, wages, cash crops, and masses of goods for purchase had automatic effects on the values, goals, and life strategies of Baganda. What happened in Buganda in the early twentieth century does not confirm the perception of missionaries, traders, and colonial officers—clearly resonant in the discourse of marxist thinkers and neoliberal development planners in more recent times—that cash and consumer goods had an intrinsic weight that would pull people toward individualistic motivations and displace the logic of production for the purpose of maintaining social relationships. Rather, people in Buganda used cash money, obtained through wage labor, sale of cotton, or independent trade, to pursue the acquisition of wealth in people. Land-rich Ganda chiefs and relatively poor Ganda tenants both attracted followers in the form of migrant laborers from other parts of Buganda and the Belgian colonies. Ganda adherence to noncommodified forms of social relationships gave the Baganda a consistent advantage over foreign employers in attracting and keeping labor.

The intense, overwhelming demands on Ganda productive activity, more than any other factor, exerted pressure on Ganda social institutions that reduced their range and effectiveness. In a society that defined and perpetuated social institutions through exchanges of labor and produced goods, extraordinary calls on people's labor made the maintenance of these institutions impossible. The relationship of chiefs and their people, and the strength of links among clan members, was stretched beyond endurance by multiple demands. These included labor for chiefs, the king, and the local community, and labor for colonial building projects and maintenance. At the same time, trade, education, and cotton cultivation offered Baganda new ways to invest their productive capacities. There were simply not enough people in Buganda, particularly after the demographic decline caused by war, plague, famine, and sleeping sickness, to do the work to sustain all these relationships.

The constant, enervating labor demands of the first decades of colonial rule had permanent effects on Ganda society. The institution of chiefship split in two: appointed chiefs remained but lost much of their credibility as protectors of people, while thousands of people replicated chiefship on a tiny scale by becoming owners of relatively small amounts of land and offering a reduced level of protection and patronage to followers. The power of lineage networks and clans to take care of people was reduced by the colonial control of the paths to political power. Lineage networks were also fundamentally challenged by women's increasing ability to set up households independent of men, and the possibility that heirs might choose to commodify the assets of a lineage for their own personal benefit.

World War I and the boom in commodity prices after the war further intensified demands for labor. Finding people to do all the work required coercion: consequently fines, rather than gifts, came to dominate the language of exchange. By 1920, things people would have taken for granted only a few years earlier—that courtesy would characterize interactions with the powerful, that food would be available if they traveled, that women would remain dependent on husbands or brothers, that a nearby chief would provide decent living conditions if their own chief did not—were no longer necessarily true.

Ganda leaders who launched an articulate protest against the changes in Buganda (described in Chapter 7) claimed that a cash economy and British overrule were not incompatible with Ganda forms of organizing society. They stated that what had ruined Buganda was chiefs who did not rule well, and they asked for the return of authority figures, such as clan leaders, who would do a better job. In the context of the enormous pressures exerted on Ganda social institutions after 1900, their diagnosis makes sense. In this chapter I argue that incessant demands for labor by the colonial government provoked the butaka land protest. Ganda chiefs and lineage networks could not maintain their role of caring for people in the face of these overwhelming demands. The first section outlines the layering of demands on people's productive activity from the beginning of cotton production in 1904 to 1923, when *kasanvu* (forced labor) was abolished. The second section considers the effect of those demands on the relationships of chiefs and their followers, and the third section examines the deterioration of clans and lineage networks' ability to take care of people. The final section describes how Baganda responded to the demands that were being made on them: by re-creating chiefship as land ownership, by developing new strategies for clan support, and, in 1919, by protesting to the Protectorate government in Entebbe that its labor demands were unbearable and would have to change.

TOO MUCH WORK: NEW LABOR, OLD TRIBUTE, AND THE POSSIBILITIES OF CASH FOR COTTON

In Buganda before 1893, people's work expressed a relationship of allegiance with a chief or other leader. Men built broad roads and bridges over swamps that led to the capital from all directions. They made fences and houses in the chief's compound, and brought beer and barkcloth to him. People also responded when their own leader was called to do work for the king. They built fences and houses in the capital, produced goods that were the particular responsibility of that chiefship, and fulfilled the multiple work requirements of the king. Men also responded to labor calls from leaders of their clan to maintain the shrines of deceased kings.[1] Devotees of a lubaale spirit built homes and farmed in proximity to a medium. The importance of work in maintaining relationships is evident in the missionary C. W. Hattersley's description of people assembling to rebuild the tomb of Muteesa in 1907. Chiefs had been "stationed" on all the main roads, and at 3:30 in the morning the king's drums signaled that it was time to assemble. When Hattersley arrived some time after six, he found "the whole countryside" gathered and "quite two thousand men" engaged in replacing the roof. "When the squad of men belonging to a given chief had finished their part of the work they seized a reed and came before their chief, and before the Katikiro, to announce the completion of their portion, and danced up and down chanting peculiar refrains and behaving generally like madmen."[2] The Lukiiko gave Sezi Senkezi 130 rupees to thank him for supervising the work that Hattersley observed, but doing the work had been the obligation—and privilege—of everyone able to participate.[3]

How to obtain labor was a problem for newcomers to Buganda who wielded no authority over other people. Missionaries and travelers moved through the country only when it suited the kabaka; without his assent, porters and food were not available. From the 1880s onward, visitors to Buganda who needed labor of some kind made arrangements with a chief, whose men then did the work. James Miti, who as a mid-level chief at this time would have experienced the dilemma himself, explained:

> Any man chosen to do such work was bound to obey and to go wherever he was required without being paid for his labour. African labour was cheap in those days and porters used to be obtained free of cost to transport luggage belonging to a Government official or to any other member of the European community in the country to places such as far-off Nimule and others . . . it was almost as difficult a task for the chief to obtain the necessary number of porters required from him from among his men as it was for the latter themselves to leave their homes and families and put in a spell of compulsory labour in a foreign country and for an indeterminate period under the most trying conditions.[4]

The Catholic and Protestant missions received labor given to them by chiefs who had converted, and also established the right to receive labor as "chiefs" of church-controlled land.[5] The authorities of the newly established Protectorate experimented with various means of obtaining labor. British administrators who had respectful relationships with Ganda chiefs were able to obtain laborers, but chiefs refused to supply labor to British officers like W. J. Ansorge, known to the Baganda as "Njota Vuu" (a person who is so antisocial that no one will bring him firewood and therefore he stays in the dark).[6] The Protectorate also began to pay six shillings per month to Baganda working in Port Alice in 1897. From that year missionaries were also able to find some people willing to work for wages, but continued to obtain labor through their relationships with chiefs.[7]

Taxation

Unable or unwilling to cultivate goodwill in order to receive labor, the Protectorate government circumvented Ganda moral economy by imposing taxation. As shown in Chapter 5, the imposition of hut tax in 1900 and poll tax in 1905 had immediate and dramatic consequences: thousands of people left their homes to find rupees, and the inadequate provisions made for people paying tax in labor caused great hardship and a significant number of deaths.[8] Although the Protectorate government had been the first beneficiary of people looking for ways to earn tax money, Ganda men soon found ways to participate in the cash economy to provide tax money for themselves and followers. Some began to organize trading caravans to the Congo Free State and to German East Africa, hiring their own porters.[9] They worked as traders all over the Protectorate "right away to Gondokoro." Others worked as interpreters, clerks, builders, craftsmen, and servants. The Baganda engaged in wage labor showed a keen awareness of appropriate remuneration: one collector lost his whole camp of nine hundred workers after he sent one hundred to another employer and one of them returned to tell his fellows that more pay was being offered there.[10]

At the beginning of taxation, chiefs fulfilled their protective role by finding wage labor for their people. Chiefs also sought other means for their followers to obtain tax money. The Lukiiko minutes record that in 1908 the kangaawo brought 721 "wicker bags" that had been made in his ssaza at the request of the provincial commissioner, and later the mugema's people provided one hundred of a specific type of bed; it appears that these goods were sold and the profits returned to the people who had made them.[11] Poll tax and cash wages did not by themselves undermine the kusenga relationship, although, as discussed in Chapter 5, some followers were able to use cash wages to obtain some of things they had previously received from chiefs.

Cotton cultivation rapidly became the primary source of rupees for tax. Missionaries, chiefs, and government officials all claimed credit for introducing the crop. The Protectorate authorities invested a considerable amount of energy and political capital in cotton cultivation: the agricultural officer, provincial commissioner, and district officers traveled to promote it, and from at least 1909 onward chefs were evaluated partly on the basis of the amount of cotton grown in their ssazas.[12] The British were so eager to ensure Ganda cultivation of cotton that men who had "2 good sizeable cotton shambas" were exempted from work for the government in 1908.[13] In addition to growing cotton for sale, Ganda traders with bicycles bought people's crops from them at their homes, and others ginned cotton using hand looms.[14] The work of growing cotton was at first organized as group labor for the chief: the drum was beaten, and people came to cultivate. After one or two seasons, cotton cultivation was integrated into

Ganda patterns of work as a form of household production, from which the
follower gave a portion to the chief as tribute.[15]

Less than a decade after the imposition of poll tax, Protectorate authorities became frustrated with the amount of labor the tax brought forward. As
early as 1907 the Lukiiko members fought about their responsibility to find
workers for the Protectorate. Finding people who were able and willing to
work became difficult as soon as people found alternatives to tax. The Lukiiko
announced in 1907 that all workers should be inspected first by the Lukiiko,
"so that we can select the fit and unfit ones," and "we shall pay them for the
work if need be."[16] Ganda enthusiasm for cotton was one reason people could
not be found to meet the labor calls of five hundred or more at a time; another was the continuing process of population decline.[17] Early-twentieth-
century observers estimated that Buganda had lost one-third of its population
since the early nineteenth century: the decline had been caused by enslavement, war, plague, and famine in the late nineteenth century, followed by the
devastating epidemic of sleeping sickness between 1903 and 1908. Sir Albert
Cook, medical director of Mmengo Hospital, estimated that the epidemic had
killed 200,000 of 300,000 people living in the immediate vicinity of Lake
Victoria. The katikkiro Apolo Kaggwa reported to the Buganda district commissioner that only 250 people remained alive out of 1,542 who had lived on
Bussi island.[18] The lake shore had been the richest and most densely populated area of Buganda, but it became entirely desolate; no one fished or made
canoes until repopulation began in 1918.[19]

Kasanvu Forced Labor

A diminishing population, the existence of cotton as a relatively benign
alternative to wage labor, and the uncomfortable and sometimes dangerous
conditions of work for the Protectorate combined to make volunteer workers
hard to find. Chiefs who forced people to work were in danger of losing their
followers. The Protectorate government might have responded by improving
the wages and accommodation of laborers, but instead Sir Hesketh Bell, governor of Uganda from 1906 to 1909, chose to impose a form of forced labor
called kasanvu, in which chiefs were required to supply numbers of workers
(one thousand or more) each month, based on lists of poll tax payers. The
workers received wages of three rupees per month, but they had no choice
about having to work. Exemptions were granted only to chiefs and people in
permanent employment. The word *kasanvu* means "seven thousand": the name
probably is derived from the number of workers required in one of the early
labor calls.[20]

Kasanvu was rationalized by Protectorate officials as "based on the traditional bonds between the chiefs and their subordinates," and as a means of

maintaining chiefs' control over their people.[21] Actually, it required chiefs to make their people go out to do work that everyone knew might be dangerous and unhealthy. Finding people to do kasanvu undermined chiefship, and some people's ability to avoid this obligation and make others liable for it transformed the character of relationships in clans and lineage networks. Governors and missionaries were correct in explaining that Ganda people worked for chiefs and for the kabaka in order to demonstrate their respect and allegiance. What they failed to acknowledge was that obligations to the Protectorate *doubled* the amount of work that was required of each person. In 1909, people worked for their chief for one month or two rupees, and they did *luwalo,* work for "Bulungi Bwa Nsi" (the good of the country), for one month. Poll tax for the Protectorate required five rupees or two months' labor, and kasanvu was an additional month's work. In 1912, kasanvu was increased to two months when labor needs required it.[22] The hapless Ganda followers who had no means of engineering exemptions for themselves were therefore obligated to demonstrate their respect and appreciation for being ruled by laboring for five to six months out of every year, or else to work for three to four months and pay their tax by selling cotton grown by their wives or other subordinates.

In addition to the five to six months a Ganda man was expected to devote to labor for the chief, the kabaka, and the governor, Christians were expected to provide labor to maintain churches and church estates, and candidates for baptism had to perform personal services, such as garden labor and carrying firewood, for their catechist. Chiefs, from the ssaza chief in charge of a whole province to the lower ranks of chiefship, were also responsible for finding people for the army, the Carrier Corps, work on the railroad, and various Protectorate schemes such as training of policemen or apprenticeship in the public works department. In August of 1914, for example, fifty army recruits brought by Kasujju to the Lukiiko were told "to return to their homes and keep a sharp ear for the drum calling them out, so that they can come quickly, without delay."[23]

The Objects of Work in the "New Buganda"

People called up for kasanvu helped make colonial rule possible by facilitating the tours of government officials. On his first trip to Kampala in 1906, Governor Bell took sixty-six porters. On a longer journey, his caravan consisted of more than two hundred porters to carry tents, furniture, baggage, and stores, plus twelve servants and forty policemen.[24] Provincial commissioners, district officers, and agricultural and veterinary officers also traveled with an entourage.

Most of Entebbe was built with poll tax or kasanvu labor. Governor Bell described his surprise at the "evidences of comfort and refinement" he found when he first arrived in 1906. The grounds of the deputy commissioner's house were almost "an old established English garden" with closely mown lawns, and "masses of splendid roses and other familiar flowers growing in profusion."[25] Entebbe was maintained, another observer noted, by a "perfect army of native water-carriers [who] keep up a constant stream between the Lake and the town."[26] Governor Bell considered Government House, not more than seven or eight years old at the time, "as ugly and prosaic a building as one would not wish to see," and sold it to South Africans to make a hotel. He built instead "a really comfortable English house . . . the big 'villa' type with very spacious verandahs on the ground floor. The reception rooms are large and lofty and nearly every bedroom has its own private little balcony commanding views over the lake that will make early breakfast a pure delight."[27] The governor explained in his diary that "a similar house could not be built in England for double the money" (seven thousand pounds sterling). He attributed his success to the presence of excellent building materials, the availability of skilled Indian artisans at low wages, and the fact that "all the unskilled labour has been supplied by natives glad to work for threepence a day [to pay their tax]."[28]

In Buganda, service to chiefs included some tasks that counted as contributions to the one month "luwalo" obligation, and others that had to be performed whenever the need arose. Building roads was a "luwalo" service. Excellently kept, broad roads had been a sign of good government in Buganda, and road building had been an event that involved everyone in an area. Hattersley observed that "thousands of people—indeed all living within a few miles on either side of the road"—came with "earth in a basket to heap up the raised track."[29] The kinds of work that had to be performed "for the good of the country" increased in colonial Buganda. In 1907 and 1908, chiefs had to use the labor owed them to remove everyone from the shore of Lake Victoria in an effort to end the sleeping sickness epidemic, build four huge hospital settlements for the thousands of infected people, and provide food for all of them.[30] In 1910 the Lukiiko announced its decision that all residents of each *ggombolola* (an administrative unit of the newly rationalized Buganda administration—smaller than a province and larger than a parish) were required to construct the ggombolola office and private latrine, clear a site for European or other distinguished visitors to camp, and clear a site for porters; the printed announcement admonished that "the place must be kept clean to prevent disease spreading among those who come to the site to work."[31]

Any man unlucky enough to live in a ssaza where mailo land was being surveyed might be required to cut boundary lines for the surveying team. Two thousand people had been involved in this work for the six months in 1910 and 1911 when the survey passed through Busiro.[32] One of the early surveyors described the departure of a surveying party from Entebbe:

Figure 6.1   A survey caravan, ca. 1908. (Royal Commonwealth Society Archives, Cambridge University)

After much shouting by the headmen and with much harmless flourishing of whips the procession would be got under way, led by a drummer with a leopard-skin apron and befeathered cap, and flanked by three *askaris* carrying ancient Snider rifles. For a mile or so a jog trot would be kept up, the more exuberant of the porters dancing from the head to the tail of the line and back. But soon the safari would settle down to a steady march, spirits being kept up by a song from the vocalist of the party with a chorus in which all joined.[33]

In 1914 the Lukiiko discussed the problem of chiefs' inability to find people willing to do the heavy labor involved in the survey. They forbade recruitment of laborers for any other purpose in any area where the surveyors were working, and discussed paying the workers. The Lukiiko members (who were the owners of the land being surveyed and who would have had to find the money for wages) in the end decided that the difficult labor of boundary cutting was part of the kusenga obligation: "It has been found impossible to pay these men. Because they themselves are Baganda and use the land for the growing of crops from which they derive cash. Further, they have been doing the job very well in the past, without any trouble." If there were not enough tenants on some estates to do the work, they would have to be surveyed at a later time.[34]

Ganda chiefs had, in the past, been responsible for feeding people traveling through their territory on the kabaka's business. Gifts of food were a token of allegiance, and the exact components of gifts were carefully noted by the Lukiiko: "Stanislaus Mugwanya has presented the Kabaka with 800 bunches of matoke and seven goats"; and on another occasion, "14 cattle, 46 goats, 300 chicken, and 700 miwumbo of food" were presented to the ssaza chief and Leaky.[35] Ssaza chiefs wrote to Entebbe to inform Protectorate officers of the insult they had suffered when rival chiefs had presented gifts that were too small. However, it was clearly impossible for chiefs to continue to feed everyone who passed through their territory. Chiefs developed complex new rules regarding who received food freely and who was obliged to pay. Disputes over feeding travelers were heard in the Lukiiko in 1905: a subsidiary chief who had refused to supply food to Simon Bitalo, sent out by the Lukiiko "to catch bugs and ticks," was summoned to account for his failure. Another representative of the Lukiiko told that he had been denied food by the chief Nankere, who told him to look for it himself. But then he was stopped by a European, who "told me to stop looking for food myself as people would say it was the European himself getting the food by those methods."[36] In 1907, "an up-country postman" carried strings of cowrie shells around his neck for buying food.[37] Lower-level chiefs were responsible for organizing the food for a rest camp, but travelers were expected to pay for the food that was provided.[38] Women followers provided the food and cooked it; it is difficult to determine whether women received payment for their work, or whether requiring followers to supply food was another source of income for chiefs. Finding, preparing, and carrying the food required by large numbers of travelers was a significant new burden on Ganda chiefs and their followers, even when they received a token cash remuneration. Daudi Basudde explained to the English-language readership of the *Uganda Herald* in 1921 that peasants expected to hear from their chiefs "that next month you will go to give your turn at the Government's forced labour, now you must take a bunch of bananas to where the District Commissioner who is on tour has camped, a distance of fifteen miles away, and get in return one penny for it!"[39]

Within the calculus of reciprocal obligation, it was essential that Ganda chiefs show proper hospitality to visiting Protectorate officials, and to this end their people made elaborate preparations to accommodate visitors. A. R. Morgan, the first cotton inspector, described the protocol: he was met at the border of each ssaza by the chief, taken to the rest camp, where he was given chickens, eggs, and bananas, and, after his visit, escorted to the boundary of the ssaza, where he was met by the next chief. He remembered that "the courtesy and kindness of the chiefs was at times almost embarrassing."[40] On one occasion when a lower-level chief felt he had not been assisted by others to provide hospitality to the visiting governor, the Lukiiko responded:

> Thanks for your letter in which you accuse the chiefs in your county. We have already decided the case against them. They were very wrong. And

we, Lukiiko members, were very wrong for not sending chiefs in the county to meet Mr. Balozi. We understand our guilt, next time we shall send them to greet Balozi. Thank you for doing so many jobs and for seeing the Balozi safely out of your county. Kibali told us how much work you had to do.[41]

A properly greeted official was provided with quantities of food, and lodging suitable to the prestige of the guest had to be built for the occasion. Governor Bell described his camp on a safari in 1906:

The camp we are occupying tonight is very pretty and has been constructed specially for me by the Chief of the locality. It is a very elaborate affair. Although we are only to occupy it for a night, a very handsome kibanda has been built for my own accommodation, and is substantial enough to last for a couple of years. It is about 25 feet by 18 and made of logs and reeds. The roof and walls are beautifully thatched and the floor of beaten clay is strewn with a thick layer of sweet-scented lemon-grass. Smaller pavilions have been provided for my staff and such a number of huts, for kitchens and servants, that the place is quite a village. I am told that, all through my journey, I shall find similar accommodation, wherever I stop, even if it be only for a few hours' rest.[42]

In Ganda terms of the meaning of work, the investment of a chief's people's labor in building elaborate camps for "Bwana Balozi" ought to yield returns of gratitude and an obligation to demonstrate reciprocal consideration on the part of the ruler. The Ganda intention that labor would maintain social connections did not translate well, however, and Bell recorded in his diary that the chief who had provided the camp "would expect no payment beyond a few words of thanks" and speculated that "these delightful conditions" would last "only so long as labour costs practically nothing."[43]

Responding to Overwhelming Labor Demands

Buganda underwent tremendous transformations in the decades following the consolidation of power by Protestant chiefs and their British allies. European residents tended to explain these changes in terms of the presence of things familiar to them: brick houses with tin roofs, everyone in church dressed in cloth, commerce in Kampala, and jam for sale at a reasonable price.[44] For Baganda, the most significant change in this time was not cloth or the substitution of rupees for cowries, but the vastly increased amounts of work people had to do. Women had incorporated planting, weeding, harvesting, and carrying cotton into their agricultural work calendar. Men had added months of productive work for the Protectorate to the months of productive work they had already been doing for chiefs. Adding to the strain on Ganda productivity was a partial withdrawal of the productive capacities of children: 35,000 were reported to be in school in 1909, and 80,000 in 1913.[45]

The increased work meant a deterioration in people's standard of living. Missionaries, more than other outsiders, noticed the changes in daily life for Baganda created by these intensified work demands. One Mill Hill Father observed that conversion decreased precipitously with taxation, because men no longer had time to attend religious instruction.[46] In 1910 the Church Missionary Society annual report to the Protectorate regarding religion and education stated that the number of baptized Christians and of people offering to teach had declined as a result of "the forced labour and numberless calls on the common people."[47] Ganda houses, which had been admired by foreigners in the 1870s for their sturdy construction and neat appearance, now seemed to be poorly made. The production and quality of domestic products, such as mats, baskets, pottery, and bark cloth, declined.[48] Sources of protein and variety in the Ganda diet were reduced when women eliminated one of two annual plantings of millet and simsim and men stopped fishing in floodwater during the rainy season in order to find time for cotton cultivation.[49]

Baganda found a number of different ways to circumvent excessive demands on their labor that were making it impossible for them to maintain the quality of their lives. In an unusual case in 1915, a young man refused the request of the assistant of the ssaza chief Kaggo to carry loads of dried bananas for the provincial commissioner. He insisted on being brought before the Lukiiko, where he claimed he was from Busoga, named Tenywa son of Kikwaku, and therefore he should not have to carry the loads. But one member stood up "to say how the boy was brought up at his home and is perfectly a Ganda and that the names he has given are not his correct names." His uncle and mother testified against him, he admitted he was lying, and the Lukiiko then "imposed ten lashes to be beaten to the boy for his resistance, bad behaviour towards his superior and hypocrisy."[50] A more common strategy was emigration. Bishop Tucker, whose articulate and passionate defense of African rights often discomfited his own missionary flock, claimed that in its first year kasanvu had led to the depopulation of Buganda due to the migration of large numbers of young men.[51] This trend continued. In 1914 a district officer reported, "The natives find that so much is required of them, what with labour obligations to the chiefs and the Government and increased taxation that life is scarcely worth living in their own country. Many therefore go to East Africa [Kenya] and neighbouring Provinces where less is required of them."[52] Moving onto church land was at first a means of mitigating the kasanvu obligation, because the church controlled kasanvu labor of its tenants until 1917, and asked them to do work that was close to home. When church tenants had to perform kasanvu as well as church labor, people considered living on church land to be a disadvantage and began to leave.[53] People migrated to avoid kasanvu labor as long as the law was in force; the year following the abolition of kasanvu, statistics collected on the population of Buganda showed an increase for the first time.[54]

People also tried to obtain exemptions from kasanvu labor, which was the most onerous labor obligation because it took people far away from their homes, disrupted their ordinary life, and entailed staying in uncomfortable and often unsanitary conditions. Unlike poll tax, kasanvu obligations could not be bought off with a payment of income from cotton. People therefore tried to turn themselves into "permanent employees," as three consecutive months of employment was the one legal means of exemption. One strategy was to take employment at a sugar or rubber plantation: apparently many people attempted to obtain documentation of their employment without actually working.[55] Owning land automatically conferred the status of a chief, and obtaining this exemption from kasanvu was probably the most compelling motivation for purchase of small plots of land. Holding the position of a lower-level chief, steward of an important chief, or "church katikkiro" gave a man exemption from kasanvu. People volunteered to be teachers, church wardens, and catechists because these were considered forms of permanent employment. (When kasanvu was abolished in 1922, the churches experienced serious difficulties filling these positions.) Artisans skilled in new trades and crafts were considered self-employed, but specialists in Ganda crafts apparently did not obtain exemptions. Thus, bricklayers, tailors, and carpenters could labor at their trades instead of performing kasanvu, but wood carvers, smiths, and canoe makers could not.

Workers to Replace Missing Men: Immigrants and Independent Ganda Women

Immigrants from other parts of Uganda, and later from the Belgian Congo, became a major part of the workforce in Buganda. In his detailed study documenting this process, P. G. Powesland suggests that immigrants working for low wages and for food fit into the place in Ganda households that had formerly been occupied by slaves captured from neighboring peoples. Like slaves a generation earlier, immigrant workers were treated as extensions of the family and gave prestige to the person who employed them.[56] Powesland estimates that in 1913, three thousand Banyoro were working for Baganda or for settlers in Buganda. During World War I, Baganda employed Basoga, Banyoro, Batoro, and Bagishu and Kavirondo, according to Hamu Mukasa. Banyarwanda began to emigrate from the Belgian Congo following famine in 1923 and the imposition by Belgian authorities of a policy of compulsory cultivation of particular crops in 1924. Immigrants came to Buganda from every direction, passing up employment opportunities elsewhere in the Protectorate because they preferred the conditions of employment with Baganda.[57]

The doubling of labor demands, along with the new possibilities created by cash payment for cotton, caused a profound shift in the pattern of Ganda households: women began to control land independently. Although Baganda already had the word *nnakyeyombekedde* for a woman who controlled land independently of men, female landholding appears to have become much more common in the first decades of the twentieth century. With the advent of cotton cultivation, chiefs and landowners began to give *ebibanja,* the plots of land to farm that indicated a relationship of reciprocal obligation, to women who were not attached to men. For example, Erinama Sebanditira explained that her mother had been widowed in 1909, and the brothers of her husband were hostile to her, so she found a chief who gave her a kibanja in return for her commitment to grow cotton for him.[58]

Concern in Luganda newspapers over chiefs giving land to women suggests that this became a common practice. In 1925 a writer to *Ebifa* complained that the number of *bannakyeyombekedde* (women who control land independently) was the same as the number of men in the villages, and that all women wanted to leave their husbands and to be free to grow cotton on their own behalf. He urged that authorities should prevent women from moving freely and growing cotton if they had no husband.[59] Complaints in *Munno,* the Catholic newspaper, in 1927 describe the threat of bannakyeyombekedde to families: women who left husbands to grow cotton on their own were reluctant to return to their husbands, and their fathers and brothers had no influence over them. The writer blamed the problem on chiefs who gave land to women.[60]

Women may have chosen to become the tenant of a chief/landowner over being the wife of a tenant as a result of household tensions created by the new work of planting, weeding, harvesting, and carrying cotton. At first, cotton cultivation was women's work because it was agricultural and therefore in women's sphere: in 1910 the agricultural officer reported matter-of-factly that women grew the crop.[61] Twenty years later, agricultural officers recorded that women in Buganda were no longer growing cotton for their husbands: Lucy Mair wrote that women grew cotton for themselves, but a wife could leave a husband who expected her to cultivate cotton for him.[62] This fundamental transition in the assignment of domestic labor suggests a struggle between Ganda men and women that might well have motivated women to choose to control land on their own account when the option became available. The renegotiation of the gendered division of labor in which women succeeded in freeing themselves from the obligation of growing cotton for their husbands must have been acrimonious: it drew comments from foreign men, a group not usually attuned to conditions within the Ganda household. Writing in 1907, C. W. Hattersley drew a parallel between Ganda women and feminine agitators in his own society: "The men have to do more, for women 'suffragettes' have appeared. These insist that, if they are not supplied with European clothing— that is, white calico or coloured clothes—the banana supply for the family will stop; they will no longer cultivate, but go off and get work as labourers, and earn money with which to clothe themselves satisfactorily."[63] Eighteen years later, the American Raymond Buell responded to the concern that "the burden upon the native women has been increased as a result of the cotton industry" by arguing that "preparing the ground for cotton planting, as well as cotton picking require very little work of an exacting nature." He suggested, "In view of the growing indolent 'feminism' of many Buganda women, which has been produced by sudden wealth, it would seem that a little honest work [cultivating cotton for their husbands] would do them good."[64]

Although there are no direct references to cotton in the slim documentation of gender relations in Buganda before 1920, domestic tensions are very apparent. In 1905, Bulazi Bulezi bit off his wife's ear because she had fed her lover twice in his house, and received three hundred cowries from him; Balironda was speared to death when he attempted to set fire to the home of the man he thought had taken his wife; Adamu Kiyonagu was fined by the Lukiiko for tying his wife up with ropes to get her to confess that she had had an abortion.[65] Zakaliya Maganga tried for months to get his wife to return to him, and never succeeded, although he got the Lukiiko to threaten to imprison the wives of the brother with whom Zakaliya thought she was hiding, if they failed to produce her.[66] In 1909, Lwabaka Nambi, the daughter of Kisingiri, one of the most powerful chiefs of the time, left her husband and refused to return unless he stopped bringing beer and women into her house and beating her, or until he gave her five hundred rupees in compensation.[67] A laconic notation in the Lukiiko record in 1916 tells the story of a woman named Muwanika who got into a quarrel with her husband in 1916. He asked her to bring him ten cents (one-tenth of a rupee), but "because the wife was feeling unwell, she did not wish to give it to him in a respectful manner (kneeling down on both knees)." Instead, she threw it out the door toward him. "This resulted in a quarrel between the parties for not respecting him." The neighbors were compelled to separate them, but "a little while later" Muwanika picked up a stick and hit her husband on the head, then she ran into the house, hid behind the door, and stabbed him in the chest with a knife when he entered. He died while the neighbors were raising an alarm, and Muwanika set the house on fire.[68] The Lukiiko noted in 1916 that "a lost woman has been found on Nakasero road," and it decided to return the woman to her father, where her husband could find her if he was still interested. The "lost" woman had apparently been taking care of herself for the two years since she had "disappeared from her husband," but her own intentions for the future were not considered by the Lukiiko.[69]

The woman who had disappeared from her husband two years earlier and the wife Zakaliya Maganga was unable to recover may have been among the women who obtained ebibanja from chiefs and mailo owners. People who controlled land had many good reasons to include independent women among their followers. Giving land to women who wanted it increased the income of the land-allocator: at this time landlord/chiefs received one-tenth (and some-times more) of a tenant's cotton crop.[70] Competition to attract followers was intense: men had left Buganda in order to avoid labor and taxes. Wage labor for the colonial government and trade also removed men from rural life. Each mailo purchaser needed to populate his land with followers, so the accelerat-ing process of land sale also increased the need for followers. Women ten-ants may have been preferable to men, because women were not called up for kasanvu or obligated to pay poll tax, so they were more available to do the chief's work. Although luwalo had traditionally been a male obligation in the Ganda gendered division of labor, women were observed to be doing most of the road work in 1910.[71]

It is possible that chiefs were motivated to acquire female tenants at this time because there were more unattached adult women than there had been previously. The sleeping sickness epidemic was said to have killed seven times more men than women.[72] Sexually transmitted diseases, which had become rampant in Buganda with the caravan trade, probably caused women to be cast off by their husbands because they had not had children. Men also avoided marriage and a settled home as a strategy to avoid poll tax and kasanvu obli-gations. Women may also have become independent controllers of a plot of land after traditional divorce imposed as a requirement for their husband's baptism. Christian men had to divorce all but one wife in order to be baptized. Although the regents and missionary leaders claimed that this would cause no hardship for the women who were to be divorced, a few renegade mission-aries argued that women who were discarded ceased to be under the control of any men.[73] In a social context in which women felt aggrieved by the new burdens of cotton cultivation, men were absent to avoid labor or absent doing labor, and chiefs were looking for followers, it makes sense that women be-gan to attach themselves to chiefs on their own.

In addition to becoming followers of chiefs, women were sometimes granted mailo or bought mailo, giving them the chieflike status of other mailo land holders. The Lukiiko recorded sales of land to women, the granting of surpluses after survey to women who asked for them, and transactions in which one woman land owner passed on her land to another woman land owner.[74] Petero Kyegulumiza, a lower-level chief in Ssingo, sold land to a woman, Azedi Nakaima, but then brought two cases against her in the Lukiiko, claiming that "she went and took all my headquarters." The Lukiiko resolved the case in her favor in February 1914: it had sent representative to look at the land and did not think Petero had any cause for complaint.[75]

Royal women had always controlled land independently in Buganda, but those women had not had children. Women's ability to attach to a chief by themselves, and not as the productive workers attached to husbands, posed challenges to Ganda society that were not easily resolved. When women pulled away from husbands and brothers to become the tenants of chiefs independently, who was responsible to take care of those women in hard times? If women who had attached to chiefs by themselves had children, to which lineage units did the children belong? The partial unbinding of the household was one of the most profound consequences of the intensification of labor demands in colonial Buganda.

Perhaps the most poignant miscommunication between Baganda and their British friends-turned-protectors had to do with the meaning of labor. Ganda chiefs trusted Hesketh Bell, the governor who initiated kasanvu. James Miti, the katikkiro of Bunyoro, remembered that "he was very much liked by the people on account of his consideration and attention to their needs. He would on all occasions consult the interests of the people of the Protectorate. His laws and other official pronouncements were a true reflection of the sympathetic interest that he took in the people of Uganda."[76] Chiefs showed their positive feelings for Bell through offering him huge numbers of well-mustered workers. Bell, on his part, had the sensitivity to notice what was being done for him: he searched out the back of his camp, where "quite a small mountain" of food was being prepared, and he appreciated the beauty of the accommodations made for him and the quality of the roads that were built. The labor made available by the Ganda chiefs was one half of a pledge of mutual assistance; but what Bell perceived, and wrote about in his journal, was cheap labor, wonderful productive work that cost practically nothing. Yet the costs for Buganda of kasanvu—Bell's formalization of the labor that had been offered to him by chiefs—were extremely, almost incalculably high.

On May 1, 1909, Bell left Uganda after a Baraza in Kampala. The Ganda regents and chiefs had arranged a special farewell surprise—as he stepped out of the subcommissioner's house, "a big drum was beaten on one of the Kampala hills, and in an instant thousands of torches broke into a blaze." For the entire six-mile journey to the Kampala port, his car passed under an arch made by thousands of Ganda men holding up torches of flaming reeds and shouting *"Webale"* (thank you).[77] Torch light had represented the power of rulers in Buganda: the chiefs had made use of the allegiance they had cultivated in their followers and their organizational skills to create a stunning statement of the importance of the governor and the place of the Baganda as his loyal followers. Neither Bell nor the government he represented

Figure 6.2   Governor Bell's farewell, 1909. Governor Bell failed to recognize the request for reciprocal respect and consideration implicit in the Ganda chiefs' command of the labor required to create a six-mile-long torch-lit arch to bid him farewell. Governor Bell experienced thousands of men calling out "thank you" as a remarkable contrast between his own modernity and the Baganda "still in the earliest stages of social progress." The *Illustrated London News* carried a picture of the scene, as described by Bell, on October 9, 1909. (C. Cuneo, reproduced in Bell, *Glimpses of a Governor's Life*, 205)

recognized the social contract inherent in the action of the Baganda, and the implementation of kasanvu over the following years entirely undermined the patterns of assistance and obligation that had made that event possible.

THE DETERIORATION OF RECIPROCAL OBLIGATION

When chiefs began to implement poll tax and kasanvu, they did so following the expectations of reciprocal obligation: a chief had to treat his followers reasonably well in order to prevent them from seeking better conditions under a different chief. Abundance of land had increased because of population decline; even though the creation of mailo had turned chiefs' followers into tenants, land scarcity was not a factor in Buganda until much later in the century.[78] Chiefs therefore had to offer protection in order to retain followers. In the 1890s, chiefs had protected followers by refusing to provide labor to Europeans who had reputations for being excessively harsh.[79] During the negotiation of the Uganda Agreement, one of the regents' first queries had concerned exemptions for sick, old, and disabled people. In 1904 Samwiri Mukasa exempted three thousand people for age, disease, or physical deformity. The district commissioner found this number unacceptably high and insisted that all the exempted people report to Kampala to prove their disability; but then when the people came to him, in groups of several hundred, he relented and upheld Mukasa's exemptions.[80]

Retaining followers by treating them well was impossible for chiefs in the new Buganda. Protectorate authorities countered chiefs' tendency to grant large numbers of tax exemptions by making chiefs' salaries a proportion of the taxes they collected. Chiefs had actually supported this change, which conformed with their notion of chiefship. However, calls for incidental labor, poll tax, and especially kasanvu led to such massive emigration that many chiefs lacked people to tax. In 1910, Lukiiko members made accusations that others had allegedly collected tax from old people and "made sick men go to Kampala."[81] These complaints suggest that older and less healthy people had begun to be taxed.

Meeting the incidental labor requirements of the Protectorate, especially as demands intensified during World War I, also undermined the protective role of chiefs. In 1914 the ssaza chief Kasujju wrote to ask the Lukiiko whether he should give food to the contingent of soldiers in his district or to the land surveyors. In some ggombololas of his province, people were eating banana roots, and "this reason is why I want the Lukiko to decide."[82] The same chief wrote reporting that he had only obtained four of the eight men he had been ordered to find for police duties, because "they fear being beaten while under training." He suggested that it would be better for the kabaka to find someone to train the police there in his ssaza. The Lukiiko replied that "we have not been pleased about that excuse" and decided to reprimand him.[83] In February 1916 the ssaza chief Kitunzi was reprimanded for "selecting" men for recruitment into the army but then failing to provide food for them while they were waiting for transportation, which did not arrive.[84] The ssaza chief Kaggo came into conflict with nine men whom he had "selected for enlistment in the forces." The medical officer had disqualified them as unfit, so Kaggo sent them to the district commissioner to carry his loads. The men complained that if they were disqualified from the army, they were unfit to do any hard work, but the Lukiiko agreed with their chief and told the men to report back to the kaggo and then go to carry the district commissioner's loads.[85] In these circumstances, Ganda men experienced few incentives to remain the followers of their chiefs.

A further disruption of the practice of power through pledged obligation occurred through a series of actions by Protectorate authorities that had the effect of removing followers from chiefs by administrative fiat. In 1909, Protectorate authorities rationalized the varied, complex hierarchies of lower-level chiefs into a uniform system of ssazas (provinces), ggombololas (districts), and mulukas (parishes).[86] Chiefship became entirely territorial, replacing the previous system of overlapping allegiances that was only partially related to where people lived. In Ganda political units of the past, tribute and taxes had flowed through chains of allegiance from tax and tribute payers to their particular superiors, who were not always the tax or tribute superiors of their neighbors. Ganda logic about taxation endured for a few more years despite the profound intervention by the Protectorate: purchasers of land continued to be able to choose which chief they would be under for administrative purposes. Thus in 1912, D. W. Cooper complained, "shambas situated in the center of one division are not ruled by the chief of the division in which they are situated, but arbitrarily placed under the administration of the chief chosen by the owner of the land."[87] Many people also managed to hold chiefships in more than one ssaza where they owned mailo land until 1917, when the British authorities insisted that people resign all but one official position.[88]

After the district commissioner pushed territorially based chiefship through the Lukiiko, a procession of chiefs who had lost their followers pleaded for their return. Nsege, the *mumyuka* (second most important chief) of Bulemeezi, brought a case against his superior, the kangaawo, saying, "in the beginning I had many people but when Gombolola Mutuba IV was deducted off my saza I remained with only 1,847 Poll Tax payers also 40 people of mine were transferred to Mukuma." The kangaawo argued that Nsege had accepted the changes when they were made in front of the Lukiiko and the district commissioner, adding, "now I don't see any reason to alter this arrangement and I don't accept this alteration." The Lukiiko sided with the chief who felt he was wronged, however, and transferred back to him the 40 people who had been given to another chief, and 353 from Kikabi "because of his old age," giving Nsege 2,200.[89] People who were third, fourth, or lower in the chiefly hierarchy of a province pleaded to have their inferior chiefs, and the people underneath those chiefs, restored to them.[90] The Lukiiko counted, hoarded, and assigned tax-paying followers carefully: when one parish ceased to have enough people to merit a chief, it tried to reassign that chief to another parish.[91] Some of the cases concerned disputes involving people whose authority in the old Buganda had come from a remembered relationship with the kabaka. Balazi, of Kasebuti village, complained that Ppookino, ssaza chief of Buddu, should have made him a second-level *mutuba* chief, because "he was a long time servant of the Kabaka." The ppookino's representative protested that Balazi did not have any people in his area, and "it could not have been fair to appoint him a chief when Kasiyaine who had already 10 people in his area was also a chief."[92]

Forcing people to do all the work demanded by the Protectorate made chiefs unpopular and motivated people to leave the district, but not forcing them to do it incurred the displeasure of British officials. The ssaza chiefs were caught in the middle, as Stanislaus Mugwanya complained, "treated like a pad (the coil of banana fiber which people placed on their heads to carry loads) which is pressed on both sides."[93] For example, Joswa Kate Mugema, one of the most popular chiefs, was reprimanded, along with his subordinates, for "slackness in the collection of Poll Tax and carriers for the Belgian Carrier Corps."[94] There is some suggestion in the records of the Lukiiko and in the Buganda annual reports that the Lukiiko chiefs solved their dilemma by blaming lower-level chiefs, but leaving them in power.[95]

Lower-level chiefs were required to implement demands for work to be done or labor to be supplied. When they failed, they were reprimanded and fined. Chiefs reported on the inadequacies of their inferiors to their fellow Lukiiko members: "Mumyuka (second-level subordinate) is lazy in his official duties, does not obey the orders, and when ordered to pay fines does not pay same. When instructed to provide kasanvu he does not move very quickly."[96] The ssaza chief of Kyaggwe reported that his *sabagabo* (third-level subordinate) "who is supposed to select men of kasanvu from his area has not cared to do so for at least three years."[97] The ssaza chief Mukwenda reported to the Lukiiko that all his ggombolola (subdistrict) chiefs were doing well except the sabagabo, who "when ordered to present kasanvu . . . only presented 5 compulsory porters and 2 askaris"; the same subchief was deficient in his obligations because "all 'bulungi bwansi' [customary communal labor] roads in the area are fully covered with grass."[98]

While higher-level chiefs readily criticized their subordinates for failure to supply labor, it is revealing to note that they were more hesitant to impose fines. Almost all harsh fines seem to have been imposed at the specific request of Europeans, or in response to a failure at work that was immediately apparent to Europeans. Ggombolola and muluka chiefs were fined for not supplying food to surveyors, for not weeding around government rubber trees (a five-rupee fine in 1908), for arresting "permanent people" because they had not done kasanvu (a twenty-rupee fine that was specifically requested by the "very annoyed" district commissioner in 1914), for not placing surveyors' beacons (a twenty-rupee fine in 1915), for not being present at the auditing of the ggombolola's books because of attending a funeral (a fifteen-rupee fine in 1915), and for taking too long to find people to carry the luggage of three Europeans staying at a rest house (a twenty-five-rupee fine commuted to ten rupees by the Lukiiko in 1916).[99] In contrast, the fine on a chief whose men got into a fight over an insulting comment that should have been taken as a joke was five rupees in 1915.[100] Conflicts arose in the Lukiiko over who should pay particular fines: the chief responsible for having the work done, or the deputy who was to execute his orders. Ssaza chiefs were fined by the provincial commissioner, or part of their portion of poll tax was withheld, if their performance was considered "unsatisfactory."[101]

Competition among chiefs for followers in the context of constant Protectorate demands eventually undermined the fundamental premise of the Ganda practice of power: that people could leave a chief who made onerous demands. Freedom of movement was progressively restricted, so that it became quite difficult for people to leave a chief, however badly he treated his followers. An early step in this process was that those planning to move could not leave their old homes until they had paid their poll tax and *busuulu,* as Apolo Kaggwa explained to Lukiiko members, "because the government is very fond of taxes." At that time, in 1909, a fine of two rupees was added to the five-rupee tax if people had not paid on time.[102] In 1914 the Lukiiko decided to require people to carry tax receipts with them at all times from November 31 to March 31; anyone who did not have a tax receipt would be arrested. The upheaval of World War I apparently created alarming possibilities: the Lukiiko records note a warning to the ssaza chiefs "to take special precautions to see that tax money should not decrease because of 'soldiers.'" The kangaawo, head of the Buganda military volunteer corp, was told to find out "whether in the army of soldiers there are some who have not yet paid their taxes. These should be made to pay quickly before going out to fight."[103] Since people could leave districts where the Lukiiko's rules were applied strictly in favor of districts whose chiefs were more lenient, a further layer of coercive measures was implemented specifically to restrict people's movement. In February 1916 the ssaza chief of Buyaga received permission to follow men to their new homes in Kyaggwe to collect the poll tax they had failed to pay before they migrated from his ssaza.[104] Kezekiya Gamyuka left Busujju when he was selected for kasanvu in 1917, and went to Butambala. However, his former chief found him there and arrested him: the Lukiiko gave the former chief, the *kitunzi,* permission to try him for moving away.[105] In 1918 the Lukiiko passed a resolution providing that any person leaving Buganda had to have a permit from his ggombolola chief.[106]

One cost of colonial labor was that Ganda chiefship deteriorated into something that had the same set of names but meant something entirely different than it had meant in the past. The premise of reciprocal obligation disappeared when people were legally constrained from moving. Attaching oneself to a chief had little meaning if there was no possibility of leaving that chief. At the same time, the chiefly role of balancing labor demands against the ability of followers to supply it had been replaced by a new chiefly role, described by the provincial commissioner as "using to the full the powers given them to enforce obedience and respect to the authorities."[107] The new chief was part of a vertical flow of power from the Protectorate down to the people, enforced by fines, imprisonment, and lashes. The orientation of older chiefs toward each other, seeking alliances and assessing the relative strength and attractiveness to followers of their peers, had been entirely effaced. The records of the Lukiiko from the first years of colonial rule reveal the independent thought and action that had characterized an earlier generation of Ganda rulers. At that time, chiefs' superiors begged for their cooperation, they did not assume it. The Lukiiko wrote to a chief who had disappointed them, "You should come as soon as you have read this letter with the numbers of people you have evicted from the lake, the numbers are wanted. Because you have been called to come so many times but you never came, you must come as soon as you can this time."[108] Stanislaus Mugwanya made a show of his disagreement with the Lukiiko in 1908, when during a quarrel he refused to attend or even to send a message. His explanation, when he was asked for one, was that "he had no pencil at the time to reply."[109] As the colonial order of things became entrenched, the Lukiiko did not make requests so politely, and chiefs did not dare to show any reluctance to obey.

Land was the one arena of authority that the Lukiiko kept firmly in its grasp throughout the first decades of the twentieth century. During the years in which Ganda chiefs attempted to develop a workable relationship with the Protectorate, the Lukiiko was vigilant in its control over land. In 1909 Protectorate authorities forced the land law (survey) through the Lukiiko, which would have made all pieces of land unclaimed at survey into Crown land. The Lukiiko responded to this threat by prearranging Ganda owners for any land that might be declared surplus in the areas being surveyed. They also engaged a lawyer who argued that the new law was contrary to the Uganda Agreement of 1900. In 1911 the newly appointed governor, Sir Frederick Jackson, took the Ganda side against his own legal advisers, saying, "we now find that we have, from the point of view of the quality of the waste and uncultivated land, got the worst of the bargain. But that bargain was of our own making."[110] The Lukiiko continued to assign leftover pieces of mailo until the mid-1920s, adjudicated between rival claimants, decided who could or could not sell their mailo, and divided out all the small pieces that became available as the land survey passed through each ssaza. As colonial involvement in taxation and in the government of Buganda diminished the power of chiefs in some areas, the members of the Lukiiko continued to demonstrate their authority through their total control over the allocation of land.[111]

Despite their control over land, chiefs lost the esteem of their people when they took actions that seemed uncaring and unjust. Stuck between British and Ganda criteria of chiefly behavior, Ganda chiefs tried various strategies to hold on to their status. Joswa Kate Mugema—chief of an important and populous ssaza who also had considerable traditional authority—was one of a handful who maintained their prestige by treating followers well and refusing to follow directives that they considered wrong. Apolo Kaggwa attempted to create a Ganda equivalent of the House of Lords that would enshrine the special status of the largest landowners. A more common strategy was for chiefs to demonstrate their high position with objects: they rode bicycles (a few followers ran behind to push them up hills), and later motorcycles; they built brick houses with tin roofs, they had clocks and crockery.[112] The governor's uniform had "a good deal of gold lace on the chest and coat tails," and the dark silk *kkanzus* of the Lukiiko members were "trimmed with gold braid."[113] Chiefs' attempts to symbolically assert the position of honor that they had lost in reality were not successful. Displays of wealth might demonstrate a chief's authority, but they could not create authority when chiefs were not behaving according to Ganda social expectations.

Chiefs were scandalized in 1917 when Y. Muwamirembe, a muluka (parish) chief's assistant, refused to represent his senior in the Lukiiko, "unless he was paid Rs 25 per month, also a coat and shoes and a chair." The case had been sent up to Mmengo from Bulemeezi because "it was too much for that court." The Lukiiko decided that the man making the request was unequivocally guilty: "There is no Muluka chief, appointed by his senior who should refuse this order, and never has there been a Muluka chief who demanded salary when appointed by his senior, to represent him." He was fined thirty rupees and warned that if he ever tried such an act again he would be dismissed from chiefship.[114] In a way, Muwamirembe was correct. In 1917 a lower-level chief did need European clothes and furniture to underline his right to call up labor, collect tax, and pass down directives from above. The Lukiiko refused to accept these new circumstances of chiefly office, however, and insisted that a lower-level chief should serve his superior for the rewards inherent in reciprocal obligation.

THE DECLINE OF LINEAGE NETWORKS AND THE THREAT OF "BAD HEIRS"

The overwhelming demand for labor that transformed the character of relations between chiefs and followers also had profound effects on the extensive, horizontal networks of protection and sustenance of Ganda clans, lineage networks, and local communities. These networks contracted when people had too much work to be able to maintain them, and people's differential success in obtaining exemptions from obligatory labor created a wedge between privileged people and others that had not existed previously. Furthermore, the legal and ideological primacy given to individuals over corporate groups by colonial authorities and missionaries deeply threatened the ability of clans and lineage networks to take care of their members.

At the turn of the twentieth century, Baganda had conceptualized people as parts of groups rather than as individuals. A family, lineage, or community was responsible for the actions of its members: for example, when a woman was stripped of her garments on a road and no one from the area came to her aid, a collective fine was imposed on the neighbors.[115] Access to resources to the means of maintaining life, such as land and building materials, had to be available to all who needed them: the Lukiiko found it difficult, and then impossible, to decide whether people could be allowed to sell stone and sand, which other people needed, from land that they owned.[116] Membership in a group provided protection from death or enslavement—Ganda students of Christianity wanted to know how Christ could have been put to death as a sacrifice when his parents were known.[117] The Lukiiko relied on clan obligations in its resolution of problems. The unfortunate Magazi Omwanga was burdened with an excessive hundred-rupee fine for not providing food to a foreigner as quickly as that man had wanted it. Magazi had not paid and would not be able to, but the regent Stanislaus Mugwanya had already paid in his stead, so Magazi "was handed to S. Senkezi in the name of Walusimbi and charged with the duty of finding the Rs 100 from among the members of the clan."[118]

An early, dramatic failure of clan and lineage networks had to do with food. The fundamental responsibility of clan members to provide hospitality to travelers who shared their clan names became impossible with the massive movement of people working for tax money or in kasanvu. In nineteenth-century Buganda, daily food, in the form of matooke bananas, was not usually purchased. No establishment where people lived was without a banana garden. Chiefs sent representatives to maintain banana gardens near Lake Victoria so their people would have food when they went to fish, or on main roads where the chief would break a journey to the capital.[119] Travelers who were not making a journey on behalf of the kabaka found food and shelter with someone in a local community who shared their clan name; according to a Ganda saying, "kinship is eating."[120] This system broke down in the 1890s when hundreds, then thousands of workers descended on Entebbe: their clan relatives did not have enough food to feed them all.

People who went to work in Entebbe suffered terribly from hunger: it was said that some died upon returning home.[121] The Protectorate government offered to sell workers maize flour, but people did not want to eat it and did not want to work longer in order to pay for food. In 1907 the Lukiiko designated seven villages "that will sell foods and matoke to Entebbe," but offering this preferred food for sale did not cause people to shift their perception that eating matooke ought not to involve money.[122] As long as Baganda had to leave their homes to work on government projects, they suffered for lack of food. Protectorate plans to make food available for sale do not indicate an awareness that traveling workers might expect to be fed by fellow clan members. Yet clan members did have the obligation to feed their relatives, the number of people needing food at colonial work sites would have surpassed the capacity of those living nearby to supply hospitality, and the hunger of workers is well documented. The experience of being a laborer away from home, needing food, and not being able to obtain it from clan relatives must have been a constant disappointment that undermined people's confidence in clans and lineages.

The onerous burden of kasanvu labor led to a more permanent rupture in clan and community networks. Exemptions from performing kasanvu were seen as valid for luwalo also. Therefore, all the people who had found ways to escape from kasanvu no longer had to participate in communal work for "the good of the country." Chiefs complained in 1910 that they were losing control of labor because of the exemptions obtained by "servants and employees."[123] While Hattersley had described thousands of people working together in 1907, by 1919 chiefs with a tax-paying population of one thousand might be able to find no more than two or three volunteers for luwalo work.[124] The large number of exemptions granted by chiefs meant that the same people— those with the least influence, the least income, and the fewest resources— were called up for communal labor over and over again, beyond the limit of one month per year.[125] This caused a widening gap between Baganda with and without access to resources, as those required to do more than their share of obligatory labor fell further behind their relatives and neighbors.

People who already had privileged access to education were able to obtain exemptions from kasanvu and luwalo. In theory, exemptions were granted to people in "permanent employment," including self-employed people practicing essential trades. In practice, however, exemptions went to people employed by Europeans or people with skills learned in mission schools: clerks, carpenters, tailors, and printers.[126] Those skilled in Ganda forms of manufacture were not exempted in labor drafts. Yakobo Tabula, a bed maker, and ten men who were the kabaka's blacksmiths challenged their selection for the military, because they felt their work entitled them to exemptions. The blacksmiths were excused, with the admonition to "work even harder," but the bed maker was enlisted.[127] The insidious, divisive aspect of poll tax labor and kasanvu (and luwalo after it lost its character of a whole group effort) was that the work would only get done if some people remained too poor to be able to pay tax instead. The district commissioner for Kampala in 1910 put this bluntly: "without this control [by chiefs over labor] many Bakopi would be too rich from other sources to need to work."[128]

The creation of a group of people obliged to do more than their share of forced labor led to the class differences that became obvious to concerned observers in the 1920s and 1930s. The wide gap that emerged between rich and poor Baganda was not primarily a consequence of landowners extracting high tithes in the form of cotton from their tenants. On the contrary, Baganda with all levels of resources used the possibilities of growing cotton to their own advantage. The people who had to do everyone's forced labor lost their health doing kasanvu labor and lost the opportunity to work for their own benefit during those months. The people who obtained exemptions benefited doubly from the advantages that gave them the exemptions in the first place.

The multiplication of demands on people's productive capacities had another subtle but corrosive effect on clan and lineage networks: the more new labor people had to do, the less time and energy they had to invest in maintaining clan and lineage networks. When people gathered together for feasts and ceremonies to observe birth, the birth of twins, naming, children's growth, marriage, death, and succession, they solidified social connections in concrete as well as spiritual ways. The people whom one met at ceremonies were the people one could rely on in difficulties. Mair observed that only funeral and succession ceremonies continued to be fully observed in 1931: some ceremonies had been replaced by Christian rituals for baptism and marriage, while others had fallen into disuse because people did not have the time or financial resources to observe them.[129] One of the lapsed ceremonies, performed three days after the birth of a child, was called "to protect all the people of the clan." When lineage networks stopped meeting together, and communities stopped celebrating life events, networks of mutual assistance weakened. One evidence of this is the difficulty people experienced in rebuilding their homes: instead of being rebuilt in a day by a work party, by 1930 a building often stood half finished for months as people tried to find time to complete it without any outside assistance.[130] Foreigners in Buganda actively discouraged clan and lineage ceremonies. They saw clan ritual as indulgence in drinking, eating, and dancing: "the indolent life led by all Africans" was one reason given by the Uganda chamber of commerce for labor shortages.[131] What foreigners could not see were the bonds of social security being forged in those events.

At the same time that new amounts and forms of work destabilized Ganda ways of maintaining connections, Christianity and Islam offered alternative explanations of morality that justified the neglect of clan and family obligations. This was partly the effect of turn-of-the-century European Protestant thinking regarding spiritual success. Lucy Mair regretted, in 1934, that mission education overemphasized "the advantages to the individual of commercializing his possessions," and did not encourage "the growth of a spirit of corporate loyalty" to the village.[132] A more fundamental challenge was that people's strong allegiances to new religions came into direct conflict with their allegiances to clan and lineage. After their relatives had failed to protect them during some of the most devastating battles of the late nineteenth century, Muslims sang, "those who believe in and expect protection from clansmen are the ones whose skulls we see on the roads."[133] Conflict between Catholics and Protestants led to divisions between family members. A Catholic father wrote to his son who had become Protestant while attending Mmengo High School, "let me congratulate you, my son, thanking you for leaving me in the fire. I am your father, and you my son ran away . . . it had been better that both of us should enter into the fire together. . . . I beseech you come not at all to my burial, I am not your father."[134]

Legal challenges added to the assault on clan and lineage networks in the early twentieth century. Poll tax had to be paid by individuals, and Protectorate law attempted to make it impossible to extend fines or punishments from the accused person to his relatives. Women's rights to purchase and inherit land, promoted by missionaries, were strongly contested by lineage networks. When women owned land, it was lost to the lineage and clan, because women passed it on to their children, who belonged to the lineages of their fathers. Clan elders faced the problem of what to do about women owning land when men failed to have male children. In 1914 the Book of Inheritance noted indecision about a particular case:

> And he had fathered two children, only girls. The clan leaders chose this heir of their clan [a male relative]. About this issue, the members of the Lukiiko saw that girl children ought to share the land of their father. This matter caused a disagreement among the members of the Lukiiko, that is why it is ordered to put it with what will be discussed in April 1915. Whether it is appropriate for girls to share in things of inheritance.[135]

Clan elders in a lineages sometimes fought the possibility of a female heir by proposing male heirs who were argued to be the secret, hitherto unknown children of the deceased.[136]

A greater threat to clan and lineage networks were "bad heirs." Since British law protected individuals but not lineages as corporate entities, an heir who received a position and property as the custodian of the assets of his lineage might choose instead to see that property as his alone. Some chiefs' sons proved to be ill-equipped to assume the role of heirs to their fathers. They had grown up in a time of cotton wealth, they had received the anticlan bias of mission education, and the "new" Buganda did not offer them the avenues of developing leadership that had been available to their fathers. Older Baganda worried that men who had become adults in the 1920s did not know how to behave. In a meeting of the Board of Governors of Budo College, Hamu Mukasa claimed that young heirs, and not old people, failed to pay their contributions to the school.[137] James Miti concluded his history of Buganda with the observation that "under the new law the old Kiganda filial reverence seemed to lose somewhat of its former grip."[138]

Conflicts between the generation that had survived the crisis of the late nineteenth century and forged the new Buganda and their children began even before the moment of succession. Samwiri Mukasa Kangaawo wrote to his sons:

One of you has deserted his job of being a Muluka chief and serving his Kabaka and country and has joined the company of people who feed him on fattened animals and stand intoxicating drinks for him. It is lucky of your generation that when brothers see such a thing of one of them, they never try to talk it over with him so that he improves, but flatter him and he is pleased with them. It is like a calabash with holes in the bottom, nobody can put their beer in it; nobody trusts him any longer.[139]

The desperation Mukasa and his generation felt is apparent in his conclusion, "you people have every now and then shown your disobedience to me and have actually told me that you are your own fathers and are not obliged to obey anybody. True, the way you have treated me is not as from a son to a father." Joswa Kate Mugema's son attempted to lease butaka land, with graves on it, to a European.[140] Apolo Kaggwa's son Sepiriya Kaddumukasa, who had been sent to England to school, impregnated a student from the Gayaza girls school and ran up huge bills for liquor. Kaggwa made provisions in his will reflecting his fears regarding succession, which specified what should happen "if the head of the butaka begins to go mad, making debts causing the sale of the butaka," and "if the head of the Butaka has sold the land in secret and has already eaten the money." In that case, according to Kaggwa, whoever had bought the land would be forced to return it and would lose his money, "because he had bought land which was not supposed to be sold," and the Lukiiko would appoint a new heir.[141] Kaggwa's worst fears were realized when his heirs sold his massive estates and ate up his wealth in legal suits against each other. The searing and bitter conflicts over inheritance that began to arise in the 1920s and 1930s, in which the prerogatives of lineage networks were pitted against the legal rights of "bad heirs" who acted as though their inheritance was their own individual property, were the inevitable consequence of the direct and indirect attacks on the social institutions of clan and lineage networks.

INNOVATIONS TO MEET THE RESPONSIBILITIES OF CHIEFS AND LINEAGE NETWORKS

In the half a generation that followed the introduction of poll tax, forced labor, and cultivation of cotton for cash, the institution of chiefship was transformed, and clan and lineage networks were severely strained. Ganda ways of perceiving the world and organizing productive activity, however, demonstrated remarkable resilience. One of the first economic interventions of the colonial government had been to try to replace cowrie currency with rupees and pice. "Several million" cowrie shells were burnt, and the lime was used in the building of the district commissioner's house in Kampala, which came to be known as *"enyumba y'ensimbi"*—"the house of money."[142] People continued to use cowries, however; Hattersley described being unable to make purchases when he offered pice instead of cowries in 1907. Thirty years after the initial attempt to eliminate it, cowrie currency was still in use.[143]

Baganda also re-created the logic of reciprocal obligation on a smaller scale by turning land ownership into a form of chiefship. The Lukiiko granted land owners a tribute of two rupees or one month's labor, indicating in the language of exchange that tenants were the followers of landowners. More important, the Lukiiko determined that mailo owners *could not* give produce or money to the chief of the area in which their land was located. This meant, in symbolic terms, that the mailo owner had no superior.[144] Mailo owners were not obliged to perform kasanvu or luwalo, nor could they be compelled by chiefs answerable to Kampala to "volunteer" for any other work. Thousands of Baganda used profits from wage labor or cotton to buy plots of "10, 20, or 30" acres in order to escape excessive labor demands.[145] Land purchase, according to social critic Daudi Basudde, enabled people "to free themselves from the chiefs' pernicious outside influences they adopted and brought to bear on the men who are living on their land."[146] On their land, mailo owners became chiefs by allocating plots to tenants and hiring immigrant laborers to grow cotton for them, in return for food and a place to live. For decades, Ganda cotton growers were able to attract more labor than plantations, ginneries, and government departments because the Baganda incorporated laborers using a form of reciprocal obligation. Immigrants attached to Ganda households followed a work rhythm that was familiar, ate the same kind of food as their employer, and might sit in his or her doorway participating in conversation with visitors.[147] Ganda landowners were so successful in maintaining non-commodified relationships with immigrant workers that the Protectorate government was forced to admonish European employers "to demonstrate a keen human interest in the welfare of their employees."[148]

Even though the enactment of community that had come from hundreds of people assembling to work together on community projects was irreparably undermined by kasanvu, Ganda community networks continued to be valuable. Despite the real threat that "bad heirs" might ruin the inheritance of a lineage, clan members found new ways to use the broad range of resources that clans and lineage networks made available. Clan members with means paid for the education of promising young relatives, and people placed their children in the homes of relatives where they would have access to better education.[149] Having clan relatives in positions in the chiefly hierarchy was also useful, and clan members could be expected to contribute: when Musa Serwajokwota was appointed to a chiefship, for example, he was not allowed to take it up because he owed a debt of seventy rupees. The Lukiiko announced, "if these rupees find someone to pay them, he will be allowed to

Figure 6.3 A cotton-weighing station, ca. 1908. Ganda cultivators employed immigrant labor to cultivate cotton and purchased small amounts of land with cotton income. (Royal Commonwealth Society Archives, Cambridge University)

receive the office."[150] Identifying strangers as clan relatives through recognition of their names ceased to be a means of finding hospitality, but a new strategy of mutual assistance arose when rural members of lineage networks began to supply food to urban members, especially in difficult times.[151]

In 1898, some of the men who had fled Mmengo to fight alongside Kabaka Mwanga against the British warned Apolo Kaggwa that his new allies would ask of him more than he might want to give. Comparing the British imperial entrepreneurs to the Ganda war god Nende, they wrote, "the Kampala European dedicates sacrifices as well as god Nende does."[152] Kaggwa and the other Protestant and Catholic chiefs who had aligned with the foreigners were inclined to disagree. As colonial interference intensified, however, Baganda who did not fight might have begun to see wisdom in that assessment. There were limits to the sacrifices Baganda were willing to make to "the Kampala European." In 1908 the Lukiiko had found men to be carpentry and brick-making apprentices in Entebbe at the request of the subcommissioner, but in 1914 the Lukiiko objected to a similar request, explaining, "this is a very difficult matter under the stated agreement between the employer and the employees."[153] In 1916, specific chiefs began to object to calls for labor, and to request that "the

Lukiko consider the matter over again."[154] After World War I, the colonial administration attempted to raise poll tax to seven and a half rupees, but the Lukiiko succeeded in convincing the Colonial Office that it had the power to veto the increase.[155]

In 1919, eleven chiefs and one of the three ministers wrote to the governor about the problems caused by kasanvu. They claimed that it was leading to continual discontent and causing migration. They said that "weak people and those . . . nearing old age" were forced to do most of the labor, and people who performed kasanvu were despised. Kasanvu meant, they said, that freedom was only for chiefs. The only resolution was to abolish the system. In 1921, all the chiefs in the Lukiiko determined that their role in calling out labor for the colonial power was untenable, and informed Entebbe that the Lukiiko was abolishing labor for the Protectorate. They stated, "After the most careful consideration, the Lukiko have decided unanimously that they do not desire kasanvu of any kind . . . to exist in Buganda . . . we pray you inform the Secretary of State for the Colonies that the Full Lukiko has finally decided to do away with kasanvu as from 31st December, 1921, as it is no longer fitting that it should be enforced."[156]

Kasanvu was abolished in January 1922, but its consequences endured. The intense labor demands of the first twenty years of colonial rule permanently altered the relationship of chiefs and followers, and of clan, lineage, and community members with each other.

CONCLUSION

Buganda changed in powerfully visible ways between 1900 and 1920, but neither the fact of a colonial presence nor the establishment of a cash economy can fully explain these changes. Wage opportunities, money, consumer goods, and private property in land gave Ganda men and women new ways of obtaining the prestige and power inherent in control over other people that had been a goal of work in the past. Baganda and other observers have explained the changes in Buganda as "a loosening of bonds" or the emergence of "greedy chiefs" and "petty capitalist farmers." These descriptions are not adequate because they do not begin on the inside of the Ganda social institutions that were changing. I have argued in this chapter that excessive demands on people's labor wore down the social fabric in Buganda because chiefs and clans could not do for people what they had always done. Chiefs were supposed to protect their followers, but in the new Buganda, in which ultimate decisions were made outside the Ganda hierarchy of power, chiefs were forced to call their people to work even when it undermined people's ability to take care of themselves at home. One of the fundamental functions of extended clan networks was providing for clan members when they traveled, but it was impossible for members of a clan to feed thousands of their fellow clansmen when they arrived to work in Entebbe, passed along a main road, or gathered at the site of some other colonial work project. Exemptions from labor demands, granted to some people but not to others, created an uncrossable divide in Ganda society that had not existed previously. The new demands for labor meant people no longer had time to put labor into maintaining connections with lineage networks and local communities. When people started to do kasanvu, in addition to the month of work required for tax, on top of work for the chief and for the king, communal building parties and lineage gatherings decreased. The institutions of chiefship and clan changed in subtle but important ways. The multiple connections that had been cultivated by people—horizontal ones between lineage and clan relatives and between various authority figures with different kinds of power, and vertical ones between people and the leaders to whom they paid tribute in labor and goods—had been replaced by coercive, uniform links in a vertical hierarchy of power.

NOTES

1. "Buganda Lukiiko," May 27, 1907, 80; S. M. Kangawo to Apolo Kaggwa, August 14, 1911, CB 114, Kaggwa Papers.

2. Hattersley, *The Baganda at Home,* 20.

3. "Buganda Lukiiko," December 16, 1907, 94.

4. Miti, "A History," 784.

5. Holger Bernt Hansen, *Mission, Church, and State in a Colonial Setting: Uganda 1890–1925* (New York: St. Martin's Press, 1984), 91.

6. Ansorge, *Under the African Sun,* 92.

7. Hansen, *Mission, Church, and State,* 92; P. G. Powesland, "History of the Migration in Uganda," in Richards, *Economic Development,* 18.

8. Bachelors were required to pay a poll tax of two rupees starting in 1905, and in 1909 hut tax was abolished and replaced by a five-rupee poll tax on all adult males. Hansen, *Mission, Church, and State,* 178.

9. P. G. Powesland, *Economic Policy and Labour: A Study in Uganda's Economic History,* East African Studies no. 10 (Kampala: East African Institute of Social Research, 1957), 7.

10. Hattersley, *The Baganda at Home,* 111, 113, 118–119.

11. "Buganda Lukiiko," March 23, 1908, 100; August 31, 1914, 117.

12. Ibid., November 7, 1907, 7; Uganda National Archive (UNA) A46/421, Secretariat Minute Paper (SMP) 1138), "Buganda: Annual Report for 1909–1910"; UNA A46/422 (SMP 1138 A), "Buganda Annual Report, 1910–1911"; A46/744, "Buganda Annual Report, 1919"; A46/745 1920, "Buganda Monthly Reports"; A46/746, "Buganda Quarterly Reports, 1920."

13. "Buganda Lukiiko," January 6, 1908, 95.

14. Hattersley, *The Baganda at Home,* 69, 114. The colonial interventions that eliminated the place of Ganda entrepreneurs took place after the period under review.

15. Wrigley, *Crops and Wealth,* 16, 47; "Buganda Lukiiko," March 24, 1908, 100.

16. "Buganda Lukiiko," November 11, 1907, 93.

17. Wrigley, *Crops and Wealth,* 44.

18. Bell, *A Governor's Life,* 112; Apolo Kaggwa to H. F. Leakey, November 11, 1907, CA 64, Kaggwa Papers.

19. Hattersley, *The Baganda at Home,* 131.

20. Powesland, *Economic Policy and Labour,* 18; Hattersley, *The Baganda at Home,* 118.

21. Hansen, *Mission, Church, and State,* 80.

22. Ibid., 199, 180.

23. "Buganda Lukiiko," August 29, 1914, 116.

24. Bell, *A Governor's Life,* 119, 131.

25. Ibid., 111.

26. Hattersley, *The Baganda at Home,* 63.

27. Bell, *A Governor's Life,* 114, 183.

28. Ibid., 184.

29. Hattersley, *The Baganda at Home,* 150.

30. "Buganda Lukiiko," January 7, 1907, 71; "Buganda Lukiiko," April 22, 1907, 80.

31. Lukiiko Flyer, CB26, Kaggwa Papers.

32. UNA A46/421(SMP 1138), "Buganda Annual Reports, 1909–1910."

33. H. B. Thomas and A. E. Spencer, *A History of Uganda Land and Surveys and of the Uganda Land and Survey Department* (Entebbe: Government Press, 1938), 75.

34. "Buganda Lukiiko," April 1914, 113, 115.

35. Ibid., June 17, 1907, 90, 82.

36. Ibid., October 5, 1905, 58, 60.

37. Hattersley, *The Baganda at Home,* 60.

38. "Buganda Lukiiko," January 23, 1906, 10, 65.

39. Daudi Basudde to *Uganda Herald,* December 9, 1921, UNA A46 2288 (SMP 7258); I am grateful to Glenn McKnight for this reference, missing in the UNA in 1995. The vast amounts of food required along Hoima and Mubendi roads led eventually to the establishment of special farms for supplying the food, but prices were kept low. At one camp on Hoima Road, in Kisimbili, 1,319 loads of food had been supplied in 1910, at a rate of one cent (one one-hundredth of a rupee) per average-sized bundle of cooked food. All the food required for feeding 1,500 men would not have paid enough for one person's poll tax. A46/422 SMP 1138 A, "Buganda Annual Report, 1910–1911."

40. A. R. Morgan, "Uganda's Cotton Industry: Fifty Years Back," *Uganda Journal* 22:2 (1958): 110.

41. Lukiiko to Paulo Mukwenda, "Buganda Lukiiko," October 2, 1905, 59.

42. Bell, *A Governor's Life,* 132.

43. Ibid.

44. Sir Albert Cook, "Further Memories of Uganda," *Uganda Journal* 2 (1935): 97–115, 104.

45. Hansen, *Mission, Church, and State,* 190; Powesland, *Economic Policy and Labour,* 9; Renee Louise Tantala, "Ganda Households and the Colonial Economy (1900–1939)," unpublished paper.

46. H. P. Gale, *Uganda and the Mill Hill Fathers* (London: Macmillan, 1959), 214.

47. Cooper, the provincial commissioner, enclosed the missionary's letter in his annual report, but added his own comments: the statement could not be taken seriously, was undoubtedly not the opinion of the mission in general, and not worthy of the Church Missionary Society. "What is required out here is practical religion such as is preached

by some of the finest men in the Church of England which teaches a man to work not only for his own good but for the good of his country, the people out here are only just beginning to learn that work is necessary and healthy for every man and that idleness is akin to immorality." He added his hope that the mission would support the government's implementation of kasanvu labor so the country "would advance" and "the moral tone of its people would be improved." UNA A46/421 (SMP 1138), "Buganda Annual Report for 1909–1910."

48. UNA A46/429 (SMP 1138 G), "Buganda: Annual Report for 1916–1917."

49. Mair, *An African People,* 111.

50. "Buganda Lukiiko," June 15, 1915, 173.

51. Hansen, *Mission, Church, and State,* 209.

52. Powesland, *Economic Policy and Labour,* 23.

53. Hansen, *Mission, Church, and State,* 193.

54. Raymond Leslie Buell, *The Native Problem in Africa* (1928; reprint, London: Frank Cass, 1965), 584.

55. In 1914 the Lukiiko decided that men who were absent from their permanent employment for more than three days would be sent to work kasanvu. "Buganda Lukiiko," April 1914, 112.

56. Powesland, *Economic Policy and Labour,* 25.

57. Ibid., 21, 42, 37; Powesland, "History of the Migration," 21, 30.

58. Erinama Sebanditira, personal communication.

59. *Ebifa* December 1925: 301–302. I am grateful to Mikael Karlstrom for this and the following references from *Munno.*

60. "How Single Women Living Alone Spoil People's Homes," *Munno* January 1927: 7–18; see also *Munno* September 1931: 144.

61. Powesland, "History of the Migration," 20.

62. Ibid., 38–39; Mair, *An African People,* 95.

63. Hattersley, *The Baganda at Home,* 109.

64. Buell, *Native Problem,* 624.

65. "Buganda Lukiiko," July 10, 1905, 40; "Buganda Lukiiko," July 17, 1905, 41; "Buganda Lukiiko," July 24, 1905, 48.

66. Ibid., September 4, 1905, 56.

67. Lwabaka Nambi to Kaggwa, November 11, 1909, CB 14, Kaggwa Papers.

68. "Buganda Lukiiko," January 8, 1916, 188–189.

69. Ibid., March 16, 1916, 206.

70. Wrigley, *Crops and Wealth,* 53.

71. Powesland, "History of the Migration," 18.

72. Hattersley, *The Baganda at Home,* 113–114.

73. Hansen, *Mission, Church, and State,* 272; Bell, *Native Problem,* 201.

74. "Buganda Lukiiko," February 14, 1905, 52; "Buganda Lukiiko," March 23, 1908, 100; "Buganda Lukiiko," October 9, 1914, 130; "Buganda Lukiiko," January 12, 1915, 148; among others.

75. Ibid., October 2, 1914, 126.

76. Miti, "A History," 990.

77. Bell, *A Governor's Life,* 206.

78. Henry W. West, *Land Policy in Buganda* (Cambridge: Cambridge University Press, 1972), 5; Wrigley, "Changing Economic Structure," 32–33.

79. Ansorge, *Under the African Sun,* 92.

80. Twaddle, *Mind of Buganda,* 59–60.

81. Kaggwa to Bishop, February 25, 1910, CB 59, Kaggwa Papers.

82. "Buganda Lukiiko," 8 October 1914, 128.

83. Ibid., 131.

84. Ibid., February 10, 1916, 189.

85. Ibid., February 24, 1916, 197.

86. R. Cranford Pratt, "The Politics of Indirect Rule: Uganda, 1900–1955," in D. Anthony Low and R. Cranford Pratt, *Buganda and British Overrule, 1900–1955* (London: Oxford University Press, 1960), 199.

87. Atanda, "The Bakopi," 16.

88. "Buganda Lukiiko," July 18, 1917, 270.

89. Ibid., November 10, 1914, 132.

90. See, for example, Lukiiko Records, November 2, 1914, 135; April 11, 1915, 170; September 1, 1914, 117; September 3, 1914, 118–119; March 24, 1917, 249; June 23, 1917, 258–259.

91. "Buganda Lukiiko," February 15, 1917, 240.

92. Ibid., March 24, 1917, 247.

93. Mugwanya, the Chief Justice, said this to the Lukiiko when it had criticized him for making a heavy fine on a man who had made a European very angry. Ibid., June 26, 1905, 23.

94. UNA A46/425 (SMP 1138 F), "Buganda: Annual Report for 1915–1916."

95. In only one case in the Lukiiko records is the dismissal of a chief upheld. Disrespect for the Lukiiko, not failure to call forth labor, was the chief's error. Simioni Sebuta, who had been the mumyuka in Burulu, asked to be reinstated. According to Kaggwa, he had been rude to strangers, and he had once threatened to spear a Lukiiko representative. Defending himself, Sebuta said that the people had insulted him and he had already been fined one hundred rupees for the offenses. He asked the Kabaka for mercy, and the Kabaka promised to consider it. "Buganda Lukiiko," June 11, 1917, 260.

96. Ibid., December 1, 1914, 141.

97. Ibid., February 1, 1916, 190.

98. Ibid., March 24, 1917, 247.

99. Ibid., October 8, 1917, 131; April 28, 1908, 102; December 18, 1914, 142–143; March 2, 1915, 160; April 30, 1915, 169; May 1, 1917, 252.

100. Ibid., February 27, 1915, 159.

101. UNA A46/422 (SMP 1138 A), "Buganda Annual Report, 1910–1911."

102. "Buganda Lukiiko," September 27, 1909, 112.

103. Ibid., September 29, 1914, 124.

104. Ibid., February 24, 1916, 197.

105. Ibid., July 21, 1917, 270.

106. Buell, *Native Problem,* 581.

107. UNA A46/429 (SMP 1138), "Buganda: Annual Reports, 1916–1917." Michael Twaddle describes people's resentment of this transformation of chiefship in "The Bakungu Chiefs of Buganda Under British Colonial Rule, 1900–1930," *Journal of African History* 10 (1969): 314.

108. "Buganda Lukiiko," February 11, 1907, 76.

109. Ibid., January 28, 1908, 102.

110. West, *Land Policy,* 23.

111. Twaddle, "The Bakungu Chiefs," 314.

112. Hattersley, *The Baganda at Home,* 149, 95; Buell, *Native Problem,* 635.

113. Bell, *A Governor's Life,* 99, 114.

114. "Buganda Lukiiko," April 27, 1916, 218–219.

115. Ibid., July 10, 1905, 28/39 (two page numbers in text).

116. Ibid., April 1914, 114.

117. Hattersley, *The Baganda at Home,* 18.

118. "Buganda Lukiiko," June 5, 1905, 13.

119. Medard, "Croissance," 166–175; Treves, *Uganda for a Holiday,* 213; "Commission," Mikairi Kidza, 401.

120. Christine Obbo, "Food Sharing During Food Crisis: Case Studies from Uganda and Ciskei," in *Food Systems in Central and Southern Africa,* ed. Johan Pottier (London: School of Oriental and African Studies, 1985), 265. Mair says that people working for the kabaka in the capital "begged" for food, unless relatives sent it to them. Mair, *An African People,* 197.

121. Atanda, "Bakopi," 7. See also Hattersley, *The Baganda at Home,* 115–116.

122. "Buganda Lukiiko," September 16, 1907, 88.

123. UNA A46/421 (SMP 1138), "Buganda Annual Reports, 1909–1910."

124. UNA A46/745 (SMP 1148), "Buganda: Annual Reports, 1919–1920."

125. Hansen, *Mission, Church, and State,* 182–183.

126. Powesland, *Economic Policy and Labour,* 27.

127. "Buganda Lukiiko," March 9, 1915, 161; "Buganda Lukiiko," January 8, 1916, 188.

128. UNA A46/422 (SMP 1148), "Annual Report for Kampala District, 1910–1911."

129. Mair, *An African People,* 44, 50, 56–57, 59, 65.

130. Ibid., 43, 126.

131. Hattersley, *The Baganda at Home,* 115.

132. Mair, *An African People,* 276.

133. Kiwanuka, *History of Buganda,* 233.

134. Hattersley, *The Baganda at Home,* 185–186.

135. "Ekitabo kya Obusika, 1908–1923," Record of Succession of Members of Clans of Buganda, currently held in the Ministry of Justice, Kampala, Uganda, January 25, 1915, 127/10.

136. "Buganda Lukiiko," September 9, 1915, 180–182; "Buganda Lukiiko," March 10, 1916, 207.

137. Minutes of Meeting of Budo Board of Governors, March 9, 1929, AR KA 2/2, Box 2, File J, Kabali Papers.

138. Miti, "A History," 1889. Audrey Richards observes that the possibility of inheriting mailo land, and the increased value of land because of cash crops, strengthened the relationship of fathers and children at the expense of clan connections. Audrey I. Richards, *The Changing Structure of a Ganda Village* (Nairobi: East African Publishing House, 1966), 24–25.

139. AR KA 2/2, Box 2, File F, Kabali Papers.

140. Mugema to Chief Secretary, August 22, 1924, UNA A46/2214 (SMP 6902).

141. "The Will Which Concerns Butaka Mailo, How It Should Remain," December 16, 1920, AR KA 43/52, Kaggwa Papers.

142. Cook, "Further Memories," 111.

143. Hattersley, *The Baganda at Home,* 42; Mair, *An African People,* 144.

144. Hansen, *Mission, Church, and State,* 184, 186.

145. Annual Report of the Department of Land and Survey, paras. 71–73, quoted in Powesland, *Economic Policy and Labour,* 35. The notoriously conservative Land and Survey Department considered that the goal was "freedom from a landlord's exactions," but, as we have seen, one-fifth or one-sixth of the obligations of a tenant was to his landlord.

146. Daudi Basudde, quoted in Wrigley, *Crops and Wealth,* 52.

147. Powesland, *Economic Policy and Labour,* 11, 38–39; Audrey I. Richards, "Methods of Settlement in Buganda," in Richards, *Economic Development,* 121.

148. Powesland, "History of the Migration," 43, 44, 46. If Uganda had not had several governors who strongly advocated peasant production and an agricultural officer who had strong radical leanings, the outcome might have been very different. Wrigley, *Crops and Wealth,* 31.

149. Hattersley, *The Baganda at Home,* 167. Mair, *An African Kingdom,* 63–64.

150. "Buganda Lukiiko," September 29, 1914, 124.

151. Obbo, "Food Sharing," 270, 277.

152. Kaggwa, *Basekabaka,* trans. Musoke, 287.

153. "Buganda Lukiiko," April 8, 1908, 102; "Buganda Lukiiko," October 24, 1914, 134.

154. Ibid., March 11, 1916, 204.

155. Hansen, *Mission, Church, and State,* 178.

156. Powesland, *Economic Policy and Labour,* 27, 32.

7

THE ORDER OF MILES ON TRIAL

Twenty years after Ganda chiefs laid out a new order of power in Buganda in the shape of individually owned land, another group of Ganda leaders put the mailo order of things on trial, charging that miles had ruined the good customs of Buganda. As cash, tax, forced labor, and fines eroded the protective and sustaining capacities of chiefs and lineage networks, these Ganda leaders demanded a reallocation of land and power, a realignment of relations between rulers and followers, and an integration of Ganda forms of authority with the forms of "these Europeanized times." Argued from 1921 to 1926 in front of the kabaka, the Lukiiko, and British officials in Uganda and England, the case against mailo offers an unusually well-documented look at the ideas of Africans who experienced the coming of colonial rule as adults and who insisted that things ought to have been done differently.

The Baganda who made the case against mailo have been misunderstood from the beginning: the only part of their comprehensive critique that received a direct response was their request for the return of butaka (clan lands). The complainants were not only bataka (clan elders), but also royal women and royal men, spirit mediums, and people who had had institutionalized remembered relationships with the kabaka; in other words, all the kinds of people who had had authority in precolonial Buganda. In a series of protests that culminated in a colonial commission of inquiry, they asserted the superiority of Ganda forms of power over those created in 1900, and insisted that Ganda practices of reciprocal obligation could be integrated with British overrule in a way that would be beneficial for everyone. They made this comprehensive critique of colonial rule before a colonial commission of inquiry only because their way of speaking about power did not make sense to their British colonial listeners.

The Commission of Inquiry into Butaka Clan Lands encompassed a fundamental misunderstanding between Ganda and British participants. As Ganda intellectuals and leaders critiqued the current order using land as an idiom of political power, colonial commissioners listened, attending to "lost land" only as a question of rights to property. Most scholarly interpretations have understood the Butaka controversy as an attempt by clan elders to regain clan lands lost in 1900, and also as a personal attack on Katikkiro Apolo Kaggwa, but it was much more than this.[1] In the case against mailo, Ganda leaders debated with each other about the nature of power in Buganda in the past. In the letters exchanged with Protectorate officials and the Home Office, and in testimony before the commission of inquiry, Ganda thinkers engaged in a battle of ideas over progress and history. The people who brought the case against mailo made a sustained and penetrating critique of colonial modernity: they argued that unobligated, bureaucratic power undermined good government and that commodified social relations enslaved people.

In making their case the complainants simplified their arguments and misrepresented the social positions that they themselves had occupied. A complex conflict over power with diverse participants became, in terms that made sense to colonial observers, a fight between clan elders who had lost land and appointed chiefs who had taken land. At the time, Baganda who testified in the case might have seen the gap between who they were and who they said they were (for example, a lubaale priest describing himself as a clan elder) as an obvious but useful distortion. Later observers and scholars, however, have perceived the strategic, oversimplified positions of bataka clan elders versus bakungu chiefs as an accurate representation of social groups and conflicts in Buganda's past.

This chapter seeks to unfold this incisive, coherent critique of colonial power that has been perceived as a request for land by a group of retrograde clan elders and malcontents. The first section considers who participated in the Butaka agitation and how they themselves understood their actions. This group was not all clan elders and included some of Buganda's most highly placed and well-educated citizens. The second section examines the argument over the nature of power in the history of Buganda pursued by the attackers and defenders of mailo. The complainants in the case focused on forms of reciprocal obligation that had been eroded in the eighteenth and nineteenth centuries. The leading chiefs defending mailo argued that kabakas had exercised single, unitary power that was never challenged, similar in form to the power they themselves exercised under British protection. The third section examines the complainants critique of modernity: their concern that multiple forms of authority created better governance, that socially unconcerned property ownership created enslavement, and that true progress required a combination of Ganda practices of power with new things from Europe.

THE BATAKA COMPLAINANTS AND THEIR CASE

The people who assembled to make the case against mailo were men and women, royals and peasants, elder statesmen from precolonial Buganda and their school-educated sons. Two had been ssaza chiefs for more than twenty years each. Some held the highest possible positions for Africans in the Protectorate hierarchy, while others had had little contact with foreigners. Some had been granted large estates of mailo, some had lost their land and been reduced to doing menial labor service for new chiefs. They were Protestants, Catholics, and Malakites, and a few held positions of authority in Ganda spiritual practices.[2]

James Miti was the highest-ranking employee of the Protectorate to participate in the case against mailo, and he served as its public representative whenever he was able to be present in Buganda. He was head of the Genet clan and had been a rising Protestant chief when he was chosen to consolidate British/Ganda control over the neighboring kingdom of Bunyoro with George Wilson in 1901. Miti, along with Wilson, designed and implemented the policy of using Ganda chiefly titles in the administration of other native kingdoms. Miti represented the quintessential success of the Ganda/British partnership: he governed effectively, devoted himself to the Church of Uganda, and entertained the members of European royalty who traveled to western Uganda on hunting safaris. He used his knowledge of British colonial culture and his status within it to position the mailo complainants as loyal Protectorate citizens: his visible participation may have been part of what motivated Protectorate officials to take the case against mailo seriously.[3]

Miti had lost his clan's butaka land in a case that stunned people because of its bizarre injustice. Miti left his clan land in 1893 at the time when Catholics took over the area, and Stanislaus Mugwanya, the Catholic katikkiro, assigned the land to Namawanja, who claimed to be a member of the proper branch of the Genet clan. But Namawanja was not actually a person who had the right within the clan to hold the butaka land, and Miti succeeded between 1894 and 1896 in reobtaining the land from Kabaka Mwanga. The case was brought in front of the Lukiiko, and Miti won again, but nothing was done to cause the decision in his favor to be reflected in documents at the Land Registry Office. In 1909 the case was brought up for a third time, because (according to Miti), the Catholic regent Stanislaus Mugwanya was insulted at the treatment he was receiving from Apolo Kaggwa, and wanted to take revenge on a Protestant.[4] This time, Namawanja said that because the certificates had been made out in his name, the land was his. Miti argued that the kabaka had decided in his favor, the Lukiiko had decided in his favor, and so had the High Court. Public opinion was with Miti: the land had been assigned to be the clan butaka, Miti was the head of the clan, and the land was morally his. If the Lukiiko invalidated the land certificates for Miti's butaka, however, everyone's certificates might be called into question. In the end, after one month of deliberation, the Lukiiko came to the conclusion that the Genet clan land belonged to the person whose name was written on the certificate. Miti explained to the Commission of Inquiry that "on the strength of my own grievances and in conjunction with the grievances of my fellow bataka we assembled together and decided to bring up our case together."[5]

Daudi Basudde was one of the most articulate spokesmen for the case against mailo: he used his newspapers *Sekanyolya* and *Matalisi* to promote it, and his letter to the English-language *Uganda Herald* attracted the attention of then secretary of state for the colonies Winston Churchill.[6] Protectorate officials described Basudde as someone who, because of his education and "modern thinking," became frustrated with members of Buganda's old guard like Apolo Kaggwa, but Basudde's role as a social critic was much more complex. He was the grand-nephew of Gabulieri Mujasi, who had amassed considerable personal power as an ekitongole chief during Kabaka Mwanga's reign, had gained a reputation for bellicosity during the late-nineteenth-century upheavals, and had led Mwanga's revolt against the British in 1897. Basudde's father, Antoni Muyimba, had joined his uncle, Gabulieri Mujasi, fighting on Mwanga's side, and consequently lost twelve square miles of mailo.[7] Basudde's deft use of English and public relations skills struck Protectorate officers as something quite new, but he was actually the third generation in his family to protest against the forms of power that developed in Buganda with the coming of the British.

The leaders of the case against mailo included a range of people who defy classification in neat dichotomies of traditional or modern, collaborators or resisters, old or young. One was the private secretary to the kabaka, Shem Spire Mukasa, the well-educated son of Kangaawo, the ssaza chief of Bulemeezi. When Shem Spire compared the socially destructive selfishness of the regents to "the Kaiser's game" in Europe, his fellow members of the Bataka community stopped the proceedings of the commission to ask for translation into Luganda.[8] His father, Samwiri Mukasa, was one of the most prominent Christian chiefs in Buganda. As the kangaawo and acting katikkiro, Samwiri Mukasa had actually made some of the mailo allocation decisions while Kaggwa was out of Buganda in 1902, but in the case against mailo his testimony benefited the complainants rather than the regents.[9] Serwano Kulubya, another school-educated young man and one of the secretaries of the Bataka association, became a muluka chief in 1923 and a ggombolola chief in 1924.[10] He was the official translator for the commission of inquiry. Yuda Musa Musoke, on the other hand, was a mituba clan leader who communicated with the provincial commissioner and governor in long, eloquent letters in Luganda legalese that overwhelmed the Protectorate's translators. Malaki Musajakawa testified in the case and also signed several important communications: he was a charismatic spiritual leader who attracted so many followers to Mugema's breakaway church (see below) that its popular name became Bamalaki, meaning "the people of Malaki."[11]

The most important instigator of the case against mailo, whose prestige and structural position in Buganda demonstrated the great importance of the case, was Joswa Kate Mugema. He was head of the Monkey clan, chief of Busiro province, and the person who had had the most independent authority in relation to the kabaka. The mugema was "father of the kabaka," and "katikkiro" of all the kabakas of the past, whose tombs and shrines were in Busiro. Joswa Kate exercised his responsibility as guardian of the power of kabakas from the beginning of British involvement in Buganda. He had the nickname "Semusota" (snake) because he had put Kabaka Mwanga in an impossible position in 1897 when he refused to accept the "East and Central Africa Medal," which Queen Victoria wanted to bestow on a few high-ranking Baganda. Mwanga could not force Mugema to accept the award from the queen, thus maintaining the fiction that all the Baganda approved of British overrule, because Mugema was his ritual parent.[12] Mugema had refused to sign the Uganda Agreement in 1900; he was the only ssaza chief to take this stance. In 1912, Mugema had complained to the provincial commissioner about Apolo Kaggwa's attempt to create a Ganda equivalent of the House of Lords.[13] Joswa Kate Mugema rejected European medicine, claiming that to use it demonstrated lack of faith in God. Although Mugema explained his assertive rejection of European medicine in biblical terms, it harmonized with his role of protecting the kabaka's position and, by extension, Ganda forms of knowledge. Mugema was an effective chief, appreciated by both his people and British administrators, with a reputation for generosity and selflessness.[14]

Joswa Kate Mugema's most significant actions came in response to the attempts by Apolo Kaggwa and Protectorate officials to stage events focused on Kabaka Daudi Cwa. Placed on the throne as an infant when Kabaka Mwanga rose against the British in 1897, Daudi Cwa had been useful as a nonking when the leading Ganda chiefs and their British allies asserted control of Buganda. At a time when the lives of ordinary Baganda were challenged by overwhelming burdens on their labor and a deteriorating standard of living, the colonial government attempted to maintain people's loyalty by new versions of the practice of "showing" the king. Mugema fought bitterly with Kaggwa over the form for the ritual of the "coronation" of Cwa in 1910. That year he broke with the Church of Uganda and established his own alternative, Katonda Omu Ayinza Byona ("those of God who can do all things").[15] His church emphasized belief in the power of God, disavowed the use of medicine, and did not discriminate against the illiterate and poor. Ninety-one thousand Baganda had enrolled by 1921.[16] Joswa Kate, who had been chief of the ssaza of Busiro for more than twenty years, was forced to resign his

ssaza chiefship in 1919 because of his stand against colonial medical practice. He retained his position as mugema, head of the Monkey clan, and
"father" of the kabaka. A serious invention of tradition ensued, as a ssaza chief
for Busiro had to be appointed who was not head of the Monkey clan—the
new title invented for the new chief could not cover up the repudiation of the
order of the kingdom this represented.[17] Joswa Kate's church offered people
new religion without aspects he considered to be European impositions: his
efforts catalyzing the case against mailo also offered the possibility of an integration of Ganda forms of authority with the needs of the present.

Four years after the 1910 "coronation" that precipitated Mugema's schism,
Kabaka Daudi Cwa came into his majority with another improvised ritual. The
new order of power in Buganda was dramatized as homage was paid to the
king, in an event given a colonial gloss by the presence of representatives of
the missionary societies and Protectorate government officials in dress uni-
forms. First came the prime minister, then the ssaza and ggombolola chiefs,
then the male members of the royal family, and last the female members of
the royal family.[18] A generation or two earlier, the substantial autonomous
authority of the nnamasole (queen mother) would have kept her out of the
king's presence and princes would have been banished from the court to prevent coalitions of chiefs using them to mount rebellions.[19] Clan elders and
spiritually powerful individuals would have been present among those with
authority. Chiefs would not have been a group with identical responsibilities
and status in distinct geographical units, but a network of people with overlapping roles and statuses. Kabaka Daudi Cwa, as a seventeen-year-old monarch, could accept the obeisance of the new equivalent of "all of Buganda,"
but he could not function as the center of the web of connections that had been
his kingdom in the past. The flow of goods, actions, and prestige that defined
relationships in the nation had been disrupted by long-distance trade and enslavement, and undermined by cash wages, forced labor, and taxation. The
many figures of authority who supported him had been replaced by newly
defined hierarchies of ssaza, ggombolola, and miruka chiefs. These administrators knelt to young Kabaka Cwa, but they collected taxes that went to the
Protectorate and received salaries that came from Entebbe.

Intense, convoluted struggles for power at the top of the Ganda hierarchy
characterized the years immediately following Cwa's coming of age. Protectorate officials tried to use the period of transition to replace older Ganda
chiefs with more pliable young men. Kaggwa, Mugwanya, and Kisingiri became "the three ministers" instead of "the regents," and they maneuvered to
maintain the power that they had held in the name of the king. The young
kabaka tried to assert his authority over these ministers, and against the provincial commissioner and the governor. For several years it appeared that
Apolo Kaggwa was winning and the kabaka was losing in these struggles.

Kaggwa had even reprimanded the kabaka in front of the ssaza chiefs and had not been punished.[20] The kabaka was also humiliated by the British. In 1920 the "three ministers" attempted to undermine each other in a case that began when the new treasurer, Musajalumbwa, flogged a worker who then appealed to Mugwanya, the chief justice. The British used the case as an excuse to alter the structure of Ganda government at the top. Kabaka Daudi Cwa became angry, because he believed that changing the structure of the Ganda hierarchy was his prerogative. When the kabaka protested to the governor, he was told to accept the new arrangement. Mugwanya, who had held the highest office in Buganda after Prime Minister Kaggwa, resigned in protest in December 1920.[21]

The furor over land of the early 1920s can be understood only in the context of these struggles over power: the timing of the case against mailo was completely logical in Ganda terms. The potential for conflict inherent in the early years of a reign was enshrined in the installation ritual, in which the kabaka fought a mock battle while ascending Budo hill. As John Rowe has pointed out, young kabakas often had to struggle to free themselves from the influence of the katikkiros who had put them in power.[22] Offering or returning land to groups who had fallen out of favor at some earlier time was one strategy available to kabakas in consolidating their rule. In the context of Cwa's obvious lack of power in relation to the katikkiro and the Protectorate, the case against mailo offered Kabaka Cwa an opportunity to assert himself using an ultimately meaningful idiom of power over people in Buganda—the allocation of land.

Joswa Kate Mugema acted in his capacity as "father" of the reigning kabaka and prime minister for the dead kabakas when he mobilized people to make the case against mailo. In November 1921 he wrote to "all my friends, the Bataka who were robbed of their clan estates in Buganda," calling them to a meeting in January to discuss the issue of butaka, "as our king, whose coming of age we have hitherto been waiting for, has now attained his majority." According to Miti, this meeting had to be postponed because of poor attendance, but on the second attempt, on January 27, 1922, "a record number of men and women" gathered to discuss the issue, make contributions, and choose secretaries.[23] Kaggwa tried to have Daudi Basudde arrested for collecting an illegal tax, but the provincial commissioner ruled that voluntary contributions to the Bataka cause were acceptable.

The form of the appeal made by Mugema, Miti, and the rest of "the Bataka Federation" is a key to understanding its meaning. When they asked Kabaka Daudi Cwa to address the land issue in 1922, they asked him to hear a case: "We, your Bataka . . . pray you most humbly to kindly consent to hear mercifully to the following our complaints which we are representing before you."[24] When the same group took the case to the colonial authorities, they

spoke of "the points in dispute ... which we would like His Britannic
Majesty's Government to decide."[25] The regents who had made the mailo allocation clearly saw themselves as defendants in a case against them. Apolo
Kaggwa wrote to all the ssaza chiefs on March 4, 1922, that a "great event"
had taken place in the Lukiiko: "Chiefs Mugema and Jemusi Miti in company
with all the bataka had us tried on a charge of having distributed the mailo
land badly by giving large shares to our friends and to our children."[26]

The forms and processes of okusala omusango (cutting cases) incorporate
the motivations that observers have attributed to the Bataka Federation (so
named although not all its members were bataka) as well as the goals that they
themselves articulated. The disputed issue in the case was control of land, and
the large incomes landowners were obtaining from tithes on cash crops produced
by their tenants has to be considered a factor in the case: some of the bataka
complainants may have been seeking rents. The leaders of the bataka, however,
were already very large landowners. Okusala omusango was a mechanism
through which competing Ganda chiefs had ascertained their relative power; the
case against mailo sought to right the wrong of lost lands, to diminish Kaggwa's
prestige, and to realign power relationships in the kingdom.

The young king responded to the opportunity organized by Mugema and
the so-called Bataka Federation to assert his authority by reallocating land.
He heard arguments presented by thirty-five heads of clans and counter-
arguments by Apolo Kaggwa and Stanislaus Mugwanya, the surviving regents,
for one week in March 1922. On June 6, 1922, Cwa gave his decision that
some of the bataka land had been unjustly taken and ought to be returned. He
determined that the majority of the clans were still in possession of their
most important (kasolya) butaka, although they had lost part of the land related to them. Some of the clans' secondary (massiga) butaka had been taken
by chiefs claiming land, and all of the land that had been given by a kabaka
to a specific person had been lost. He instructed the Lukiiko to figure out a
way to give the land back. Apolo Kaggwa was obviously frightened, as he
wrote to the governor that the Bataka's action set "a very unfavorable pre-
cedent" that might undermine the prestige of the native government.[27]

Over the next few months people waited to see whether Kaggwa would
surrender the authority that belonged to the king. People stopped cultivating
land that they feared might change hands.[28] The governor called together
Kaggwa and the other ministers, the ssaza and some ggombolola chiefs, and
lectured them on solving their own problems.[29] Daudi Cwa began to make
individual land decisions, and the Lukiiko ignored them.[30] The first turning
point in the case against mailo came when the Lukiiko refused the kabaka's
request to return land to the bataka in 1922. Kaggwa emphasized his humili-
ating defeat of the kabaka and his supporters by drafting a bill that allowed
the sale of butaka to strangers after the land had first been offered to clan

members, and allowing clan elders to live on clan land as long as they behaved as respectful, obedient servants of their landlord.[31] Kaggwa's victory exposed a process that had begun a half century before when his predecessors began to trade and amass wealth independently of Kabaka Muteesa. The loss of the kabaka's power to Kaggwa, which had been neatly hidden by the regency, was now perfectly obvious. The degree to which the new power of the katikkiro obscured a permanent loss of power to the "Protecting Power" had yet to be fully demonstrated.

The kabaka's failure to restore their butaka land did not cause people to lose confidence in the power of their king. Nor did they blame their frustration and distress on the deepening Protectorate presence in Buganda. Instead, the Ganda leaders of the case against mailo asked the colonial government to restore order in Buganda by putting everyone back in their proper place. In streams of letters to Entebbe, the Bataka Federation and a splinter organization of massiga bataka asked that the government hear the case and settle it in their favor, against the allocators of mailo.[32] The governor initially tried to scold the Baganda for not solving their own problems and insisted that the issue had to be resolved by the native government, but the outpouring of articulate protest from the leaders of the Bataka movement to their friends in England and to important figures in the home government eventually forced the Protectorate authorities to capitulate. After some discussion of what form the intervention should take, the decision was finally made to hold a commission of inquiry in Buganda in April 1924.

In the first phase of their case, the bataka had called upon the king to act justly and reallocate land. In the second phase, they specifically asked the British government to restore Ganda forms of government in order to allow the kabaka to govern. The booklet they published in English to influence public opinion explained:

> [U]nder the 1900 Treaty our Kabaka's time honoured and immemorial prerogative of being himself an adjudicator in disputes and allotter of unoccupied land has been destroyed, further because our native kingdoms and its land policy and social economy were inseparable connected with the preservation of our native system of land tenure, and since all these were changed and since the Government failure to comprehend our indigenous social views on the land question, we find the consequences to have led to much misunderstanding and our Native Government is now falling to pieces.[33]

The failure of the new forms of authority and the necessity of incorporating old ones formed the basis of the case that the Bataka brought to the Protectorate Commission of Inquiry in 1924.

The Uganda police provided a hundred-man Guard of Honor when the Commission of Inquiry first met on April 10, 1924. The two commissioners, Provincial Commissioner Sturrock and Chief Justice Griffin, were greeted with a salute of guns and music by the King's African Rifles Band, and then opening speeches were made in front of "distinguished Government personages."[34]

Colonial support for a critique of colonial rule happened because Baganda made statements about injustice and power that their British listeners heard as statements about injustice and land ownership; if the Protectorate authorities had followed the implications of the arguments on Ganda terms, it is unlikely that the argument could have been made on a public stage. The gap between Ganda and British meanings for butaka can be traced all the way through the case against mailo. Bataka complained that they "virtually became peasants," a statement that encapsulated a loss of authority and status as well as land; but it was understood as only a complaint about lost land.[35] Daudi Basudde described the ceremonies of asking for and receiving a barkcloth tree to mark the creation of subclans, a ritual that, like the opening of the British parliament, defined political relationships through actions, not written words. What the colonial officers understood from his description, however, was that the barkcloth trees marked the ownership of the land.[36] Butaka had the array of meanings for Ganda leaders that "the crown" had for British officers, but throughout the case against mailo, the British responded to something smaller; as if the Baganda were calling for a restoration of "the crown" and intending only the return of a piece of elaborate jewelry.

ARGUING ABOUT THE HISTORY OF POWER IN BUGANDA

While British listeners thought they were hearing a case about ownership of graveyards, the participants argued with each other about the nature of power in Buganda in the past. The terms of the debate were set on the first day of testimony when Prince Kyamagwa accused Apolo Kaggwa of disinterring a kabaka in order to solidify his claim to land.[37]

> [H]e made us unbury the bones of the dead, our relatives the princes and princesses who died a long time ago and he drove them away from those butaka villages which he had finished snatching. And he did not stop with those bones only, but there were the bones of a Kabaka (king) himself which he removed from the grave. The words we say are that it can never be forgotten in Buganda.[38]

Kaggwa was given an opportunity to cross-examine the prince, who then made his condemnation even more specific:

Kaggwa: The skull [of Kabaka Tebendeke, eighteenth king of the Buganda dynasty] you are talking about was buried in the grave and I removed it?

Prince: You ripped it out of the place where it had been for all those years and you removed it.

Commissioner: Did you put it outside?

Prince: You told us "You put it in another place you want, I have taken the land."[39]

Kaggwa had not in fact done the abominable thing of which he was accused; he had not unburied the skull of a kabaka, nor had he told people he did not care what happened to it as long as he owned the land.[40] Prince Kyamagwa's testimony evoked memories of an actual event in 1906, when Kaggwa had unburied the bones of Grasshopper clan elders (and incurred the anger of both Ganda and British authorities).[41] The accusation of an unthinkable crime, with resonances in a reprehensible act that people remembered well, made the claim that mailo land had utterly violated the order of the kingdom, physically embodied in the jawbone shrines of deceased kings. The defense put forth by Kaggwa and Mugwanya, the other former regent, was that the mailo allocation conformed to Ganda practices and expressed the dignity and power of kabakaship. Both sides grounded their arguments in Ganda history and ignored dimensions of that history that did not suit them. The conflict was not about tradition versus progress (everyone wanted progress), or about the presence of the British (everyone said the queen had been on their side in 1900). The real issue was what actions maintained the honor and dignity of Buganda.

The essence of the regents' defense in the case against mailo was that the absolute power that the victorious chiefs had drawn to themselves in the nineteenth-century upheavals and in their collaboration with the British was actually the kabaka's power. Mailo was merely the newest manifestation of a normal Ganda practice: "it was the usual custom for the Kabaka to change about people's butaka land and give it to other people; following this custom the Regents in the name of the Kabaka distributed all estates among the chiefs and people whether butaka or not."[42] The regents emphasized the strand of Ganda political thought that recognized the role of a strong ruler in curbing competition. However, they attributed to all kabakas the unobligated power kings had achieved when Semakookiro began the practice of killing princes at the end of the eighteenth century: "the Kabaka had power to give or deprive any butaka land, and to create any chieftainship or discharge anyone from his chieftainship, and to kill any people, chiefs, or bataka, or to raid them." This was an accurate description of kabakas' relationship to other figures of authority for the past century, but Kaggwa and Mugwanya's letter to Kabaka Cwa told the whole history of Buganda in terms of land being taken from "bataka" and given to "chiefs," "warriors," and other clients of kings. This remembered history left out the stories of kabakas backing down as a result of pressure from chiefs, or any sense that figures below the kabaka took any action but submission. In their version of history, the king, like the ruling chiefs under the British, could not be challenged: "the Kabaka had every power to do whatever he liked with any kind of land."[43]

The leaders of the case against mailo argued that kabakas had exercised power in interaction with other authority figures, and that the mailo agreement undermined the kabaka's power to create and realign relationships. They claimed that a kabaka's action in taking land away was always followed by that kabaka or another one giving the land back. Complainants referred to the proverb "The Mutaka is a cockroach which does not die in the smoke" to prove people could make the kabaka respond to their wishes. Basudde explained that

> as soon as a Mutaka was deprived of his butaka land, he together with the other bataka of the same clan would at once appeal to the Kabaka for the restoration of their butaka land; and if that particular Kabaka would not hear them they would wait till that Kabaka died and would then appeal to his successor. Any particular Kabaka who attempted to seize butaka lands his reign was never peaceful or prosperous. Moreover the mode of deprivation of butaka land of the old days is not the same as the present one brought about by the introduction of the "mailo" system of land tenure. . . . [T]his new method of depriving the bataka of their butaka lands brought about by the "mailo system is absolutely final."[44]

This view of the past ignored memories of clans driven underground through an angry kabaka's persecution: it is true that people fought back and destabilized the reigns of kings who took their land, but they did not always win.

Jemusi Biriko pursued the difference between the mailo allocation and a kabaka's allocation, explaining that the Lukiiko under Kaggwa refused to hear appeals

> because it had already decided to destroy the customs of our country of Buganda, and had deprived the Kabaka of his estates and us the bataka of our butaka lands. All the Kabaka's estates had already been taken away from [him] and given to other people, such as the estates in Kisalosalo, and Kibulusi and Kiwuliriza; and the whole of the Kibuga had been divided up among them. The counties had been divided into two parts, one part consisting of the official estates of the Saza Chiefs and the other part the private estates of the Chiefs, whereas in the old days the whole of the County consisted one form of land tenure and that was the official estates of the Native Government.[45]

Reigning kabakas had previously demonstrated their authority by creating new ebitongole chiefships, such as those Biriko mentioned, but mailo prevented kabakas from restructuring the order of the country.

The Bataka framed their case in a way that pointed to the regents' failure to fulfill the just intentions of the British. They continually argued that the Uganda Agreement, in paragraph 15, stated that everyone was to receive the miles that he possessed at that time. "The representatives of the Good Queen Victoria made the agreement to certify that every one shall remain on his land of which he was in possession at that time."[46] The problem, they said, came when the regents misrepresented the Agreement in order to take all the land for themselves. Kaggwa and Mugwanya claimed that the Bataka community could not blame the regents for changing the customs of Buganda, "since the country was already in a state of chaos due to the Civil Wars, change of the Kabakas and other circumstances." They specifically stated in their own defense that the mailo allocation had expressed a new order of power: "the allotment of land at that time was not subject to the native custom of the clan system of Buganda, but was mainly for the benefit of the principal chiefs." They claimed, however, that their actions in making the mailo allocation had restored butaka to the clans: "It was only the Lukiko which took into consideration the system of butaka land tenure when the allotment of land was being made, and revived this ancient custom which had become obsolete due to the Civil Wars which were then raging in the country brought about by the religious frictions."[47] Both sides claimed Queen Victoria as their ally and accused their opponents of destabilizing social order through destructive self-interest.

Both critics and defenders of mailo encapsulated their arguments about the nature of power in Buganda in narratives concerning the writing that appeared on land certificates. According to some of the massiga bataka, the most powerful chiefs had told people applying for mailo to write "this is my old butaka land" on their applications. This was wholly wrong, the massiga bataka complained, because the land they were asking for had not been their butaka, it had been land they received because they were chiefs. Naming the land in the wrong way, in writing on the certificate, subverted the authority of the kabaka, who ought to have been able to give the land out as he chose. It also detracted from the station of the true bataka. They wanted all the land certificates with the inscription "this is my old butaka land" to be changed to read "this is my old chieftainship land."[48] Their complaint about the writing on land certificates encapsulated many of the arguments in the case against mailo: the new order had deprived essential figures of their place; it had undermined the kabaka's ability to regulate and shape his kingdom, and it had caused people who held power to wield it in an arbitrary and unjust manner, which they would not have done if they feared the kabaka could remove them by giving their land and position to someone else.

Kaggwa and Mugwanya also explained the fundamental meaning and consequences of mailo with a story about what was supposed to be written on land certificates. The regents defended themselves by saying that the Lukiiko's power to give out land came from the 1900 Agreement, "which contains such good provisions which maintain peace and guard our nation, and which have enlarged Buganda considerably."[49] In their story, the legitimacy of all the remembered relationships that had explained land allocation in the past had been specifically disavowed. Instead, at the instructions of the British Protectorate, legitimate authority to grant land was to reside in the Lukiiko. According to Kaggwa and Mugwanya, the chief Jemusi Kisule Kajugujwa had written on his claim for mailo, "This estate is my butaka land, it was given to me by Kabaka Mawanda!" The British government authorities refused to approve the land allocation because the chief had claimed the land from the time of a kabaka living two centuries earlier. The Protectorate authorities told the chief to make a new inscription on the top of the certificate: "This is my Butaka land, given to me by the Lukiko!"[50] Apolo Kaggwa and Stanislaus Mugwanya argued that the changes brought by the British had been beneficial, and that the mailo allocation followed Ganda custom. They claimed that the regents had acted in the name of the kabaka, giving the land to powerful chiefs as kabakas had always done in the past, and that the mailo allocation had actually restored the status of bataka that had been confused by the civil war. Kaggwa and Mugwanya argued that their opponents were disloyal: "it is well known in Buganda as well as in other nations that he who despises the Kabaka's representative despises the Kabaka himself."[51]

The intentions of the British in negotiating the Uganda Agreement and the consequences of more than twenty years of British overrule appeared to be irrelevant in the debate, which the participants framed around contradictory claims regarding how kabakas had ruled the kingdom. Each side used the remembered history of the kingdom selectively and strategically. The Bataka complainants disregarded the severe loss of agency most Baganda suffered as social order deteriorated with the wars of expansion; the regents ignored any moment in Ganda history when kabakas had been forced to compromise.

A CRITIQUE OF COLONIAL MODERNITY

The people who brought the case against mailo argued that the 1900 Agreement undermined the patterns of reciprocal obligation that made Buganda great. Writing to Kabaka Cwa in 1922, they explained that when the regents allocated mailo,

> they upset everything and as the results of that mistake caused the present
> ill feeling which exists among our people as a whole, shattering also our

country from its former foundation and destroying all our good customs of helping and loving each other, thus putting us under a form of Government which we cannot understand. We feel as if we were under the hybrid customs.[52]

Shem Spire Mukasa, the private secretary to the kabaka, summarized the case to the commission of inquiry two years later using the same logical connection between mailo land and social well-being:

Our main points of contention in this dispute are as follows:

1. The first one is that we have been deprived of our Butaka estates, and this point is the direct cause of the second point which is this:
2. That the native customs which are the guardian of the importance and prestige of our nation have been entirely destroyed.[53]

Good government, they said, required love, which entailed more contributors to the process of decisionmaking and greater social responsibility.

The leaders of the case against mailo asked for a return of the complex, multiple structures of power that had characterized Buganda in the past. In their original appeal, they asked Kabaka Daudi Cwa to return land to those who had held it in 1900; implicit in that request was a return of the authority associated with control over land. "What we request is to put each and every individual back within his old boundaries known up to the present day." In their appeal to the kabaka, the complainants mentioned land that had been associated with powerful figures in Buganda that was not butaka land: the royal marketplace in the kibuga, the land of Ganda deities on Bussi and Buganga Islands, estates belonging to the kabaka, "which they knew very well that from time ever immemorial had never been alienated by anybody else," and the estates of princes and princesses.[54] The Bataka community made their claims for a return of power more explicit as the case progressed. Daudi Basudde and Yuda Musoke informed the chief secretary that the purposes of the National (Buganda) Federation of Bataka included "to make a new start to put our butaka on a proper footing such as it was before H.M. Government came to Buganda," and "to restore our clans to the position they used to hold and that every clan should send its representative to speak for it in the chief judicial assembly of our nation as used to be the custom."[55]

The hierarchy of chiefs had been drastically streamlined by the British Protectorate as it strove to implement what it considered to be efficient administration. Thirty or forty years previously, chains of chiefs of different ranks had collected taxes and apportioned shares among themselves in complicated ways before passing the rest on to the capital. "All of Buganda" had consisted of a complex and layered system of people holding many different ranks, in which one individual often held more than one position. Some people in this system derived authority from their clan positions; some held one of a variety of forms of royal status; some had unique positions of power that had been created by the gift of a kabaka in the past; others had been appointed by the reigning kabaka or his predecessor. How these figures ranked in relation to each other had been subject to negotiation, and varied according to the relative strength of different components at any moment in time.[56] It was not, as observers have imagined, a simple situation in which those appointed by the kabaka sat at the top of hierarchies of people with ancient clan positions. The thousands of people who participated in this multilayered structure of government had been rationalized into a much smaller structure composed of three tiers of ssaza, ggombolola, and miruka chiefs.[57] By the 1920s, thousands of positions of authority had been eliminated.

Some of the people who testified in the case against mailo had been cut out of power: but not all of them had been clan leaders, although that is how they defined themselves before the commission of inquiry. Juma Omawanyi's experience demonstrates the narrowing space of authority in Buganda. Omawanyi had controlled about a square mile of land as part of his office as tailor to the kabaka; he was "the Kabaka's man." This minor office did not entitle him to receive mailo, so he became the "private man" of Mugwanya and was ordered to work on his dhow. He said, "I do not quite know the actual date when this took place, as I cannot count." He accused Mugwanya of rejecting his request to be given mailo: "It was you yourself [Mugwanya] who called us to give us miles, but when I came before you, you did not even deign to look at me but said that if you gave us miles where would you find people to rule over."[58] Omawanyi's story suggests that his land had been a form of obwesengeze—land granted to mark a particular relationship with the kabaka, rather than butaka—land that marked the identity of clans. That Omawanyi and others called themselves bataka when they had actually held land in other capacities demonstrates the loss of locations of power that had taken place in Buganda. Ganda society no longer had a place for someone who had authority over other people because of the particular work they performed for the kabaka: if they were not chiefs acknowledged by the Protectorate government, the only position that could explain their status was clan eldership.

Even priests asked for the restoration of the land that had been dedicated to their lubaale deities by calling themselves bataka. The principal medium of the lubaale Musisi appealed to the Protectorate authorities for a return of his land, although—perhaps because his land had been taken by Mugema— he did not participate in the case against mailo. In 1924, he wrote:

> I lost my position at the hands of the three Regents, and not at the Kabaka's.
> I asked . . . the reason for my dismissal, but they could not give it. Along

with my dismissal from my position, my principal Butaka estate known as Guludene was also taken from me. . . . What new commands have been substituted by God authorizing the usurpation of our Butaka lands whilst they (the ministers) had their own Butaka estates which had not been taken away from them?[59]

Guggu, the priest of the shrine of the lubaale Mukasa, testified before the Commission of Inquiry on behalf of the Bataka. Half a century earlier, Alexander Mackay had observed that Kabaka Muteesa seemed to be cowed by Guggu's predecessor and always complied with his demands. Guggu did not describe himself as the heir of a powerful spiritual position, however. He told the commissioners: "I am Guggu, the principal mutaka of the Sesse islands. I was in possession of three islands but I was not given a single one. . . . All these islands were taken possession of by the Late Gabunga Yosiya Kasozi. He turned me out of them at the time of the miles."[60] The regents challenged his definition of himself as a mutaka; they said the islands had belonged to the Lubaale Mukasa, and when Christianity was introduced "the heathen customs of 'lubale' died out, and consequently this Mutaka Guggu naturally lost all his importance and power which he merely possessed on account of being a priest of 'Lubale' Mukasa."[61]

Guggu had been a fundamentally significant member of the old order because of his spiritual responsibilities, not because he had controlled large amounts of land before 1900. His former spiritual power was entirely elided in his own speech and that of others on his side. Was this because the spiritual power of lubaale priests could no longer be spoken of in public, or because it did not matter? The regents and also the kabaka claimed that land dedicated to lubaale deities had been given to the chiefs as mailo because no one still believed in the power of lubaale forces. This was not entirely true, however. Land dedicated to the lubaale Kibuka in Mawokota had been assigned as mailo to members of the lineage responsible for Kibuka's shrine.[62] It is possible that Guggu was included in the case because the Bataka Federation believed Guggu's presence offered some kind of admonishment to the regents. The presence of an important Ganda spiritual figure among the complainants, a group led by educated elite Christians, suggests that the transition from lubaale worship to new religions was not as abrupt as has been supposed.

In addition to asking for the return of power and authority to those who had lost it, the leaders of the case against mailo also criticized the ways that power was exercised in the new Buganda. Fewer people participated in the Lukiiko as chiefship was rationalized following the 1900 Agreement, and fewer points of view were acknowledged. The massiga bataka wrote, "we the natural Bataka, were driven away from the Lukiko, we had no voice or anyone to intercede for us."[63] Even the ssaza chiefs who continued to be members of the Lukiiko did not have the capacity to make decisions that went against the regents, as the kangaawo Samwiri Mukasa testified: "The Lukiko appointed three Representatives to inquire and settle various claims and grievances but you did not listen to the decisions of these Representatives, but you did everything by virtue of your powers, and you put the Lukiko down under your feet. We had a Lukiko, but it was not a Lukiko in reality."[64] This accusation regarding the sham quality of the Lukiiko under Kaggwa echoed Daudi Basudde's description of "our existing dry-bone, lifeless native government, which is reduced from its real meaning and its old sanctions, to a mere shadow or rather an artificial symbol of its former self."[65] The mailo complainants expected the Lukiiko to be more accountable and responsive than it had been under Kaggwa's supervision and British overrule.

The mailo complainants said Kaggwa divided Baganda into two categories, those who had power and those who did not. This violated the Ganda practice that brought many voices into decisionmaking. In their original appeal to the kabaka, they stated that when the case was first mentioned in the Lukiiko, Kaggwa "started to disregard us and he shouted at us, then he started making us into two Classes; one class consisted of those who were not 'Abekitibwa' [people of honor] and the other of those who were of Ekitibwa [honor]. Why should the Katikiro do like this as though he was the accusing, whereas he was the accused and he had no power to treat us in such a way?"[66] They complained that the katikkiro was "spoiling everything in this whole country" by taking sides in clan disputes. In his questioning of Bataka witnesses, Kaggwa did divide people into categories of those with honor and those without. For example, he asked one witness, "If you did not receive any allotment of miles, how could you have come before the Lukiko to complain?" Yokana Lubanda replied, "That is the very weapon with which you used to beat us, as soon as we stood up in the Lukiko—just as I am standing up now—you would speak to us roughly and order us not to speak again."[67] Kaggwa did not have to be courteous because his followers could not leave: to stay in power, he had to please the Protectorate authorities in Entebbe, not the Baganda.

The people who brought the case against mailo argued that the forms of power they remembered would work better than colonial ones. They wanted those in power to treat others with consideration and dignity—a behavior that they asserted had been manifested by Ganda rulers in the past. To achieve that end, they wanted people to occupy the positions of authority they had previously occupied, to participate in discussions and in cases, and to have some traction in relation to their superiors. Mikael Karlstrom points out that people were not being heard was a recurrent theme in discussions of cultural malaise in Ganda newspapers in the 1920s. One writer asked, "Is this ruling the people, not to hear what they have to say?"[68]

The Bataka community argued that mailo land turned people into slaves. This strong and evocative accusation might seem to have been calculated to evoke the sympathy of European observers, as rescuing Africa from slavery was one of the rationalizations for British empire taught to Africans in school. In the case against mailo, however, the mailo case complainants used the image of enslavement to identify significant aspects of life in the new Buganda that they could not accept. Most concretely, they stated that the mailo allocation enslaved people because it prevented them from carrying out the rituals essential to social reproduction. In a more general sense, people with power were not treating their subordinates in an appropriate way: people were enslaved when landowners treated the land they owned as a means to make a profit and ceased to show concern for its residents.

A popular song expressed the sentiment that associated mailo with slavery: *"Buto-dene bagenze Entebbe okutunda abana"* ("the men with paunches have gone to Entebbe to sell their children").[69] The song refers to the signing of the 1900 Agreement: the "men with paunches" were the regents and ssaza chiefs who had benefited from mailo, an action that "sold their children." The Bataka called themselves "slaves of those who took our lands" in their original appeal to the kabaka to hear the case in 1922. This document elaborates the connection of mailo land and enslavement:

> Our graves are being removed from their places where they were laid for generations in case the present owner of the land feels inclined to exercise his power which is just like that of a tyrannous conqueror exercises against those whom he has conquered. All our children for whom from time ever immemorial we used to keep our Butaka lands and live happy, are now suffering through this bad attitude which is spoiling all our customs and power on our hereditary lands. Our children are now being sold along with the land as part of it. Whereas we in accordance with our Butaka lands being held communally, possessed our own share of the land in our respective clan and each head of a clan used to treat all his relatives as his children and likewise they in turn called him their father, and nothing of the present landless class ever existed.[70]

As everyone in Buganda in the 1920s had access to land as tenants, the term "landless class" may have implied people who, as discussed in Chapter 6, were experiencing diminished access to the forms of protection and sustenance that they had experienced in the past.

The accusation that mailo caused enslavement had specific meanings regarding connections between the members of a lineage group, and between a ruler and his subjects. Lazalo Byuma Seryenvu explained to the Commission of Inquiry that Hamu Mukasa, the ssekiboobo, or ssaza chief of Kyaggwe, had obtained the butaka of the Njovu clan: at first his clan members thought he was saving the land for the clan, because it had appeared that their clan land would be marked for the kabaka, but then the ssekiboobo "marked out his own miles on these estates in the name of Hamu Mukasa." As a consequence, "he converted all these bataka whom he had deprived of their butaka land into his private tenants, and those who refused to become his private men had to leave their butaka land" and become "private tenants" on other people's land. This transition in status was not linked to slavery: the people who lost their status as land controllers became "servants" not slaves. Seryenvu said that the mutaka called Sentemero "became the Sekibobo's servant and carried the Sekibobo's coffee up to the time of his death." However, because the clan did not have access to the butaka, they had been unable to perform the appropriate rituals on the death of the mutaka. The inability to perform kwabya olumbe, the ceremony that ends mourning and marks succession, had turned the children into slaves. "Up to the present day the funeral rites in connection with the burial of this Mutaka have not yet been performed, as his children have no place where they can gather together and perform them, since they have now become just like slaves and outcasts."[71]

The burial of clan elders in the appropriate clan burial grounds named a family and maintained the links between people and their ancestors. People whose elders could not be buried with the appropriate attention in the appropriate palace were perceived to have no family—they were outcasts and slaves. The kwabya olumbe ceremony, which transferred a person's living status to his heir and confirmed his place among the dead, was so important that some bataka chose to give up the possibility of owning mailo in order to remain on the land that contained their graves. Yona Magera received butaka, but continued to press for the return of the burial place of the principal mutaka of the clan. Saulo Lugwisa testified that he had had to bury his father "in the jungle" because he had not been allowed to bury on the proper butaka, and Zedi Zirimenya had faced the same horrible dilemma, carrying the body of an elder to his correct burial place, only to be turned away by the steward of the mailo owner.[72] The bataka community complaint that mailo owners had behaved like conquerors—who took captives away from their own people and turned them into slaves—because to be deprived of graves was to be deprived of the means of maintaining essential social connections.

Mailo land also turned people into slaves because the appropriate relationships between land-controllers and land-receivers were distorted when land could be bought and sold. In their statement "our children are now being sold along with the land as part of it," the bataka described the commodification of social relationships that had occurred over the past twenty years along with the commodification of land. "Tyrannous conquerors" did not show any concern for the social place of the people they conquered, and landowners likewise acted in their own interest without concern for others. The original appeal to the kabaka accused the regents, who "own now hundreds of square miles," including misappropriated butaka, of being "prepared to sell to foreigners at any time." They specifically linked the sale of butaka, which were "really being sold up to now," with the rejection of standards of reciprocity by the land-owning chiefs, "who are interested in selling and buying all the land on account of their wealth which is derived from us through their salaries and so forth." A further evidence of their violation of Ganda patterns of interaction was their refusal to discuss the issue: "[T]hey do not even want to hear a single word appertaining on the subject. They merely trample on it." They claimed that the 1918 transfer scheme to redeem butaka did not succeed because of "profiteering" by landowners.[73] As the case dragged on with no resolution after the Commission of Inquiry, the Bataka appealed to the Protectorate to do something, claiming the Lukiiko was encumbered by self-interest. They cited the onerous Nvujo law, a conversion of tribute to rent, originally drafted by the Lukiiko as 20 percent of the value of cash crops. According to the Bataka, the Lukiiko "looked upon the question as money making scheme by which they are themselves benefitted and have not considered the evils and difficulties this Nvujo brings to bear upon the peasants."[74]

The mailo complainants expressed concern that mailo land led to greed, and greed led to ill will in society: "on account of the Regents misusing this Agreement through their mere intention of getting land to which they were not entitled to, they upset everything and as the results of that mistake caused the present ill feeling which exists amongst our people as a whole." The good customs that had been "destroyed" were "our good customs of helping and loving each other," and the Bataka community requested Kabaka Cwa's intervention because "we cannot help keeping evil thoughts" and "should Your Highness not find any means of settling up this question, our ill feelings shall never come to an end, although we shall feel as if we had committed an offence against your Highness."[75] The negative atmosphere was a problem that had to be resolved.

The people who made the case against mailo warned the kabaka that "this friction may remain for generations unless your Highness hears and settles this friction" and they suggested a resolution: "to put each and every individual back within his old boundaries known up to the present day." The simplicity of their solution—to restore every controller of land according to the description of clan estates in Apolo Kaggwa's *Ebika bya Buganda*—may have contributed to the accusation that the proposals of the Bataka were "retrograde" and "increasingly impracticable under the conditions of 20th century life and progress."[76] However, the Bataka community themselves deliberately asserted that their goals were not incompatible with the positive aspects of the new order in Buganda. Many of them were "new" men who received salaries from the Protectorate, participated in church leadership, and marked their status in the forms of the new culture of consumption. Several of them had obtained the highest possible levels of education for themselves or their children. They clearly articulated what they considered to be the failures of the current order, but they asked for reform, not a return to the past.[77] Their own statements about their intentions, and the explanations they provided to Protectorate officials about how they would implement a return of clan lands, define the possibility of a modern Buganda built on the foundation of good Ganda customs. The Bataka community envisioned a Buganda in which rulers were powerful but also accountable, in which many people participated in government, in which people controlled amounts of land that were not excessively large, and in which those with power demonstrated concern for the people they ruled. They did not see any inherent contradiction between these things and land title, literacy, and the new patterns of life that they practiced without any comment.

The mailo complainants explained their aspirations to Protectorate authorities in terms of foundations. Daudi Basudde and Yuda Musoke wrote to the chief secretary, explaining why the governor had to pay attention to the Bataka's case:

> We humbly beg to state that we see that it will be difficult for this land of ours to advance in the way forward as the Government has promised to all of us as we see that as regards the foundation on which our country has been built since 1900 it has proved a foundation of progress on the shorter side of the building but on the other side the foundation is not level and this side is with its good customs on which Buganda rests. . . . In creating this league we are not actuated by a desire to rush our country forward but a) to provide for it a sound foundation from which it can go forward slowly [and] b) to go into the matter of this wrong while our elders who made the 1900 Agreement are still with us for later when they have gone it will be difficult for the younger generation to settle these differences.[78]

If the goal of the Protectorate was to lay the foundation of good government, then the British needed to pay attention to the structures of Buganda that had caused it to function effectively as a nation.

The leaders of the case against mailo wanted people with authority to be accountable. They complained that "people who are totally demoralized (without morals) through crimes and drunkenness, who under native law and customs, could never be tolerated to lead the destinies of the people on the land, in the present case they are left as they are, because they hold personal titles on the land according to Sir H.H. Johnston's benevolent agreement."[79] The circumstances of the case allowed the Bataka community to openly mention mailo landowners, but their criticism might also have applied to chiefs responsible for excessive labor calls and collecting onerous taxes.

A critical aspect of the Bataka community's view of an alternative order in Buganda was that there was enough land for all, if everyone had the appropriate amount. They stated in their original appeal, "We humbly beg to assure Your Highness that we are not in any way partisans of dislodging our compatriots from their real lands, if they have got any and ultimately acquire them." The extremely large amounts of land taken by the largest landowners had caused a land scarcity that otherwise would not have been a problem. The witness for the Civet Cat clan said, "I would like this Commission to note this that Gombolola and Miruka Chiefs were allotted as much as 12 to 20 square miles, while the bataka who are considered as the fathers of these chiefs were only given two square miles."[80] Daudi Basudde pointed out that when it was discovered that twelve hundred miles remained unallocated, Kaggwa, who already had fifty square miles of private property, was given another twelve, and other large landowners were also given more large allotments. Basudde asked, "Of those 1200 sq. miles, was it right or not to have allotted to the chiefs [smaller chiefs who received no mailo] some official miles attached to their Chieftainships?"[81]

The Bataka community did not anticipate that land allotted in the appropriate way would ever be exhausted: "If there is no land available on that part of clan land that member will find it on other branches of the clan, and in this, we question very much whether there will be any possibility of having any scarcity of land in this way, as this never happened before in this country."[82] They argued that the needs of Kaggwa and Mugwanya to control large amounts of land to demonstrate the importance of their offices ought to have been met by their obtaining permission from the king to open up new lands. Opening new lands was the Ganda way of solving the problem: "if there were no estates available for him he would have opened up new land, since it is the usual custom for the Katikiro to open up new land."[83] With this statement, the Bataka witness indirectly traced the crisis in Buganda to colonial policies: chiefs could not hope to open new land because colonial demands for workers drained away the necessary labor. Furthermore, there was no more waste land, because the 1900 Agreement allocated it to the British.

Although many of the leaders of the Bataka community functioned successfully in a wage economy, they imagined that relationships between landowners and people on the land would not necessarily be mediated by cash. They articulated a revised expectation of reciprocity: if people on the land had a relationship with the landowner that involved kinship ties, which implied protection and assistance, then it was fair to ask them to work without wages. If they had no relationship with the landowner, rent might be an alternative. The spokesman for Walusimbi, head of the Civet Cat clan, explained to the commission: "The members of my clan residing on my land have definite duties which they perform for me even from the old days and they perform these duties for me still now, so I do not collect rent from them instead of payment of rent they build my house." He added that other people, who were not members of his clan, had settled on his land, and he collected rent from them "unless they agree to work for me in lieu of payment of rent."[84]

The Bataka community stated that they wanted to preserve individual land tenure, but they rejected the notion that land as property could be detached from social concerns. As they pointed out, in other places private property was subject to restrictions, such as provisions that land could not be executable for debt, or could not be transferred without permission. In Buganda, they wanted a form of private property that acknowledged the rights of clans, so that clans could obtain their lands and a lineage could be protected from the inclination of one of its members to live improvidently and sell land.[85] Their defense of their request for clan lands suggested that the social dimensions of land had greater salience for them than its transferability. Miti and others wrote that the British were wrong in thinking that the mailo owners deserved to keep the land because they had improved it: not only had they taken no trouble to develop the land, but they had doubly ignored the social responsibility inherent in control of land, first by collecting rents from tenants without providing anything in return, and second by selling the land. The Bataka claimed that their request to be allocated clan land should not have been any more difficult than a transfer from one owner to another. They asked, "How many certificates have been changed from one owner to another in case original owner feels inclined to get money out of his land by means of sale?"[86]

The people who brought the case against mailo envisioned a Buganda that integrated what they remembered to be the good customs of the past with the realities of the present. They imagined a Buganda that had both a cash economy and free exchanges of labor and service, both Christianity and the expression of the importance of clan ancestors, both private land ownership and social responsibility. The Ganda leaders who rose to speak against mailo in the 1920s suggested it might have been possible to maintain British protection and reestablish the webs of power which people remembered as just and workable in the past.

CONCLUSION: BEYOND BAKUNGU VS. BATAKA

A much narrower, much less interesting history of the conflict over land in Buganda in the 1920s can be found in a superficial reading of the records of the case. Both the claimants and the defendants participated in the simplification of the issues into bakungu chiefs with land versus bataka clan elders deprived of land. Perhaps they expected "bataka" to imply all the forms of authority that had been part of precolonial Buganda; perhaps they presented a dichotomy because they did not think their British audience could follow more complex histories. In the heat of the conflict, the debate became intensely polarized: landowners who had been willing to accommodate bataka on their lands began to drive them away, and bataka witnesses usually failed to mention the portion of their clan lands that they had received in the mailo allocation.[87]

Apolo Kaggwa's written defense of the regents, which included a history of Buganda told entirely in terms of conflict between bataka and kabakas in which the kabakas were always victorious, has been the most significant legacy of the case against mailo for the writing of Buganda's history.[88] The Bataka community also simplified the Ganda political order into bataka and their opponents who were chiefs appointed by the king, even as they argued that centralized power was not good for the nation. They constantly invoked the loss of butaka, even when they were speaking about royal land, lubaale deities' land, and land given by the king to commemorate a particular relationship. They also spoke about a past in which bataka and kabakas were the only important participants.

The simplified dichotomy of the public debate in the case against mailo, combined with the gradual erasure from 1891 onward of forms of authority that were neither bataka nor bakungu, crystallized overly simplified perceptions of Buganda in the past. In their summary of the issues in the case, Commissioners Griffith and Sturrock wrote, "No one else except the Bataka had any right over land in Buganda and in our opinion no one other than the Bataka had any rights infringed when occupied land was converted into the freehold property of a Regent or Chief."[89] It is not surprising that later scholars conceptualized Buganda's history as a conflict between territorially based clan heads and appointed chiefs who were ultimately victorious.[90]

As we have seen, the Ganda polity was much more complex and subtly articulated than the model of top layers of bakungu and lower layers of bataka. This system, which can be conceptualized as a web, can be reconstructed from the evidence collected by Roscoe and Kaggwa in 1905, from the explanation of Ganda land tenure produced by Morris Carter in 1911, from the histories of Buganda recorded in the nineteenth century, and from the witnesses before the Commission of Inquiry whose personal stories revealed many layers of complexity. Guggu's presence (not his words) testified to priests' and spirit mediums' power over land and people.[91] The utility and importance of ebitongole came up in testimony regarding the position of the kauta, and in complaints about the kabaka's loss of control over other ebitongole and the kibuga.[92] The loss of land that had marked a specific remembered relationship with the kabaka was discussed by several witnesses, who had their land by virtue of the favors they did for the king, but who called themselves bataka during the Commission's proceedings.[93] Members of the Abalangira, the clan of princes, voiced their complaints as "bataka," but their statements before the Commission never touched on the role of royal women and their male relatives in sustaining and checking the power of a reigning kabaka.

The perception of the controversy in the 1920s as part of a tradition of conflict between bataka and bakungu obscures the accomplishment of the Ganda thinkers who brought the case against mailo. These Ganda leaders, who called themselves the Bataka community but included many diverse authority figures, asked for a return of everyone to their former positions. They criticized the overreaching power of the central chiefs, and moved strategically to support the young kabaka in establishing his authority. When that initial effort failed, they made a sustained critique of colonial power. They were leaders of the kingdom who had in their own careers experienced the loss of Ganda control over the production of wealth and the loss of Ganda political autonomy, and they were familiar with Ganda political order. They articulated their vision of how things could be different by decrying the destruction of customs that facilitated well-being, by calling for a return of diverse forms of authority, by criticizing "enslavement" inherent in commodified social relationships, and by asserting that British overrule could be combined with effective Ganda government as they remembered it.

It was perhaps inevitable that their case ultimately failed (as success would have entailed unraveling the colonial state), but even so it is remarkable that in the 1920s they succeeded in articulating a series of arguments that attracted and maintained the attention and concern of Uganda Protectorate officials and those of the British government. Ironically, the dichotomized discourse of the case against mailo set the political agenda for Buganda for the following half century; but inside those documents, it is possible to glimpse the complex, multilayered system that the people who brought the case against mailo remembered when they spoke of "the good customs of Buganda."

NOTES

1. The loss of clan lands dimension is described in Mair, *An African People,* 165–166; J. M. Fortt, "Land Tenure and the Emergence of Large Scale Farming," in Richards, Sturrock, and Fortt, *Subsistence,* 72; Low, *The Mind of Buganda,* xviii; Pratt, "Politics of Indirect Rule," 234; and Mahmood Mamdani, *Politics and Class Formation in Uganda* (New York: Monthly Review Press, 1976), 123–124. Animosity toward Apolo Kaggwa is highlighted as the essence of the controversy by Audrey Richards, Henry West, and A. B. Mukwaya. Audrey I. Richards, "Authority Patterns in Traditional Buganda," in *The King's Men,* ed. L. A. Fallers (London: Oxford University Press, 1964), 301; West, *Land Policy in Buganda,* 142; Mukwaya, *Land Tenure in Buganda,* East African Studies No. 1 (Kampala: East African Institute of Social Research, 1953), 21. Glenn McKnight demonstrates that the actions of the Bataka Federation significantly shaped Protectorate agricultural policy for the following decades. Glenn McKnight, "Land, Politics, and Buganda's 'Indigenous' Colonial State," *Journal of Imperial and Commonwealth History* 28:1 (2000): 65–89.

2. My evidence for this assertion, explored below, comes primarily from a careful reading of testimony before the Bataka Land Commission, and also correspondence in Entebbe Secretariat Archives (ESA) Secretariat Minute Paper (SMP) 6902, filed in the Uganda National Archives as A46 2213 and 2214. I refer to the Commission papers as SMP 6902 below, because the files had been combined when I consulted the UNA in 1995. At that time some parts of the SMP 6902 file had been misplaced. The records of the Commission itself can be found in translation in the Public Records Office in CO 536/ 133. Guggu, the principal medium of the Lubaale Mukasa spoke before the Commission of Inquiry, and the medium Guludene wrote to the governor asking for the return of his land.

3. Miti to Kabaka, March 4, 1922, UNA SMP 6902, suggests that Kaggwa may have tried to delay hearings of the case so that Miti would not be able to be present to lend his prestige.

4. Miti, "A History," 781, 993.

5. "Commission," Jemusi Miti, 500.

6. McKnight, "Buganda's 'Indigenous' Colonial State," 77; Governor Archer to Secretary of State, April 20, 1924, UNA SMP 6902, 9.

7. Twaddle, *Kakungulu,* 73, 82; F. B. Welbourn, *East African Rebels: A Study of Some Independent Churches* (London: SCM Press, 1961), 21–22, n218.

8. "From this Chief down to the less important Chiefs all did the same. Just as Chief Katikiro did so did his good friend Hamu Mukasa follow his footsteps. And just as Chief Mugwanya did so did our brother Yakobo Musajalumbwa. So all the other Chiefs were compelled to join in this game. It was a great game to them, but on the side of the Bataka it was one which ruined our lives. It was a game of so great importance in our country just like the game Emperor Kaiser played in Europe." "Commission," Shem Spire Mukasa, 381–382.

9. "Commission," Samwiri Mukasa, 490–491.

10. Sturrock to Secretary of State for the Colonies, January 8, 1925, UNA SMP 6902.

11. Musajakawa had an intensity reminiscent of Ganda spirit mediums of earlier generations. Imprisoned for refusing to pay a tax to fund local medical services in 1921, he refused to eat prison food or wear prison clothes. He died of self-starvation nine days after his deportation from Buganda in 1929, after a riot caused by Malakite refusal to be vaccinated. Miti, "A History," 1842–1847.

12. *"Semusota guli mu ntamu: bw'oguta tolye, bw'oguleka tolye"*—"The snake's in the cooking pot: kill it or leave it you'll have nothing to eat." Welbourn, *East African Rebels,* 11, 25.

13. Twaddle, "Bakungu Chiefs," 318.

14. Welbourn, *East African Rebels,* 24.

15. Ibid.

16. Ibid., 34. Mugema's church was commonly known as the Malakite Church after its most vigorous promoter, Malaki Musajakawa. It deserves more scholarly attention.

17. Welbourn, *East African Rebels,* 43, 217.

18. Miti, "A History," 1003.

19. A few years later, when it appeared that Kabaka Daudi Cwa might side with the Bataka, Kaggwa's son and some friends published a statement claiming the kabaka's immorality impeded the progress of the nation. Having discussed his illegitimate children, they moved on to the topic of princes who were not imprisoned: "how then can we

refer to such sons as princes when we know not of the existence of such a place for their confinement?" Miti, "A History," 1070.

20. Twaddle, "Bakungu Chiefs," 315.

21. Miti, "A History," 1039–1041.

22. Rowe, "Revolution," 38.

23. Miti, "A History," 1052–1053.

24. Bataka to Kabaka, February 1922; Bataka Community, *The Baganda Land Holding Question* (for private circulation only) (Kampala: Uganda P. and P., n.d. [1923]), 17 (cited hereafter as *Land Holding Question*).

25. Ibid., 4.

26. Miti, "A History," 1066.

27. Kaggwa to Governor, June 12, 1922, UNA SMP 6902.

28. Mugema et al. to Governor, May 30, 1922, UNA SMP 6902.

29. Ibid., July 11, 1922, UNA SMP 6902.

30. Cwa to Lukiiko, September 18, 1922, reproduced in Miti, "A History," 1088–1089.

31. Miti, "A History," 920–921, N.B. this comes after p. 1090.

32. The "Masiga Bataka," including Yuda Musoke and Malaki Masajakawa, began to write independently to Protectorate officials, in long, intricate impassioned Luganda, starting in August 1922.

33. *Land Holding Question,* 29–30.

34. Letter to Commissioner of Police, April 4, 1922, UNA SMP 6902; Miti, "A History," 1102–1103.

35. *Land Holding Question,* 4.

36. "Commission," Daudi Basudde, 350–351.

37. Two years earlier, Kaggwa had had Prince Kyamagwa imprisoned for forgery, because he had signed a document on behalf of the Abalangira (clan of princes), even though he was not ssabalangira (head of the princes). Masiga Bataka to Governor, December 14, 1922, UNA SMP 6902. Unfortunately, documents describing this case have been removed from the file in the Entebbe Secretariat Archives; all that remains in the file is the transmittal slip.

38. "Commission," Yosiya Mawanda Kyamagwa, 479.

39. Ibid., 480 (retranslated from the original).

40. "Commission," ex-Sabalangira, 482.

41. This action, discussed in Chapter 5, infuriated Ganda and British authorities and may have contributed to the attempt to disbar him from the clan in 1910. Miti, "A History," 995.

42. Kaggwa et al. to Daudi Cwa, March 18, 1922, UNA SMP 6902.

43. "Commission," Apolo Kaggwa, 580.

44. "Commission," Daudi Basudde, 351–352.

45. "Commission," Jemusi Biriko, 378.

46. "Commission," Malaki Musajakawa, 341.

47. Kaggwa et al. to Kabaka Daudi Cwa, March 30, 1922, addendum to "Commission," 582. Daudi Basudde insisted when questioned by Mugwanya that the "things which took place in 1892 or 1893" were irrelevant to the case, and he would only answer questions about what happened in 1900. "Commission," Basudde, 489.

48. Masiga Bataka to Governor, August 1, 1922, UNA SMP 6902; "Commission," Serwano Kiyaga, 470–471; "Commission," Zakayo Semakade, 366–367.

49. They also explained, "In the old days our country was self-governing, but now it

is under the protection of the British Government, having been handed over by Kabaka Mwanga." Kaggwa et al. to Daudi Cwa, March 18, 1922, "Commission," 576.

50. Kaggwa and Mugwanya to Daudi Cwa, March 18, 1922, "Commission," 571–572.

51. Ibid., 577.

52. Bataka to Daudi Cwa, February 1922, *Land Holding Question,* 18.

53. "Commission," Shem Spire Mukasa, 381.

54. Bataka to Daudi Cwa, February 1922, *Land Holding Question,* 24; also Miti to Kabaka, "Further Resolution re Bataka Question," March 1, 1922, UNA SMP 6902.

55. Basudde and Mukasa to Chief Secretary, May 15, 1922, UNA SMP 6902.

56. Insightful and vivid accounts of competition among figures of authority in Buganda characterize John Rowe's "Revolution in Buganda 1856–1900"; and Michael Twaddle's, *Kakungulu and the Creation of Uganda,* 33–65 passim.

57. Questioning Apolo Kaggwa, Daudi Basudde referred to "the sub-chiefs who were in existence then and who have now been converted into Gombolola Chiefs." "Commission," Daudi Basudde, 524.

58. "Commission," Juma Owamanyi, 429.

59. Gologoli Guludene Mutasi to Governor, August 14, 1926, "An Explanatory Statement of Our Ancestry," UNA SMP 6902, 56.

60. "Commission," Guggu, 384.

61. "Commission," Yosiya Sajabi Semugala, 385.

62. "Commission," Daudi Cwa, 592; "Commission," Apolo Kaggwa, 513; "Commission," Daudi Basudde, 440. Welbourn notes that the statement that the new oligarchy suppressed worship of the old gods "is frequently made but difficult to substantiate from documentary evidence." He cites Kaggwa's son, Kwalya Kaggwa, stating that the Lukiiko used the mailo allocation to suppress lubaale worship. Welbourn, *East African Rebels,* 218.

63. Masiga Bataka to Chief Secretary, December 20, 1922, UNA SMP 6902.

64. "Commission," Samwiri Mukasa, 492.

65. Daudi Basudde to *Uganda Herald,* December 9, 1921, UNA A46 2288 (SMP 7258).

66. Bataka to Daudi Cwa, February 1922, *Land Holding Question,* 23; Miti to Kabaka, "Further Resolution re Bataka Question," March 1, 1922, UNA SMP 6902.

67. "Commission," Apolo Kaggwa and Yokana Lubanda, 415; Michael Twaddle explores this in "Bakungu Chiefs."

68. *Ebifa mu Buganda,* December 1919, 269, quoted in Karlstrom, "The Cultural Kingdom in Uganda," 99.

69. Welbourn, *East African Rebels,* 19.

70. Bataka to Daudi Cwa, February 1922, *Land Holding Question,* 20.

71. "Commission," Lazalo Byuma Seryenvu, 485–487.

72. "Commission," Valanta Batanude for Yona Magera, 361; "Commission," Saulo Lugwisa, 448; "Commission," Zedi Zirimenya, 357–358; "Commission," Antwani Kikuzi, 425.

73. Bataka to Daudi Cwa, February 1922, *Land Holding Question,* 19–22.

74. Jemusi Miti for the Bataka Community to Governor, April 26, 1926, UNA SMP 6902.

75. Bataka to Daudi Cwa, February 1922, *Land Holding Question,* 20.

76. Ibid., 20, 23; Minutes of J. de G. Delmege, Acting Provincial Commissioner, after May 27, 1926, UNA SMP 6902.

77. Mikael Karlstrom points out that a sense that development requires awareness of the past as well as innovation characterized Ganda royalists in the 1990s. Karlstrom, "Cultural Kingdom in Uganda," 287.

78. Daudi Basudde and Yuda Musa Mukasa to Chief Secretary, May 15, 1922, UNA SMP 6902.

79. *Land Holding Question,* 30–31.

80. "Commission," Lew Nsobya, 466.

81. "Commission," Daudi Basudde, 524.

82. "Answers to the Questions of the Provincial Commissioner, Discussed by the Executive Committee of the Bataka Community," May 27, 1926, UNA SMP 6902.

83. "Commission," Aligizanda Mude, 338.

84. "Commission," Lew Nsobya for Walusimbi, 467.

85. *Land Holding Question,* 30–31.

86. Miti et al. to Governor, April 26, 1926, UNA SMP 6902.

87. The testimony of Pasikale Bambaga illustrates the polarization of the argument: he failed to acknowledge that the regents did actually try to allocate land to the clan, but made a mistake, and he also neglected to mention that he received a mailo elsewhere in compensation. "Commission," Pasikale Bambaga, 458, 461. However, in their attack on him, the regents glossed over the fact that the kasolya butaka ended up in the wrong hands. See the testimony of Nkuwe for evidence of the controversy changing the relationship between mailo claimants and landowners. "Commission," Nkuwe, 392.

88. "The Lukiko's Reply to the Question of Allotment of Land in Buganda Brought Up by the Bataka," Kaggwa et al. to Kabaka Daudi Cwa, March 18, 1922; "Commission," 561–578.

89. Quoted in undated Minutes after May 26, 1926, UNA SMP 6902.

90. Low, *Modern History,* 15, 140; Southwold, *Bureaucracy and Chiefship,* 10; David E. Apter, *The Political Kingdom in Uganda: A Study in Bureaucratic Nationalism* (Princeton: Princeton University Press, 1961), 105.

91. "Commission," Guggu, 385–386.

92. "Commission," 385, 437, 439, 505, 521, 531.

93. For example, "Commission," Nkuwe, 388–391; "Commission," Matayo Serubuzi, 422.

8

CONCLUSION

This book has traced the history of the habit of thought that love ought to characterize social relations and that exchanges of land, service, and gifts bound together the members of a polity. The practice of reciprocal obligation marked in permanently cropped banana lands enabled the inhabitants of the region north of Lake Victoria to weave a supple social fabric. The Buganda kingdom grew through multiple, linked iterations of the relationship of obligation contracted between a chief and his people, and the active agency of followers in this practice gave ordinary people a substantial role in the creation and maintenance of social order.

People built relationships through exchanges that created mutual obligation from the earliest origins of the kingdom. Ancient regional cults drew together clans that each offered particular services essential to worshiping Kintu and tending the spiritual medicine Mbajwe. Chiefships multiplied as leaders mustered the labor of followers to open new land for intensive banana cultivation. In the distant past, authority figures who eventually became clan elders, chiefs, and kings drew each other into relationships of obligation that gradually gave those institutions their familiar form. The names of the oldest Ganda chiefships demonstrate that chiefs linked themselves to the king through services they performed, and the new kind of king named kabaka established a place at the center of the polity through receiving gifts and bestowing prestige. Carefully regulated gifts from particular chiefs to particular royal wives structured relations in the kingdom from the reign of Kateregga in the seventeenth century, and two hundred years later, Baganda gained the support of missionaries and British imperial entrepreneurs through their hospitality and the labor they offered. Ganda chiefs and peasants used imported goods, cash wages, and the possibility of purchasing land to attract followers to themselves and re-create chiefship on a smaller scale. The relatively benevolent terms of employment offered by Ganda cultivators attracted thousands of migrants from Rwanda and Burundi whose labor helped to create the prosperity of colonial Buganda.

That followers compelled their rulers to govern well through withholding their support was another principle of the Ganda practice of power visible over many centuries. The vast, overlapping web of thousands of chiefships gave followers choices, and those in power had to be responsive to the concerns of their subordinates or risk losing them. According to dynastic tradition, chiefs refused to allow Kabaka Mutebi to dismiss two important chiefs in the mid-seventeenth century, and Baganda withdrew their support from Kabaka Kagulu half a century later because of his unbearable cruelty. Kabaka Muteesa could not obtain canoe transport after he angered the lubaale Mukasa through his excessive kindness to his missionary guests. In 1893, Catholics and Muslims expressed their displeasure at the land settlement after the civil war by refusing to offer laborers for work in the capital, and their action led to a renegotiation of the allocation of land to the religious groups. The overwhelming labor demands of early colonial rule led thousands of Baganda to leave the kingdom; chiefs who could not retain their followers through treating them well began to punish men for leaving. Rural Baganda explained in the 1990s that the elected local governing councils established by Museveni's National Resistance Movement were like Ganda chiefship because they made authority figures accountable to the community they served.[1]

Reciprocal obligation facilitated intricately complex, overlapping power structures. Constant competition among chiefs for followers made the kabaka's role as impartial arbiter essential, but kabakas were not alone at the center of power in Buganda. Queen mothers and queen sisters, lubaale deities, the katikkiro and the kimbugwe all controlled land and received tribute that gave them autonomous authority, and other chiefs, such as the mugema and the kibaale, had a role in checking the king's power. The authority of these figures eroded in the nineteenth century as trade in ivory and slaves weakened the kingdom's center, and the autocratic rule of the regents under Protectorate supervision entirely erased their role as counterweights to the kabaka's power.

When the allegiance of followers no longer mattered to their superiors, the logic of reciprocal obligation ceased to function. The massive importation of war captives that accompanied the kingdom's expansion in the eighteenth and nineteenth centuries eroded the status of free followers and led to bloody competition for the kabakaship. Kabaka Semakookiro resolved the crisis by killing all potential kabakas, an action that made his life safer but fundamentally undermined Baganda capacity to curb the excesses of their monarch. The order of Buganda unraveled when trade in ivory and slaves allowed the king and chiefs to form ekitongole chiefships entirely removed from the web of reciprocal obligation; chiefs restored order after the civil war that ensued through a reconfiguration of chiefs' power over land that incorporated new religions into the logic of the kingdom.

The British failure to comprehend the implications of the labor offered by Ganda chiefs had lasting consequences for Baganda. When ssaza chiefs called on their followers to build sturdy, commodious guest houses and hold up thousands of torches to welcome visiting Protectorate officials, they expected the British to respond with material demonstrations of their appreciation. Instead, the Protectorate institutionalized a form of forced labor service whose onerous demands undermined the legitimacy of chiefs and the capacity of clan members to care for each other. Since people who owned land or had mission education were exempt from forced labor, the burden of this obligation accelerated the emergence of class differences among Baganda. A vocabulary of fines replaced a vocabulary of gifts as Ganda chiefs "treated like a pad (for carrying headloads) which is pressed on both sides" attempted to get work and taxes out of their followers without giving anything in return.[2]

Followers lost the capacity to wield obligation for their own benefit in incremental stages. The reestablishment of chiefly order over people and territory in the 1890s involved some diminution of people's agency because royal women, lubaale forces, and some categories of chiefs lost their role in government, narrowing followers' options. Colonial taxation transformed the productive dimension of people's connections with chiefs, as the Lukiiko secretary wrote in 1900: "Ever since the European made the Buganda Government a well which he drains at its spring—I mean the collection of taxes— what water do you expect to find in the well?"[3] The elimination of thousands of positions from the chiefly hierarchy in 1909 destroyed most opportunities for people to listen and offer their perspective in the judgment of cases, and to speak their concerns directly to their rulers. In the context of labor and tax obligations that could add up to more than five months' labor in a year, the Busuulu and Nvujjo law placed a limit on rents and gave tenants "protection" from eviction—a total inversion of their right to leave a ruler who made excessive demands.

Active submission to Ganda authorities—only one half of the exchange that had constituted reciprocal obligation—was all that remained for nonelite Baganda by the late colonial period. In 1953, Michael Nsimbi wrote, "It was out of such training, submission to being ruled and obedience . . . that the nation of Buganda, in which we all take such pride today, arose."[4] The call by some Ganda politicians for "federo" (a federation of semi-autonomous regions that would include the Buganda kingdom as a political unit) evoked a rosy picture of prosperity in the mid-twentieth century, a time when the capacity of Ganda followers to exert pressure on their rulers had all but disappeared. Kabaka Ronald Mutebi, installed in 1993, received generous gifts from his people, but had few means for reciprocating in a tangible way. The diminishing social agency of Ganda followers evident in these examples originated, to some degree, in deliberate transformations of structures of power.

Ugandans and others inquiring into the utility of no-party, multiparty, and other mechanisms for just and equitable governance may find encouragement in the long history of debate about the nature of good government that characterizes the African past. In Buganda, those arguments preceded, encompassed, and followed a colonial presence. During the controversy over land and power in the 1920s, one side emphasized the ultimate authority of the kabaka and the other side focused on multiple voices in decisionmaking, but neither side questioned the utility of Ganda forms of governing for shaping a dynamic and progressive society. The people who brought the case against private property in land argued that market relations destroyed the social order, and progress could only happen when rulers and followers expressed love for each other. They wanted gradual development, to find ways to combine useful knowledge from Europe with practices of power that could curb harmful selfishness. They had complete confidence that, with time and effort, their goal could be achieved.

NOTES

1. Karlstrom, "Cultural Kingdom in Uganda," 436.
2. "Buganda Lukiiko," June 26, 1905, 23.
3. Lukiiko to Jemusi Miti Kibuka, "Buganda Lukiiko," July 30, 1900, 68.
4. Quoted in Karlstrom, "Cultural Kingdom in Uganda," 324.

AFTERWORD:
WHAT HAPPENED
TO MAILO LAND?

A snake in the cooking pot is an irresolvable dilemma. Kill the snake and the meal is lost because the pot breaks; leave the snake and the meal is lost because the snake spoils the food. Mailo land was a "snake in the cooking pot" for the entire twentieth century: no resolution to the problem it posed for the Ganda polity could be implemented without destroying things that seemed essential to Buganda.[1] The request for a return of multiple Ganda power-holders to their former positions made in the case against mailo of the 1920s was irresolvable, because mailo had inscribed the logic of power and the locations of power that facilitated the colonial state. Giving back the land, and the authority that people wanted along with it, would have exposed the fiction of Ganda self-rule.

For the people who brought the case against mailo, change was impossible because they wanted to maintain their fealty and obedience to the British, and also to reorder power. They continued, for years, to politely ask for the return of their land, then the survivors channelled their energies into more overtly anti-British political activities starting in the 1940s. The most volatile crises in Ganda politics concerned the issues raised in the case against mailo—control of land and the power of the kabaka.

For Apolo Kaggwa and the other large landowners, ownership of mailo also entailed a snake in the cooking pot dilemma: they wanted the prestige that control of land had always implied, but they could not maintain that prestige and also use land as a source of profit. The many square-miled land holdings of the larger chiefs could not be sustained. In a real-life sequence of events that seemed to follow the plot of a morality play, much of Apolo Kaggwa's excessively large mailo allotment was sold to pay lawyers fees for a family quarrel and for the debts of his heir.

In the years immediately following the case against mailo, Protectorate and Home Office officials vacillated between sympathy for the people who had been unjustly deprived of their land and concern for the preservation of the order of power inscribed in the allocation of mailo land. The actual resolution of the case against mailo ignored the irresolvable political issues and addressed the less-emphasized complaint about the deterioration of reciprocity. The Busuulu and Nvujjo law, forced through the Lukiiko by Protectorate authorities in 1928, quantified the tribute paid by people on the land (now tenants) to their landlords, and spelled out the landlords' obligations to tenants. The Busuulu and Nvujjo law transmuted the labor and goods given by a tenant to a land owner into a fixed amount of money: ten shillings per year in place of labor tribute, and four shillings per acre on the first three acres of crops, in place of gifts of produce. These amounts represented about 10 percent of the value of a year's production in 1928, but they soon lost their economic meaning.[2] Tenants continued to give landlords bark cloth and some beer every time they brewed it, and part of what they hunted: this was economically valuable, but these exchanges gradually became less significant. Landowners or their representatives had to judge cases that arose among tenants, and good landowners offered hospitality to tenants and "took care" of them through intervening with officials, arranging school places for talented children, and so forth. In the 1930s Lucy Mair noted that "the younger generation" of mailo owners were less likely to meet these obligations.[3] The Busuulu and Nvujjo law established a tenant's right of occupation, curtailing a statutory right of eviction that landowners had previously possessed but rarely used.[4]

The law thus completed the process of legal commodification of social relationships that had begun with the creation of private property in land. In neither case did this process of commodification eliminate the social meanings attached to land in Buganda. As long as landowners sought to attract tenants or bought land with tenants, mailo land entailed a degree of authority over others. The Busuulu and Nvujjo law meant that followers on the land expressed their allegiance through cash payments and not through gifts. Using cash as the medium for exchanges concerning land did not obliterate people's expectations of mutual obligation.

Butaka also became commodified. Following the failed struggle to regain clan lands, butaka ceased to refer only to the burial grounds where lineage elders maintained the connections between living people and their ancestors that ensured well-being. Butaka came to also mean land owned by an individual, secured by graves of that person's immediate relatives. Like reciprocal obligation and the complex forms of authority in Buganda, the connections maintained by butaka shrunk dramatically in the circumstances of a cash economy and colonial power relationships.

Mailo land was a form of property that originally expressed rights derived from ruling, not from owning. Over the course of the twentieth century, being a landowner lost the elements of the responsibility to judge cases, to do favors, to provide hospitality and meat, to give gifts, and to know tenants well enough to fit the owner's demands to the tenants' particular circumstances. Being a tenant lost the responsibilities to provide labor, to give beer, barkcloth, and the fruits of hunting. Tenants' right to undisturbed occupation granted by the Busuulu and Nvujjo law limited mailo owners' capacity to use land for commercial purposes. In cases from the 1940s to the 1970s, land courts had a tendency to side with tenants, and it was in fact almost impossible to remove a tenant.[5]

As inflation made busuulu and nvujjo payments economically insignificant and the nominal power of landowners as rulers was eliminated, prestige became the distinguishing characteristic of mailo land ownership. Offering respect and gifts, though not a legal obligation, was an important dimension of tenancy through the 1990s.[6] Some cases of eviction hinged on the "respectfulness" of the tenant, and not his payment of busuulu and nvujjo "rents."[7]

The 1998 land law clarified landowner-tenant relations after a period of ambiguity from Idi Amin's 1975 land decree, which purportedly nationalized all land. Between 1975 and 1998, mailo landowners could not collect rent, and tenants could not give it. Receipts from rent paid before 1975 continued to have meaning, proving the tenant's legitimate right to be on the land; these receipts were passed on to a new tenant when a tenancy was sold.

The 1998 land law gives tenants a registrable interest in mailo land on which they have a tenancy, and the right to maintain a tenancy for a payment of five thousand shillings (about $2.50 in 2003) per year, as long as they remain in occupation of the plot. The mailo landowner's obligation is to leave the tenant undisturbed: the landowner cannot remove a tenant unless he can prove that the tenant has not paid rent for one year, and then he has to take the case before a district land board.

The law was criticized for providing windfall profit to tenancy holders in peri-urban areas: it made no distinction between a tenancy of a few acres in a rural area and a tenancy in suburban Kampala, which has a very high economic value. Discussion of the more efficient land use that could be expected from making tenancy registrable and transferable raised anxiety regarding landlessness. It was feared that the actual intention of the law—to "rationalize" land ownership in order to make land more productive—encoded the expectation that people who have capital utilize land more effectively. Therefore, the land law might ultimately be a mechanism for taking land out of the control of small-scale farmers and delivering it to those who had the most access to money, intensifying the gap between wealthy and poor Ugandans and undermining the high levels of access to land that Ugandans had enjoyed before the law was passed.

What is left of mailo land title and what is due to mailo landowners? These questions are complicated because forms of land control express deeply felt expectations of what people ought to do and how they ought to behave to each other. Mailo land began as an assertion of Ganda sovereignty in opposition to Protectorate aspirations of land alienation for European settlement. It preceded the solidification of colonial rule and the full establishment of a cash economy, and it embodies both the Ganda chiefs' expectation that land control bound people together and Johnston's expectation that land control prioritized the exclusive rights of owners. Over the course of the twentieth century, mailo land has furthered these often contradictory purposes.

In the face of deliberate intervention by Protectorate authorities, people used the legal forms of mailo ownership to assert Ganda beliefs—that attracting and caring for followers was a source of honor, that land-allocators and land-receivers should feel affection for each other, and that no one should be deprived of the means of subsistence. At the same time, widespread ownership of mailo land was possible because the largest mailo owners exercised their rights as owners and sold substantial amounts of land. Many who sold mailo land used the profits to acquire education for their children, transmuting the prestige of land control into relatively secure elite status in an increasingly stratified society.[8] Professor Apolo Nsibambi's observation that "people need to know where they come from to be able to know where they have gotten to and where they are going" is particularly relevant, and particularly challenging, in thinking about mailo land.[9]

NOTES

1. Mailo land has received substantial attention from scholars. A. B. Mukwaya's *Land Tenure in Buganda: Present Day Tendencies* and Henry W. West's *Land Policy in Buganda* analyze the effects of individualization of land fifty and seventy years after the event. Exceptionally nuanced descriptions of relationships on mailo land are E. Frank Muhereza's *Land Tenure and Peasant Adaptations: Some Reflections on Agricultural Production in Luwero District* and E. B. Mugerwa's "The Position of the Mailo-Owners in the Peasantry Society in Buganda: A Case Study of Muge and Lukaya villages," which was a University of Dar es Salaam political science examination dissertation in 1973. The extremely complex character of current land rights and land use are described in two recent Ph.D. dissertations from the University of Wisconsin–Madison: Elizabeth Troutt's "Rural African Land Markets and Access to Agricultural Land: The Central Region of Uganda (Property Rights)," and Daniel Maxwell's "Labor, Land, Food and Farming: a Household Analysis of Urban Agriculture in Kampala, Uganda."

2. West, *Land Policy in Buganda,* 73–75.

3. Mair, *An African People,* 183, 276.

4. E. S. Haydon, *Law and Justice in Buganda* (London: Butterworths, 1960), 132.

5. This is discussed in Holly Hanson, "'Showing the Land,' Survey, and Registration: Mechanisms for Land Transfer in Buganda Fifty Years After the Individualization of Tenure," paper presented at the International Conference on Land Tenure and Administration, Orlando, Fla., November 1996.

6. E. Frank Muhereza, *Land Tenure and Peasant Adaptations: Some Reflections on Agricultural Production in Luwero District,* Working Paper no. 7 (Kampala: Centre for Basic Research Publications, June 1992), 41.

7. See, for example, *Sonko v. Senkubuge,* Principal Court Criminal Case 202 of 1948, Civil Appeal 75 of 1951, cited in Hanson, "'Showing the Land,'" 15.

8. Karlstrom, "Cultural Kingdom in Uganda," 198–200.

9. *Ngabo,* June 15, 1992, quoted in Karlstrom, "Cultural Kingdom in Uganda," 287.

GLOSSARY

Baganda. People of Buganda (sing. muganda).

bakopi. Peasants, a slightly pejorative term.

bakungu. Chiefs whose authority came entirely from the kabaka (sing. mukungu).

balangira. Princes (sing. mulangira).

balozi. Governor.

Baraza. Gathering of Baganda chiefs and Protectorate officials for consultation.

bataka. The heads of clans; in the 1920s, the movement of people protesting the allocation of mailo land (sing. mutaka).

batongole. Chiefs who controlled ebitongole.

Buganda. Kingdom north of Lake Victoria.

busuulu. Land rent; originally labor tribute owed to the allocator of a kibanja.

butaka. Land where important clan ancestors were buried.

cwezi. Practice of spirit mediumship promoting health and well-being.

ekitongole. Office, department, in the late nineteenth century, a chiefship created by the kabaka (or a chief) for a named purpose, often with nonfree labor (pl. ebitongole).

ekyaalo. Village; large rural estate.

Entebbe. Seat of Protectorate government.

gabunga. Mamba clan elder, keeper of the kabaka's canoes, chief of Ssese after 1900.

ggombolola. District, a category created in the colonial reordering of territory and chiefship.

kabaka. King.

kaggo. Ssaza chief of Kyaddondo, had precedence in kibuga.

kaima. Ssaza chief of Mawokota.

kangaawo. Ssaza chief of Bulemeezi.

kasanvu. One month's obligatory manual labor with pay.

kasolya. Principal clan butaka.

kasujju. Ssaza chief of Busujju.

kasumba. Chief in charge of an ekitongole of bark cloth makers.

katambala. Ssaza chief of Butambala, Sheep clan elder.

katikkiro. Prime minister.

kauta. Chief responsible for supervising cooking for the kabaka.

kibaale. Chief responsible for criticizing the kabaka.

kibanja. Land granted by a chief to a follower, its gardens fed one family (pl. ebibanja).

kibuga. The capital.

kiimba. Ssaza chief of Bugangadzi.

kimbugwe. Keeper of the king's twin figure; one of the kingdom's principal chiefs.

kinyolo. Chief with particular ritual responsibilities who had to be a son of mugema.

kitikkiro. Pinnacle of a Ganda building

kitunzi. Ssaza chief of Ggomba, Lion clan elder.

kkanzu. Long gown worn by men.

kufumbirwa. To be married by a man (lit., to become someone's cook).

kusenga. To join a chief, to contract a relationship of mutual obligation among unequals, in which land and protection were exchanged for loyalty and service.

kusenguka. To leave a chief; to terminate a relationship with a superior.

kusengusa. To send away a follower.

kuswera. To marry a woman, in the ancestor language of Luganda.

kuswerwa. To be married by a man, in the ancestor language of Luganda.

kuwasa. To marry a woman (lit., to cause someone to peel bananas).

kwabya olumbe. Succession ceremony.

lubaale. Deities with a greater-than-local influence (sing. balubaale).

lubuga. Queen sister, a significant ruler in precolonial Buganda.

Lukiiko. Gathering of chiefs to discuss affairs in the courtyard of the king; later, the parliament.

luwalo. Work performed by all ordinary people "for the good of the country."

mailo. Land controlled as private property, allotted in square miles.

mandwa. Spirit medium (pl. bandwa).

matooke. Small green banana eaten steamed as the staple food.

miruka. Parishes, lowest level in the colonial reordering of territory and chiefship (sing. muluka).

misambwa. Ancient spiritual forces associated with rivers, waterfalls, great trees, and other natural phenomena.

Mmengo. Capital in the late nineteenth and early twentieth centuries.

mugema. Ssaza chief of Busirro, "katikkiro" of the deceased kings; head of Colobus Monkey clan.

mugerere. Ssaza chief of Bugerere.

mukama. Term for king among some of Buganda's neighbors.

mukwenda. Ssaza chief of Ssingo.

mumyuka. Chief of second rank, deputy.

mutala. Village, newly acquired land.

mutuba. Rank of chiefship, also branch of clan, barkcloth tree.

muzimu. Ancestor spirit.

mwami. King in related languages, chief under the kabaka in Luganda.

mweso. Board game.

mwoyo. Life force, soul.

nabikande. A sister of the nnamasole who oversaw the birth and ensured the legitimacy of the king's children.

nnakaberenge. A female chief who provided food to the kabaka.

nnakyeyombekedde. Woman who controls land independently of men (pl. bannakyeyombekedde).

nnamasole. Queen mother, a ruler whose authority mirrored the king's.

nvujjo. Land rent, originally tribute in produce owed to the allocator of a kibanja.

obwesengeze. Form of chiefship commemorating service to a superior.

okusala omusango. To judge (lit., to cut) a case.

okweebuula obuko. Process through which a woman increases her rights in a marriage by returning to her own family until her husband has paid bridewealth.

omusango. Hearing of cases in front of a chief and people who gathered to listen and voice their opinions.

omuwanika. Treasurer, a regent in the first decades of colonial rule.

ppookino. Ssaza chief of Buddu.

regents. Three chiefs who ruled in the name of Daudi Cwa during the first decades of colonial rule.

sabagabo. Third-level subordinate chief.

second katikkiro. Chiefly title during the 1890s.

ssabaganzi. Brother of the nnamasole, uncle of the kabaka.

ssaza. Province.

ssekiboobo. Ssaza chief of Kyaggwe.

ssiga. The largest subdivision of a clan (pl. massiga).

wolungo. Keeper of the king's twin figure; a chiefly title in Bunyoro that became kimbugwe in Buganda.

SELECTED BIBLIOGRAPHY

Ansorge, W. J. *Under the African Sun: A Description of Native Races in Uganda, Sporting Adventures, and Other Experiences.* New York: Longmans, Green, 1899.

Apter, David E. *The Political Kingdom in Uganda: A Study in Bureaucratic Nationalism.* Princeton: Princeton University Press, 1961.

Ashe, Robert Pickering. *Chronicles of Uganda.* New York: Randolf, 1895.

Atanda, J. A. "The Bakopi in the Kingdom of Buganda." *Uganda Journal* 33 (1969): 151–162.

Barnes, Sandra T. "Gender and the Politics of Support and Protection in Precolonial West Africa." In *Queens, Queen Mothers, Priestesses, and Power: Case Studies in African Gender,* ed. Flora Edouwaye Kaplan. Annals of the New York Academy of Sciences, vol. 810. New York: New York Academy of Sciences, 1997, 1–18.

Bataka Community. *The Baganda Land Holding Question* (for private circulation only). Kampala: Uganda P. and P., n.d. [1923]. In possession of author. Deposited in the library of the Uganda Society in 2003.

Bell, Sir Hesketh. *Glimpses of a Governor's Life: From Diaries, Letters, and Memoranda.* London: Sampson Low, Marston, n.d.

Bourdieu, Pierre. *Outline of a Theory of Practice.* Trans. Richard Nice. Cambridge: Cambridge University Press, 1977.

Brierley, Jean, and Thomas Spear. "Muteesa, the Missionaries, and Christian Conversion in Buganda." *International Journal of African Historical Studies* 21:4 (1988): 601–618.

Buell, Raymond Leslie. *The Native Problem in Africa.* London: Frank Cass, 1965 (1st ed. 1928).

Carter, W. Morris. "The Clan System, Land Tenure, and Succession Among the Baganda." *Uganda Protectorate Law Reports* 1 (1904–1910): 99–120.

Cohen, David William. *Womunafu's Bunafu: A Study of Authority in a Nineteenth-Century African Community.* Princeton: Princeton University Press, 1977.

Cook, Sir Albert. "Further Memories of Uganda." *Uganda Journal* 2 (1935): 97–115.

Curtin, Philip D. *The World and the West: The European Challenge and the Overseas Response in the Age of Empire.* Cambridge: Cambridge University Press, 2000.

Ehrlich, Cyril. "The Economy of Buganda, 1893–1903." *Uganda Journal* 20:1 (1956): 17–25.

Fallers, Lloyd. "Despotism, Status Culture, and Social Mobility in an African Kingdom." *Comparative Studies in Society and History* 2 (1959): 4–32.

———. "Social Stratification in Traditional Buganda." In *The King's Men,* ed. Lloyd Fallers. New York: Oxford University Press, 1964, 64–113.

———, ed. *The King's Men: Leadership and Status in Buganda on the Eve of Independence.* New York: Oxford University Press (on behalf of the East African Institute of Social Research), 1964.

Feierman, Steven. "A Century of Ironies in East Africa (c.1780–1890)." In Philip Curtin, Steven Feierman, Leonard Thompson, and Jan Vansina, *African History: From Earliest Times to Independence,* 2nd ed. New York: Longman, 1995, 352–376.

———. "Africa in History: The End of Universal Narratives." In *After Colonialism: Imperial Histories and Postcolonial Displacements,* ed. Gyan Prakash. Princeton: Princeton University Press, 1995, 40–65.

———. *The Shambaa Kingdom: A History.* Madison: University of Wisconsin Press, 1974.

Fortt, J. M. "The Distribution of the Immigrant and Ganda Population Within Buganda." In *Economic Development and Tribal Change,* ed. Audrey I. Richards. Cambridge: W. Heffer and Sons for the East African Institute of Social Research, 1954, 77–118.

Fortt, J. M., and D. A. Hougham. "Environment, Population, and Economic History." In *Subsistence to Commercial Farming in Present-Day Buganda,* ed. Audrey I. Richards, Ford Sturrock, and Jean M. Fortt. Cambridge: Cambridge University Press, 1973, 17–46.

Gale, H. P. *Uganda and the Mill Hill Fathers.* London: Macmillan, 1959.

Gorju, Julien. *Entre le Victoria, L'Albert et L'Edouard.* Rennes: Oberthur, 1920.

Grant, James Augustus. *A Walk Across Africa, or Domestic Sceneries from My Nile Journal.* Edinburgh: Blackwood and Sons, 1864.

Gray, J. M. "The Year of the Three Kings of Buganda." *Uganda Journal* 14 (1949): 15–52.

Gutkind, Peter C. W. *The Royal Capital of Buganda: A Study of Internal Conflict and External Ambiguity.* The Hague: Mouton, 1963.

Hansen, Holger Bernt. *Mission, Church, and State in a Colonial Setting: Uganda 1890–1925.* New York: St. Martin's Press, 1984.

Hanson, Holly. "Queen Mothers and Good Government in Buganda: The Loss of Women's Political Power in Nineteenth-Century East Africa." In *Women in African Colonial Histories,* ed. Jean Allman, Susan Geiger, and Nakanyike Musisi. Bloomington: Indiana University Press, 2002, 213–236.

Harford-Battersby, Charles F. *Pilkington of Uganda.* 2nd ed. London: Marshall Brothers, 1898.

Hattersley, C. W. *The Baganda at Home.* 1908. Reprint, London: Frank Cass, 1968.

Haydon, E. S. *Law and Justice in Buganda.* London: Butterworths, 1960.

Hunt, Nancy Rose. *A Colonial Lexicon of Birth Ritual, Medicalization, and Mobility in the Congo.* Durham, N.C.: Duke University Press, 1999.

Iliffe, John. *A Modern History of Tanganyika.* Cambridge: Cambridge University Press, 1979.

Kaggwa, Sir Apolo. *Empisa za Baganda.* 1907. Partially translated by Ernest B. Kalibala under the title *The Customs of the Baganda,* ed. May Mandelbaum. Columbia

University Contributions to Anthropology no. 22. New York: Columbia University Press, 1934.

———. *The Kings of Buganda.* Trans. and ed. M.S.M. Kiwanuka. Nairobi: East African Publishing House, 1971.

Kato, L. L. "Government Land Policy in Uganda: 1889 to 1900." *Uganda Journal* 35:2 (1971): 153–160.

Keech McIntosh, Susan, ed. *Beyond Chiefdoms: Pathways to Complexity in Africa.* Cambridge: Cambridge University Press, 1999.

Kingdom of Buganda. *Customary Law Reports, 1940–1955: Being a Digest of Decisions on Customary Law Made by the Principal Court of His Highness the Kabaka of Buganda During the Years 1941–1951.* Comp. E. S. Haydon and I. S. Lule. Nairobi: E. A. Printers, 1956.

———. *Customary Law Reports, 1940–1955: Being a Digest of Decisions on Customary Law Made by the Principal Court of His Highness the Kabaka of Buganda During the Years 1940–1955.* Comp. E. S. Haydon and I. S. Lule. Nairobi: E. A. Printers, 1956.

Kiwanuka, M.S.M. Semakula. *A History of Buganda from the Foundation of the Kingdom to 1900.* New York: Africana, 1972.

Kottak, C. P. "Ecological Variables in the Origin and Evolution of African States: The Buganda Example." *Comparative Studies in Society and History* 14 (1972): 351–380.

Larson, Pier. *History and Memory in the Age of Enslavement: Becoming Merina in Highland Madagascar, 1770–1822.* Portsmouth, N.H.: Heinemann, 2000.

Low, D. Anthony. *Buganda in Modern History.* Los Angeles: University of California Press, 1971.

———. "The Making and Implementation of the Uganda Agreement of 1900." In D. Anthony Low and R. Cranford Pratt, *Buganda and British Overrule: 1900–1955, Two Studies.* London: Oxford University Press, 1960.

———. "The Northern Interior, 1840–1884." In *History of East Africa,* vol. 1, ed. Roland Oliver and Gervase Mathew. Oxford: Clarendon Press, 1963, 287–351.

———. "Religion and Society in Buganda 1874–1900." *East African Studies* (Kampala) no. 8 (1957): 1–16.

———, ed. *The Mind of Buganda: Documents of the Modern History of an African Kingdom.* Los Angeles: University of California Press, 1971.

Mackay, Alexander M. *A. M. Mackay Pioneer Missionary of the Church Missionary Society in Uganda.* London: Hodder and Stoughton, 1890.

Mair, Lucy. *An African People in the Twentieth Century.* 1934. Reissue, London: Routledge and Kegan Paul, 1965.

———. *Native Marriage in Buganda.* Memorandum 19. London: Oxford University Press for the International Institute of African Languages and Cultures, 1940.

Mamdani, Mahmood. *Citizen and Subject: Contemporary Africa and the Legacy of Late Colonialism.* Princeton: Princeton University Press, 1996.

———. *Politics and Class Formation in Uganda.* New York: Monthly Review Press, 1976.

McKnight, Glenn. "Land, Politics, and Buganda's 'Indigenous' Colonial State." *Journal of Imperial and Commonwealth History* 28:1 (2000): 65–89.

Morgan, A. R. "Uganda's Cotton Industry: Fifty Years Back." *Uganda Journal* 22:2 (1958): 107–112.

Muhereza, E. Frank. *Land Tenure and Peasant Adaptations: Some Reflections on Agricultural Production in Luwero District.* Working Paper no. 27. Kampala: Centre for Basic Research Publications, June 1992.

Mukwaya, A. B. *Land Tenure in Buganda.* East African Studies no. 1. Kampala: East African Institute of Social Research, 1953.

Mulira, E.M.K. *Sir Apolo Kaggwa, K.C.M.G., MBE.* Kampala: Buganda Bookshop, 1949. Manuscript translation by Dr. John Rowe.

Murphy, John D., et al. *Luganda-English Dictionary.* Washington, D.C.: Catholic University of America Press, 1972.

Musisi, Nyakanike B. "Women, 'Elite Polygyny,' and Buganda State Formation." *Signs: Journal of Women in Culture and Society* 16:4 (1991): 757–786.

Newbury, David. *Kings and Clans: Ijwi Island and the Lake Kivu Rift, 1780–1840.* Madison: University of Wisconsin Press, 1991.

Obbo, Christine. "Food Sharing During Food Crisis: Case Studies from Uganda and Ciskei." In *Food Systems in Central and Southern Africa,* ed. Johan Pottier. London: School of Oriental and African Studies, 1985, 265–279.

Perelman, Michael. *The Invention of Capitalism: Classical Political Economy and the Secret History of Primitive Accumulation.* Durham, N.C.: Duke University Press, 2000.

Perham, Margery. *Lugard: The Years of Adventure, 1858–1898.* London: Collins, 1956.

Polanyi, Karl. *The Great Transformation: The Political and Economic Origins of Our Time.* Boston: Beacon Press, 2001.

Powesland, P. G. *Economic Policy and Labour: A Study in Uganda's Economic History.* East African Studies no. 10. Kampala: East African Institute of Social Research, 1957.

———. "History of the Migration in Uganda." In *Economic Development and Tribal Change,* ed. Audrey I. Richards. Cambridge: W. Heffer and Sons for the East African Institute of Social Research, 1954, 17–51.

Pratt, R. Cranford. "The Politics of Indirect Rule: Uganda, 1900–1955." In D. Anthony Low and R. Cranford Pratt, *Buganda and British Overrule, 1900–1955.* London: Oxford University Press, 1960, 163–316.

Ray, Benjamin C. *Myth, Ritual, and Kingship in Buganda.* New York: Oxford University Press, 1991.

Reid, Richard, and Henri Medard. "Merchants, Missions and the Remaking of the Urban Environment in Bugada, c.1840–90." In *Africa's Urban Past,* ed. David M. Anderson and Richard Rathbone. Portsmouth, N.H.: Heinemann, 2000, 98–108.

Richards, Audrey I. *The Changing Structure of a Ganda Village.* Nairobi: East African Publishing House, 1966.

———. *Economic Development and Tribal Change: A Study of Immigrant Labour in Buganda.* Cambridge: W. Heffer and Sons for the East African Institute of Social Research, 1954.

———. "Methods of Settlement in Buganda." In *Economic Development and Tribal Change,* ed. Audrey I. Richards. Cambridge: W. Heffer and Sons for the East African Institute of Social Research, 1954, 119–140.

Robertson, A. F. *Community of Strangers: A Journal of Discovery in Uganda.* London: Scholar Press, 1978.

Roscoe, John. *The Baganda: An Account of Their Native Customs and Beliefs.* 1911. Reprint, New York: Barnes and Noble, 1966.

Rowe, John A. "The Pattern of Political Administration in Precolonial Buganda." In *African Themes: Northwestern University Studies in Honor of Gwendolen M. Carter,* ed. Ibrahim Abu-Lughod. Evanston, Ill.: Program of African Studies Northwestern University, 1975, 65–76.

Schiller, Lawrence D. "The Royal Women of Buganda." *International Journal of African Historical Studies* 23:3 (1990): 455–473.

Schoenbrun, David Lee. *A Green Place, a Good Place: A Social History of the Great Lakes Region, Earliest Times to the Fifteenth Century.* Portsmouth, N.H.: Heinemann, 1997.

———. *The Historical Reconstruction of Great Lakes Bantu Cultural Vocabulary: Etymologies and Distributions.* Koln: Koppe, 1997.

———. "We Are What We Eat: Ancient Agriculture Between the Great Lakes." *Journal of African History* 34 (1993): 1–31.

Southwold, Martin. *Bureaucracy and Chiefship in Buganda: The Development of Appointive Office in the History of Buganda.* East African Studies no. 14. Kampala: East African Institute of Social Research, n.d.

———. "Leadership, Authority, and the Village Community." In *The King's Men,* ed. Lloyd Fallers. New York: Oxford University Press, 1964, 211–255.

———. "Succession to the Throne in Buganda." In *Succession to High Office,* ed. Jack Goody. Cambridge Papers in Social Anthropology no. 4. Cambridge: Cambridge University Press, 1966, 82–126.

Speke, John Hanning. *Journey of the Discovery of the Source of the Nile.* Edinburgh: Blackwood and Sons, 1863.

Stanley, Henry M. *Through the Dark Continent.* Vol. 1. 1878. Rev. ed., 1899. Reprint, New York: Dover, 1988.

Taylor, John V. *The Growth of the Church in Buganda: An Attempt at Understanding.* London: SCM Press, 1958.

Thomas, H. B., and Robert Scott. *Uganda.* London: Humphrey Milford, 1935.

Thomas, H. B., and A. E. Spencer. *A History of Uganda Land and Surveys and of the Uganda Land and Survey Department.* Entebbe: Government Press, 1938.

Tosh, John. "Lango Agriculture During the Early Colonial Period: Land and Labour in a Cash Crop Economy." *Journal of African History* 19:3 (1978): 415–439.

———. "The Northern Interlacustrine Region." In *Pre-Colonial African Trade: Essays on Trade in Central and Eastern Africa before 1900,* ed. Richard Gray and David Birmingham. London: Oxford University Press, 1970, 103–118.

Treves, Sir Frederick. *Uganda for a Holiday.* London: Smith, Elder, 1910.

Tripp, Aili Mari. *Women and Politics in Uganda.* Madison: University of Wisconsin Press, 2000.

Tucker, A. R. *Eighteen Years in Uganda and East Africa.* 2 vols. London: Edwin Arnold, 1908.

Twaddle, Michael. "The Bakungu Chiefs of Buganda Under British Colonial Rule, 1900–1930." *Journal of African History* 10 (1969): 309–322.

———. "The Emergence of Politico-Religious Groupings in Late Nineteenth Century Buganda." *Journal of African History* 29 (1988): 81–92.

———. "The Ending of Slavery in Buganda." In *The End of Slavery in Africa,* ed. Suzanne Miers and Richard Roberts. Madison: University of Wisconsin Press, 1988, 119–149.

———. *Kakungulu and the Creation of Uganda, 1868–1928.* Athens: Ohio University Press, 1993.

————. "Muslim Revolution in Buganda." *African Affairs* 71 (1972): 54–72.

————. "Slaves and Peasants in Buganda." In *Slavery and Other Forms of Unfree Labour,* ed. Leonie J. Archer. London: Routledge, 1988, 118–129.

Uganda Protectorate. *Laws of Uganda 1951.* Vol. 6. Entebbe: Government Printer, 1951.

Walser, Ferdinand. *Luganda Proverbs.* Kampala: Mill Hill Missionaries, 1984.

Wamala, E. "The Socio-Political Philosophy of Traditional Buganda Society: Breaks and Continuity into the Present." In *The Foundations of Social Life: Ugandan Philosophical Studies,* ed. E. T. Alfovo et al. Cultural Heritage and Contemporary Change Series no. 2, Africa, vol. 2. Washington, D.C.: Council for Research in Values and Philosophy, 1992.

Welbourn, F. B. *East African Rebels: A Study of Some Independent Churches.* London: SCM Press, 1961.

————. "Some Aspects of Kiganda Religion." *Uganda Journal* 26:2 (1962): 171–182.

West, Henry W. *Land Policy in Buganda.* Cambridge: Cambridge University Press, 1972.

Wright, Michael. *Buganda in the Heroic Age.* Nairobi: Oxford University Press, 1971.

Wrigley, Christopher C. "The Changing Economic Structure of Buganda." In *The King's Men,* ed. Lloyd Fallers. New York: Oxford University Press, 1964, 16–63.

————. "The Christian Revolution in Buganda." *Comparative Studies in Society and History* 2 (1959): 33–48.

————. *Crops and Wealth in Uganda: A Short Agrarian History.* Kampala: East African Institute of Social Research, 1959.

————. *Kingship and State: The Buganda Dynasty.* Cambridge: Cambridge University Press, 1996.

PAPERS, THESES, AND UNPUBLISHED MANUSCRIPTS

Atanda, J. A. "The *Bakopi* in the Kingdom of Buganda, 1900–1927: An Analysis of the Condition of the Peasant Class in Early Colonial Period." Cyclostyled paper labeled "History Department, MSP/16." Northwestern University Africana Collection.

Gitta, Cosmas. "International Human Rights: An Imperial Imposition? (A Case Study of Buganda, 1856–1955)." Ph.D. diss., Columbia University, 1998.

Hanson, Holly. "'Showing the Land,' Survey, and Registration: Mechanisms for Land Transfer in Buganda Fifty Years After the Individualization of Tenure." Paper presented at the International Conference on Land Tenure and Administration, Orlando, Fla., November 1996.

Karlstrom, Mikael. "The Cultural Kingdom in Uganda: Popular Royalism and the Restoration of the Buganda Kingship." Ph.D. diss., University of Chicago, 1999.

Maxwell, Daniel. "Labor, Land, Food, and Farming: A Household Analysis of Urban Agriculture in Kampala, Uganda." Ph.D. diss., University of Wisconsin–Madison, 1995.

McKnight, Glenn. "A Moral Economy of Development: Transforming the Discourse of Development in Uganda, 1895–1930." Ph.D. diss., Queen's University, 1996.

Medard, Henri. "Croissance et crises de la royaute du Buganda au XIX siecle." Ph.D. diss., University of Paris, 2001.

Mugerwa, E. B. "The Position of the Mailo-Owners in the Peasantry Society in Buganda: A Case Study of Muge and Lukaya Villages." M.A. political science diss., University of Dar es Salaam, 1973.

Musisi, Nakanyike B., "Transformations of Baganda Women: From the Earliest Times to the Demise of the Kingdom in 1966." Ph.D. diss., University of Toronto, 1991.

Rowe, John. "Revolution in Buganda 1856–1900, Part One: The Reign of Mukabya Mutesa, 1856–1884." Ph.D. diss., University of Wisconsin, 1966.

Shetler, Jan Bender. "The Landscapes of Memory: A History of Social Identity in the Western Serengeti, Tanzania." Ph.D. diss., University of Florida, 1998.

Tantala, Renee Louise. "The Early History of Kitara in Western Uganda: Process Models of Religious and Political Change." Ph.D. diss., University of Wisconsin, 1989.

———. "Ganda Households and the Colonial Economy (1900–1939)." Unpublished paper.

Troutt, Elizabeth. "Rural African Land Markets and Access to Agricultural Land: The Central Region of Uganda (Property Rights)." Ph.D. diss., University of Wisconsin–Madison, 1994.

Waller, Richard. "The Traditional Economy of Buganda." M.A. essay, University of London, School of Oriental and African Studies, 1971.

ARCHIVAL SOURCES

Bataka Land Commission. Also titled Commission of Inquiry into Butaka Clan Lands. Uganda National Archives, A46/2213, A46/2214, formerly classified as Entebbe Secretariat Archives of the Uganda Protectorate, Secretariat Minute Paper no. 6902.Church Missionary Society Papers at the University of Birmingham, G3 A7/ 0 1900, no. 3.*Ekitabo kya Obusika,* 1908–1923. The Record of Succession of Members of Clans of Buganda. Currently Held in the Ministry of Justice, Kampala, Uganda.

Kabali, Ezera. Kabali Papers, Makerere University Library, Africana Collection.

Kaggwa, Apolo. Kaggwa Papers, Makerere University Library, Africana Collection.

Kaggwa, Sir Apolo. *Basekabaka be Buganda.* Typescript of English translation by Simon Musoke. Africana Collection, Makerere University Library. N.B. pagination of this document is inconsistent.

———. *Ekitabo kya Kika Kya Nsenene.* Mengo: AK Press, n.d., manuscript translation seen courtesy of John Rowe.

Katende, John. *Cases and Materials: Land Law in East Africa.* Vol. 1, Land /69/4/ (b). Cyclostyled study materials for Makerere University students of law.

Kingdom of Buganda. Buganda Lukiiko. Records translated into English by the East African Institute of Social Research, seen courtesy of John Rowe, deposited at the Makerere Institute of Social and Economic Research and the Makerere University Africana Collection.

———. High Court and Principal Court Records seen at the High Court, Kampala.

Macdonald, J.R.L. "Report on Uganda Disturbances in Spring, 1892." (1893) Public Records Office (PRO) Foreign Office (FO) Series FO s (African) F02/60.

Miti, James. *A History of Buganda,* n.d. Manuscript translation in Makerere University Library Africana Collection.

Roscoe, John, and Apolo Kaggwa. "Enquiry into Native Land Tenure in the Uganda Protectorate." 1906, Rhodes House, Bodleian Library, Oxford; Shelfmark MS Africa s 17.

Uganda National Archives (UNA) formerly Entebbe Secretariat Archives (ESA) A46 series, formerly Secretariat Minute Paper (SMP) 1138 and 1148.

United Kingdom. Public Records Office. Bataka Land Commission, also titled Commission of Inquiry into Butaka Clan Lands. CO 536/133.

———. Public Records Office. Foreign Office (FO) Series FO 2/202.

Walker, Archdeacon John Henry. Uncataloged papers in Royal Commonwealth Society Papers at Cambridge University.

White Fathers *(Société des Missionnaires de Notre-Dame des Missions d'Afrique). Chronique Trimestrielle.* Center for Research Libraries, Cooperative Africana Microfilm Project MF 2530.

Zimbe, Bartolomayo Musoke. *Buganda ne Kabaka* (Mengo, 1939). Typescript translation, "Buganda and the King." Cambridge University Library.

INDEX

About the Author

HOLLY ELISABETH HANSON is Assistant Professor, Department of History, Mt. Holyoke College.